Macready, Booth, Terry, Irving
Great Shakespeareans
Volume VI

Great Shakespeareans

Each volume in the series provides a critical account and analysis of those figures who have had the greatest influence on the interpretation, understanding and cultural reception of Shakespeare, both nationally and around the world.

General Series Editors:

Peter Holland, University of Notre Dame, USA
Adrian Poole, Trinity College Cambridge, UK

Great Shakespeareans: Set I

Volume I: *Dryden, Pope, Johnson, Malone,* edited by Claude Rawson
Volume II: *Garrick, Kemble, Siddons, Kean,* edited by Peter Holland
Volume III: *Voltaire, Goethe, Schlegel, Coleridge,* edited by Roger Paulin
Volume IV: *Hazlitt, Keats, the Lambs,* edited by Adrian Poole

Great Shakespeareans: Set II

Volume V: *Scott, Dickens, Eliot, Hardy,* edited by Adrian Poole
Volume VI: *Macready, Booth, Irving, Terry,* edited by Richard Schoch
Volume VII: *Jameson, Cowden Clarke, Kemble, Cushman,* edited by Gail Marshall
Volume VIII: *James, Melville, Emerson, Berryman,* edited by Peter Rawlings
Volume IX: *Bradley, Greg, Folger,* edited by Cary DiPietro

Great Shakespeareans: Set III

Volume X: *Marx and Freud,* Crystal Bartolovich, Jean Howard and David Hillman
Volume XI: *Berlioz, Verdi, Wagner, Britten,* edited by Daniel Albright
Volume XII: *Joyce, T. S. Eliot, Auden, Beckett,* edited by Adrian Poole
Volume XIII: *Wilson Knight, Empson, Barber, Kott,* edited by Hugh Grady

Great Shakespeareans: Set IV

Volume XIV: *Hugo, Pasternak, Brecht, Césaire,* edited by Ruth Morse
Volume XV: *Poel, Granville Barker, Guthrie, Wanamaker,* edited by Cary Mazer
Volume XVI: *Gielgud, Olivier, Ashcroft, Dench,* edited by Russell Jackson
Volume XVII: *Welles, Kozintsev, Kurosawa, Zeffirelli,* Mark Thornton Burnett, Kathy Howlett, Courtney Lehmann and Ramona Wray
Volume XVIII: *Hall, Brook, Ninagawa, Lepage,* edited by Peter Holland

Macready, Booth, Terry, Irving

Great Shakespeareans
Volume VI

Edited by
Richard Schoch

Continuum International Publishing Group
The Tower Building
11 York Road
London SE1 7NX

80 Maiden Lane
Suite 704
New York, NY 10038

www.continuumbooks.com

British Library Cataloguing-in-Publication Data
A catalogue record for this book is available from the British Library.

ISBN: 978-0-8264-4225-3 (Hardback)

Library of Congress Cataloging-in-Publication Data
A catalog record for this book is available from the Library of Congress.

Typeset by Newgen Imaging Systems Pvt Ltd, Chennai, India
Printed and bound in Great Britain by CPI Antony Rowe,
Chippenham, Wiltshire

Contents

Series Editors' Preface

What is a 'Great Shakespearean?' Who are the 'Great Shakespeareans?' This series is designed to explore those figures who have had the greatest influence on the interpretation, understanding and reception of Shakespeare, both nationally and internationally. Charting the effect of Shakespeare on cultures local, national and international is a never-ending task, as we continually modulate and understand differently the ways in which each culture is formed and altered. *Great Shakespeareans* uses as its focus individuals whose own cultural impact has been and continues to be powerful. One of its aims is to widen the sense of who constitute the most important figures in our understanding of Shakespeare's afterlives. The list is therefore not restricted to, say, actors and scholars, as if the performance of and commentary on Shakespeare's works were the only means by which his impact is remade or extended. There are actors aplenty (like Garrick, Irving and Olivier) and scholars too (Bradley, Greg and Empson) but our list deliberately includes as many novelists (Dickens, Melville, Joyce), poets (Keats, Eliot, Berryman), playwrights (Brecht, Beckett, Césaire) and composers (Berlioz, Verdi and Britten), as well as thinkers whose work seems impossible without Shakespeare and whose influence on our world has been profound, like Marx and Freud.

Deciding who to include has been less difficult than deciding who to exclude. We have a long list of individuals for whom we would wish to have found a place but whose inclusion would have meant someone else's exclusion. We took long and hard looks at the volumes as they were shaped by our own and our volume editors' perceptions. We have numerous regrets over some outstanding figures who ended up just outside this project. There will, no doubt, be argument on this score. Some may find our choices too Anglophone, insufficiently global. Others may complain of the lack of contemporary scholars and critics. But this is not a project designed to establish a new canon, nor are our volumes intended to be encyclopedic in scope. The series is not entitled 'The Greatest Shakespeareans' nor is it

'Some Great Shakespeareans,' but it will, we hope, be seen as negotiating and occupying a space mid-way along the spectrum of inclusivity and arbitrariness.

Our contributors have been asked to describe the double impact of Shakespeare on their particular figure and of their figure on the understanding, interpretation and appreciation of Shakespeare, as well as providing a sketch of their subject's intellectual and professional biography and an account of the wider context within which her/his work might be understood. This 'context' will vary widely from case to case and, at times, a single 'Great Shakespearean' is asked to stand as a way of grasping a large domain. In the case of Britten, for example, he is the window through which other composers and works in the English musical tradition like Vaughan Williams, Walton and Tippett have a place. So, too, Dryden has been the means for considering the beginnings of critical analysis of the plays as well as of the ways in which Shakespeare's plays influenced Dryden's own practice.

To enable our contributors to achieve what we have asked of them, we have taken the unusual step of enabling them to write at length. Our volumes do not contain brief entries of the kind that a Shakespeare Encyclopedia would include nor the standard article length of academic journals and Shakespeare Companions. With no more than four Great Shakespeareans per volume – and as few as two in the case of volume 10 – our contributors have space to present their figures more substantially and, we trust, more engagingly. Each volume has a brief introduction by the volume editor and a section of further reading. We hope the volumes will appeal to those who already know the accomplishment of a particular Great Shakespearean and to those trying to find a way into seeing how Shakespeare has affected a particular poet as well as how that poet has changed forever our appreciation of Shakespeare. Above all, we hope *Great Shakespeareans* will help our readers to think afresh about what Shakespeare has meant to our cultures, and about how and why, in such differing ways across the globe and across the last four centuries and more, they have changed what his writing has meant.

Peter Holland and Adrian Poole

List of Illustrations

Notes on Contributors

Gail Marshall is Professor of Victorian Literature and Director of the Centre for Victorian Studies at the University of Leicester. She is the author of numerous articles on Victorian literature and culture, as well as books on Victorian fiction and theatre, the most recent of which is *Shakespeare and Victorian Women* (2009). She is the general editor of Pickering & Chatto's series *Lives of Shakespearian Actors* and is editing *Shakespeare and the Nineteenth Century* for Cambridge University Press. Her current monograph project is on the literature, culture, and historiography of 1859.

Richard Schoch is Professor of the History of Culture at Queen Mary, University of London. He is the author of *Shakespeare's Victorian Stage: Performing History in the Theatre of Charles Kean* (1998), *Not Shakespeare: Bardolatry and Burlesque in the Nineteenth Century* (2002), *Queen Victoria and the Theatre of her Age* (2004), *The Secrets of Happiness: Three Thousand Years of Searching for the Good Life* (2006) and the editor of *Victorian Theatrical Burlesques* (2004). He is currently writing a book on the historiography of British theatre. Schoch has been awarded fellowships from the Folger Shakespeare Library, the Leverhulme Trust, the Stanford Humanities Center and the American Society for Theatre Research. His books have been shortlisted for the Barnard Hewitt Award (USA) and the Theatre Book Prize (UK).

Gary Jay Williams is the author *Our Moonlight Revels: 'A Midsummer Night's Dream' in the Theatre* (1997), winner of the Theatre Library Association's George Freedley Award. He is a co-author and editor of *Theatre Histories: An Introduction* (2nd edition, 2010) and was Editor of *Theatre Survey* from 1995 to 2001. He has been awarded fellowships from the Folger Shakespeare Library, Harvard's Houghton Library, Yale University and the National Endowment for the Humanities. He is an Emeritus Professor of Drama at the Catholic University of America, Washington, DC.

Edward Ziter is Associate Professor of Theatre History in the Department of Drama and affiliated faculty in the Departments of English and Performance Studies at New York University. He is the author of *The Orient on the Victorian Stage* (2003) and his articles have appeared in *Theatre Journal*, *Theatre Survey*, *The Wordsworth Circle* and in several anthologies. He is currently working on a study of British actors of the romantic period. His other major research interest is Syrian theatre. He has served on the Executive Committee of the American Society for Theatre Research, as book reviews editor for *Theatre Survey* and as performance reviews editor for *Theatre Journal*.

Introduction

Richard Schoch

Scholarship on Shakespeare in performance in nineteenth-century Britain and America has focused in recent years on a cluster of related concerns: the dominance of the actor-manager and the star system, pictorialism, historical consciousness, 'rational amusement,' respectability, Bardolatry (and its critics), cultural nationalism and imperialism. To frame the chapters in this volume, which both build upon and modify scholarly precedent, a brief overview of current critical investigations seems warranted. My intent is not to construct an annotated bibliography but rather to trace the contours of recent scholarship. In so doing I am aware that the issues I will survey represent a particular moment in the historiography of Shakespeare in performance—a perspective that bears equally upon the chapters in this volume. Indeed part of what unites the chapters that follow on William Charles Macready, Edwin Booth, Ellen Terry and Henry Irving is their authors' awareness of how different histories will inevitably be written out of the same archival record. So my fellow contributors and I invite you to read this volume not as a definitive account of Shakespeare on the nineteenth-century Anglo-American stage (definitiveness in the humanities being by definition a category error) but as an encapsulation of certain questions asked of certain historical objects, with both the questions and the objects necessarily determined by the subjective choices and assumptions of the historians themselves.

While a devotion to Shakespeare foretold the financial ruin of actor-managers throughout the nineteenth century, no legitimate theatre could establish a solid reputation without it. Indeed, a theatre's 'illegitimate,' but vastly more popular, offerings effectively subsidized the perceived moral obligation to produce Shakespeare: the 'despised melodrama' and the 'tight-rope dancing of the Devil Antonio' compensated for the 'loss and vexation incurred' in performing the Bard.[1] To imagine a Victorian theatre without Shakespeare, however fiscally prudent that would have been, is to imagine a theatre no longer English. And in the United States, Shakespeare was then (as so often now) the sign of cultural prestige. Of course the desire to perform Shakespeare, though embodied most vividly in actor-managers, extended to theatrical celebrities generally, from actresses like Ellen Tree, Helena Faucit and Ellen Terry to performers not principally known as long-term theatrical managers, such as the Anglo-French actor Charles Fechter and the Americans Edwin Booth and Richard Mansfield.

During his brief managerial career at Covent Garden (1837–1839) and Drury Lane (1841–1843), William Charles Macready was renowned for a noble but failed effort to establish a respectable theatre where the national drama would be produced with appropriate reverence. Achieving that worthy distinction entailed not only restoring the integrity of Shakespeare's texts (although still heavily edited for performance) but also staging his plays with increased attention to historical accuracy in sets and costumes, attracting royal patronage and expelling prostitutes from the theatre—pursuits and obsessions that lasted throughout the century.

Within a decade of the passage of the Theatres Regulation Act of 1843, which abolished the longstanding monopoly of London's patent theatres, Samuel Phelps at Sadler's Wells and Charles Kean at the Princess's Theatre embarked upon their famed series of Shakespearean revivals. During his lengthy managerial tenure (1844–1862), Phelps was lauded for endearing a local audience to legitimate drama, ensemble acting, textual restoration, ambition in performing nearly the entire Shakespearean canon (thirty-one plays) and ingenuity in making do with a paucity of stage resources. 'To that remote suburb of Islington,' Macready approvingly noted, 'we must look for the drama if we really wish to find it.'[2] Whether because of the financial constraints imposed by managing a theatre with modest box-office potential, the supposedly less refined tastes of a north London audience, or his own uncompromising allegiance to textual purity, Phelps was content to leave spectacular and antiquarian *mise-en-scène* to his West End counterpart, Charles Kean.

In only nine seasons as manager of the Princess's Theatre (1850–1859), Kean recreated the medieval and Tudor England of Shakespeare's history plays, Periclean Athens in *A Midsummer Night's Dream* and seventeenth-century Italy in *The Merchant of Venice.* Actor turned antiquary, Kean 'rummaged out old books,' 'turned over old prints' and 'brushed the dirt off old music' in preparing historically correct revivals of Shakespeare.[3] So insistent was Kean upon authentic stage accessories that his detractors at *Punch* dubbed him not the 'Upholder' of Shakespeare, but the 'Upholsterer.' Yet to Kean's relatively modest playhouse on Oxford Street in the heart of the commercial West End came some of the leading figures of the mid nineteenth century: Queen Victoria and Prince Albert (and their children), Dickens, Palmerston, Gladstone, Hans Christian Andersen, Lewis Carroll and the Duke of Saxe-Meiningen. Household names in their day, neither Phelps nor Kean is counted among the 'Great Shakespeareans' in this series—which is not so much an omission as an indication of how that greatness is now defined.

Kean's retirement from the Princess's Theatre marked the beginning of a twenty-year gap in memorable London productions of Shakespeare, a interregnum of tediousness relieved only by Fechter's *Hamlet* (1861, 1864)—audiences thrilled to his amiable blond-haired Scandinavian prince—and Squire and Marie Bancroft's *The Merchant of Venice* (1875)—a commercial failure, but memorable for E. W. Godwin's picturesque scenery and Ellen Terry's winning comeback performance as Portia. Not until Henry Irving's famed management of the Lyceum Theatre (1878–1902) was Shakespeare fully restored to the London stage. Irving inherited from Charles Kean not simply a repertoire of Shakespeare and gentlemanly melodrama but a strong taste for spectacular *mise-en-scène*. His stage partner was Terry, whom Oscar Wilde affectionately dubbed 'Our Lady of the Lyceum,' a sobriquet nicely capturing the semi-religious reverence accorded to both the actress and the temple of dramatic arts where she fulfilled the role of high priestess.

In the early summer of 1881, during a revival of *Othello*, Terry and Irving shared the stage with Edwin Booth (1833–1893), the most important American Shakespearean in the second half of the nineteenth century. Shakespeare had been performed professionally in America ever since a company of twelve English actors, led by the brothers William and Lewis Hallam, sailed into Yorktown harbor in the colony of Virginia in 1752. Prominent English performers such as George Frederick Cooke, Edmund Kean, Charles Kemble, his daughter Fanny Kemble and Macready all undertook American tours in the opening decades of the nineteenth century. But it was not until Edwin Forrest (1806–1872) and Charlotte Cushman (1816–1876) that the country claimed its first homegrown theatrical stars. A robustly muscular performer, who possessed some of the elder Kean's dynamism, Forrest incited controversies over masculinity, first by comparison with the subdued dignity of Macready, his foreign competitor, and then with the young Edwin Booth, his rival on native soil. It was the more genteel Booth, scion of a legendary theatrical dynasty, who set the standard for Shakespearean acting in America's Gilded Age. Though for a time Booth did run his own theatre in New York, his career, unlike Irving's, was not primarily as a manager. But as the greatest theatrical star of his era, he travelled endlessly across America, bringing Shakespeare to towns large and small, wherever the transcontinental railroad could take him.

Within these structures of theatrical management and touring, how did Shakespearean drama look to theatergoers? It looked like a painting sprung to life. Pictorialism, although it featured in the full range of Victorian theatrical productions from melodrama to pantomime, was especially identified with Shakespeare revivals. Pictorial *mise-en-scène* entailed not just highly elaborate scenery (both painted wings and drops and three-dimensional 'built out' structures) but also vivid costumes and properties, spectacular scenic and lighting effects and the frequent use of tableaux vivants. In short, pictorialism was not *what* actor-managers thought about when they staged their productions; it was *how* they thought. Only with great difficulty could a nineteenth-century production of Shakespeare be regarded as anything other than an animated painting.

Of course there were dissenters. In 1875 the *Athenaeum* lamented that Shakespeare's plays were being 'convert[ed] . . . into spectacular entertainments . . . not widely different from a circus.'[4] But the truth was that alternatives to pictorialism found few buyers in the theatrical marketplace. When the antiquarian and dramatist J. R. Planché and the theatrical manager Benjamin Webster presented *The Taming of the Shrew* (Haymarket, 1844) in pseudo-Elizabethan style—drop curtains, placards to indicate scene changes—*Bentley's Miscellany* denounced the novelty as anti-theatrical. If scenic 'practical economy' were taken to an extreme, the journal warned, the audience 'may be able to read a play at home, and fancy themselves at the theatre.'[5]

This largely unchallenged union of theatrical and visual culture—affirmed by the public through reading illustrated editions of Shakespeare's plays and looking at theatrical paintings, prints and engravings—made historical subjects particularly attractive. Performance was a potent agent of historical consciousness in the nineteenth century because it could realize the past with a sensuous immediacy far greater than that of literature, painting, or even photography. Indeed, the theatre's commitment to representing the past accurately was the very sign of its modernity. To prefer anachronistic productions of Shakespeare, the *Morning Post* argued at mid-century, was to prefer 'the semaphore to the electric telegraph' or 'the stage-coach to the locomotive.'[6] The measure of success for Shakespearean revivals became their ability to surpass the vivacity and precision of novels, paintings, museum collections and architectural restorations.

Archaeological eclecticism flourished throughout the century, and a lively range of historical places, personages and events was re-created for eager and expanding audiences. While Shakespeare's English and Roman chronicle plays were obvious choices, his tragedies, comedies and romances were all treated as opportunities for historical instruction, no matter how imprecise their locale or chronology. In the early 1840s Macready commissioned the antiquarian Charles Hamilton Smith to provide sketches of medieval and Renaissance costumes for possible productions of *The Merchant of Venice*, *Romeo and Juliet* and *The Two Gentlemen of Verona*. Kean, in 1857, played Prospero in *The Tempest* as a 'Polish necromancer of the 17th century'—an identity not licensed by Shakespeare—in a long black gown adorned with cabalistic characters.[7] And the Renaissance costumes for Irving's *The Merchant of Venice* (1879) were inspired by the paintings of Titian and Veronese.

For all its sensual delights, Victorian theatrical historicism was intimately tied to the middle class obsession with 'rational amusement': the education of mass audiences through popular culture. Far from sharing the critic G. H. Lewes' lament that a 'didactic mania' to 'teach, teach, teach' had overtaken the stage, actor-managers boasted that the theatre could become the 'engine for the direction of the public mind.'[8] In an 1881 lecture delivered at the Edinburgh Philosophical Institution, Irving declared that 'the stage is now seen to be an elevating instead of a lowering influence on national morality.'[9] Utilitarian views of performance became a commonplace in the Victorian era, justifying everything from 'temperance' melodramas to pedantic program essays on *Macbeth* and *Henry VIII*. Like many commonplaces it often appeared disingenuous. And thus William Bodham Donne, the long-serving Examiner of Plays, observed that the maxim 'the stage is a great moral engine for the education of the people' was but an empty platitude.[10]

Whether principled stance or tiresome cliché, the reformist agenda appealed strongly to actor-managers who mythologized themselves as gentlemanly proprietors of reputable places of amusement. Lavish revivals of Shakespeare were central to this self-promoting mythology. Through such productions, the theatrical profession acquired respectability as an agent of moral and social improvement. This upwardly mobile zeal was exemplified, above all, by the careers of Macready, Kean and Irving. So high-minded had the theatre become by the 1850s that Gladstone, who only twenty years earlier had condemned the stage as sinful, passed a leisurely afternoon touring the Princess's Theatre, engaging Kean in a 'long conversation on the question of Government subvention to the Drama.'[11]

The knighthood that Queen Victoria bestowed upon Irving in 1895 represented not a sudden escalation in the fortunes of the theatre but rather the culmination of a long campaign to legitimate a profession whose members had been branded 'vagabonds and rogues' little more than a century earlier. Shortly after receiving his knighthood Irving remarked that it 'removes, once for all, a certain shadow which has rested on our calling.'[12]

Gentlemanly proprietors of reputable places of amusement were begging to be ridiculed, and the burlesque backlash—the comic attack upon the pious pretensions of Shakespearean culture—was not long in coming. From its origins in the Restoration, theatrical burlesque had always been a powerful weapon in the critique of 'legitimate' Shakespearean culture by a seemingly 'illegitimate' popular culture. But never was it more powerful or more widespread than in the nineteenth century. From John Poole's *Hamlet Travestie* (1810) to W. S. Gilbert's *Rosencrantz and Guildenstern* (1891), Shakespeare burlesques in both Britain and the United States were a vibrant yet controversial form of popular performance: vibrant because of their exuberant humor; controversial because they imperiled Shakespeare's iconic status. Plays like Francis Talfourd's *Macbeth Somewhat Removed from the Text of Shakespeare* (1853) and William Brough's *Perdita; or, the Royal Milkmaid* (1856) critiqued what the *Westminster Review* termed the 'respectable humbug' of Bardolatry.[13]

In looking at the burlesque attack upon the pomposities of official Shakespearean culture, we can detect two main principles. First, that the object of satire is usually not Shakespeare's text as such but a specific performance. Thus, George L. Fox starred in *Hamlet Travestie* (Olympic Theatre, New York City, 1870) in order to parody the performance of Edwin Booth, 'the accepted Hamlet of the American Stage.'[14] Second, that the burlesque authorizes itself to speak on Shakespeare's behalf when the poet comes under attack (as burlesque writers saw it) from latter-day theatrical iconoclasts. Burlesques sought not merely to criticize contemporary Shakespearean performances but to correct them. The enormous appeal of theatrical parody bears impressive witness to the nineteenth century's profoundly equivocal commitment to Shakespeare and 'great Shakespeareans' alike.

Part of burlesque's appeal lay in its topicality, with scripts frequently rewritten to refer to the day's headlines. In Britain, topicality made the Lord Chamberlain and the Examiner of Plays nervous by opening the possibility of direct reference to political events, something state censors could not permit. They felt safer with Shakespeare, whose centuries-old texts, they believed, could hardly be pressed into the service of daily politics. But critics and audiences found no difficulty in advocating the political utility of Shakespeare in performance. As we might expect, those performances served the interests of both nationalism and imperialism. It would be mistaken, however, to suppose that Shakespearean performances only registered changes that occurred in some zone of reality from which the theatre was excluded. Rather, theatrical performance was one site where collective national and international identities were produced, negotiated and distributed. Victorian Shakespeare did not so much project a single coherent theory of identity as it became the playing field for the constitution of various historicist and nationalist perspectives by ideologically conscious spectators, who were themselves a large and socially diverse group.

In the United States, Shakespeare played a contradictory dual role in nineteenth-century cultural politics. As exemplified by the American tours of actors like Macready, Shakespeare could stand for a fealty toward British culture—an affirmation of monarchy and hereditary privilege—that for some observers was retrograde, neo-colonialist and downright treasonable. Shakespeare was the tyranny from which America had fought to be set free. Yet as symbolized by Edwin Forrest, Shakespeare could also stand for a proudly native approach to culture, one that repudiated British example but retained the genius of the individual artist who transcended mere nationality. Depending upon your position, Shakespeare was either the despised past or the liberated future. In 1833 James Fenimore Cooper hailed Shakespeare as 'the great author of America,' while four decades later Walt Whitman denounced the playwright as 'poisonous to the idea of pride and dignity of the common people, the life-blood of the democracy.'[15]

The transcripts of British Parliamentary committee hearings in 1832 and 1866 on theatrical licensing address at surprising length the contested issue of Shakespeare on the stage as a force for a shared national identity and social cohesion.[16] Indeed, one of the commonest arguments *against* the creation of a national theatre was that it already existed (in everything but name) through the prominence of Shakespeare in the principal play-houses of London's commercial West End. The Bard's prominence went through peaks and troughs—among the peaks were the Shakespeare Tercentenary of 1864 and the founding of the Stratford Memorial Theatre in 1879—but the national drama was regularly invoked as the expression of national identity. On the global stage, Shakespeare contributed to the extension of a British sphere of influence, whether through the overseas tours of British actors (the Huron tribe in Québec, to show their appreciation for the acting of Edmund Kean, made him an honorary tribal chieftain), foreign actors such as Tommaso Salvini and Adelaide Ristori who played Othello and Lady Macbeth in London (but never in English), or amateur performances in colonial India and Australia—all of which helped to create the first global network of Shakespeareans.

Behind the variety of events covered in the four chapters lies a set of shared methodological concerns. These concerns may be broadly termed 'post-positivist' or post-structural, given their commitment, not to performance reconstruction, but to the construction of meaning in and through performance. Moreover, the meaning of any performance, Shakespearean or otherwise, is made (and remade) retrospectively, through the evidence that survives it. Of course such evidence is not itself neutral or transparent but always the result of processes of selection and organization. Always partial, evidence only seems to point to the totality of a prior event. Far from being preserved in an archival 'state of nature,' evidence comes to the scholar and the student already saturated with meaning. Indeed it is precisely the interpretive saturation of evidence—the way in which meaning arises from it, rather than being imposed upon it—that demands rigorous archival research in the aftermath of 'theory.'

This volume represents the latest iteration of scholarly engagement with the documentary record of Shakespeare on the nineteenth-century stage. Let me close this introduction, then, with an overture toward the chapters that follow, arranged in broadly chronological order. W. C. Macready (1793–1873) was the first of the great Victorian actor-managers to make fidelity to Shakespeare a hallmark of his managerial career and to participate in the wider cult of Shakespeare worship. For all their distinctiveness, Samuel Phelps, Charles Kean, Henry Irving and Herbert Beerbohm Tree largely followed the precedent that Macready had set at the dawn of the Victorian era for what theatrical Bardolatry meant. In his chapter, Edward Ziter appropriately focuses on Macready's management of Covent Garden and Drury Lane in the years immediately prior to the 'emancipation' of Shakespeare through the Theatres Regulation Act of 1843. Ziter looks closely at the hallmarks of Macready's production style—textual restoration and historically correct *mise-en-scène*—and sets them within the context of his campaign to elevate the social standing of the theatre by aligning itself with Shakespeare's rising cultural authority. It was Macready's missionary zeal to rescue the theatre from the immemorial charge of licentiousness (a charge given renewed credibility in light of Edmund Kean's sexual scandals) that accounts for the actor-manager's deliberate attempt to give his Shakespearean productions—and, indeed, his own personal devotion to the playwright—a high degree of prominence.

Through readings of the public events of high Bardolatry—testimonial dinners, ceremonies of gift-giving, speeches, and the newspaper reports that trailed all such events—Ziter makes a compelling case for Macready's career as a pivotal instance of the Victorian theatre's reverence toward Shakespeare, one that anticipated the earnestness of Charles Kean and the celebrity-status of Henry Irving. The chapter concludes with a suggestive account of the cultural politics of the Astor Place Riot, in which the appearance of rival British and American tragedians—Macready and Edwin Forrest—in the role of Macbeth at two New York theatres led to deadly violence in the streets.

Which brings us to the United States. In his chapter on Edwin Booth, the reigning Hamlet of mid-nineteenth-century America, Gary Jay Williams begins by reminding us that the most common reaction to the actor's performance was an astonished belief that 'Booth is Hamlet' and 'Hamlet is Booth.' Using the process of 'conceptual blending,' as it has been developed in cognitive studies, Williams treats this singular response of theatergoers as manifesting the 'profoundly temporal, culturally contingent nature of the theatre' (p. 60). Through rich contextualization and deep engagement with contemporary sources, the chapter situates Booth's Hamlet at the crossroads of two phenomena: the sufferings of the United States during and immediately after the Civil War and the private ongoing sufferings of Booth himself. Williams carefully exposes the dense interlacing between the Civil War, the assassination of Lincoln by Edwin Booth's younger brother, the actor's domestic tragedies and sorrows (for him, the assassination was both a public and a private matter), his legendary performance as Hamlet, and the conscious strategy of his handlers and publicists to frame how the public would interpret that performance.

In a way that recalls the ambivalence or detachment of Hamlet at the beginning of the play, Booth appears less as the engineer of that strategy than as the field of action over which it unfolded. This is not to deny Booth agency, but rather to highlight the contrast between him and, for example, Macready and Irving. Unlike those actor-managers, Booth was much less invested in the Shakespeare trade. And yet the connection between him and Shakespeare resonated far beyond the theatre, touching the political divisions that had torn the nation asunder. By highlighting this connection, Williams challenges the dominant formalist interpretation of Booth, as exemplified in the performance reconstruction scholarship of

Charles Shattuck. But rather than simply disavowing the methods of scholars from earlier generations, Williams respectfully engages with them, and thus enables his chapter—dedicated to Shattuck's memory—to become a salutary instance of the discipline reflecting upon itself in order to clarify how and why scholarship on Shakespeare in performance changes over time.

Like Booth, the actress Ellen Terry (1847–1928) identified Shakespeare with private life. But unlike the American actor, she knowingly gave that private identification a public visibility. Unusually for an actress of the period, Terry was a prolific author, whose principal works were the autobiographical *The Story of My Life* (1908) and the posthumously published *Four Lectures on Shakespeare* (1932). A dedicated letter writer, she engaged in a lengthy and spirited correspondence with George Bernard Shaw. Departing from traditional narrative biography, and moving towards cultural biography, Gail Marshall uncovers in Terry's writings evidence of how the actress deliberately and strategically wove Shakespeare into the fabric of her life and public self-image. In fashioning her own legacy, in declaring how posterity should remember her, Terry consciously and repeatedly invoked Shakespeare.

Although feminist scholarship in recent years has helped greatly to revise our understanding of Victorian theatre and drama, it has until very recently intersected much less with the history of Shakespeare in performance, no doubt because of the deeply patriarchal structure of Victorian theatrical management and production and a reluctance among scholars to duplicate the hagiographic tendencies of theatrical biographies, often the main source of information on Victorian actresses. Marshall's chapter, which is in productive dialogue with her monograph *Shakespeare and Victorian Women* (2009), represents a welcome extension of feminist cultural history to Victorian Shakespeare. (Volume 8 in this series, which includes chapters on the actresses Fanny Kemble and Charlotte Cushman, also furthers this scholarly agenda.)

In a deft blend of chronological and thematic approaches, Marshall identifies three key moments in Terry's relationship to Shakespeare. When recalling the early years of her career, especially when living in the shadow of her elder sister Kate, also an actress, Terry depicted herself as a young woman 'at home' with Shakespeare. In so doing she drew upon the enormous emotional power of the Victorian bourgeois cult of domesticity—a cult of which Terry was not always a paid-up member, given the somewhat bohemian nature of her private life. The actress's twenty-year partnership with Henry Irving at the Lyceum placed her at the absolute pinnacle of fame, giving her an unrivaled celebrity. The key ingredient of Terry's wide appeal was her charm as a Shakespearean heroine. Yet as Marshall argues, the actress understood (in a way that her admirers, particularly male, somehow never did) that the rhetoric of charm encompassed a dangerous duality: both an unselfconscious childlike appeal *and* the knowingness of the charmer who casts a spell over all those who draw near. Terry's Portia was charming while her Lady Macbeth was a charmer—and vice-versa. So, too, would her Rosalind have been, if Irving had given her chance to play that longed-for role. In the final stage of her career, and even though she appeared in plays by Shaw and Henrik Ibsen, Terry was most highly acclaimed as a Shakespearean, not least through her many public lectures and dramatic readings. The relationship between Shakespeare and Ellen Terry was truly symbiotic, as Marshall amply demonstrates. Terry's fame and her charm gave Shakespeare a popular appeal hitherto unattained, while the dramatist's cultural authority became the means for the actress's canny project of self-fashioning.

In the closing decades of the Victorian era Terry's name was inseparable from that of Henry Irving (1838–1905), her theatrical leading man, longtime actor-manager of the Lyceum Theatre, and the first actor to be knighted. Like Terry, Irving is one of the few theatrical personalities of the nineteenth century whose reputation has survived into the twenty-first. Beyond question what secured Irving's lasting fame was his series of grand Shakespearean revivals—thirteen in all—produced at the Lyceum between 1878 (when he became manager) and 1902 (when, after financial difficulties, the theatre was sold). But that alone does not account for his place in the story of Shakespeare's theatrical afterlife. As I explain, what set Henry Irving apart from other actor-managers of the Victorian era were a distinctive aesthetic in producing Shakespeare and a distinctive outlook in appropriating Shakespeare.

The distinctiveness of Irving's theatrical aesthetic was his conviction that he was a total artist of the theatre in a way that no one else could be. Every facet of every Lyceum production—acting, scenery, costume, lighting and music—would be stamped with his individuality and his alone. Irving saw himself not as Shakespeare's indentured servant, but more the other way around. The implications of that attitude were significant. As I argue, Irving's commitment to the absolute autonomy of art helped to usher Shakespeare into the modernist age, as personified in the young director-designer Edward Gordon Craig, who was Ellen Terry's son and Irving's protégé.

Irving embraced the global cult of Shakespeare worship to an extent unmatched then or since. His ardent pursuit of the Bard outside the theatre and across the Atlantic Ocean suggests desires that reach far beyond theatrical success. Going beyond a stage-centered account, and encompassing Irving's speeches, published essays and North American tours, I expose how the actor used Shakespeare's cultural prestige to transform himself into a public intellectual for the Victorian age—a project of self-fashioning that looks back to Macready and invites comparison (and contrast) with Ellen Terry. Without question, Shakespeare found in Henry Irving a staunch defender and dutiful acolyte. But Irving must have felt that he had won the toss. Because he, the lad from a Somerset village, became the spokesman for a brand of cultural imperialism whose image was the Warwickshire lad.

Each chapter in this volume engages with conventional sources—some familiar, some fresh—but not always in conventional ways. Indeed, parts of the story of Shakespeare's theatrical afterlife that have not usually been deemed significant—Terry's sibling rivalry, Irving's lengthy American tours, Macready's ceremonial dinners, Booth's private sorrows—suddenly take on a deeper resonance. That is not because no one in the past knew anything about these episodes but because Shakespeareans today are directing new questions at them. That is another way of saying that the authors of the chapters in this volume recognize that they have constructed the object of their own inquiry by virtue of the questions that they asked and the assumptions and theoretical biases that shaped those questions in the first place. Such a perspective necessarily calls into question the very notion of a 'great' Shakespearean. All the contributors to this volume agree that Shakespearean greatness, far from being the unfolding through time of a pre-ordained master narrative, must instead be understood, if not ironically, then certainly as the product of local and topical engagements involving artists, audience and critics. How those engagements revolved around four major theatrical personalities of the nineteenth century is the subject of the rest of this volume.

Chapter 1

W.C. Macready

Edward Ziter

I have only been the officiating priest at the shrine of our country's greatest genius (immense cheers)*; and, indeed, I can honestly take credit for little more than true devotion, zeal and good intention . . .*

—*William Charles Macready, reported in* The Examiner, *July 28, 1839*

When William Charles Macready described himself as an 'officiating priest' in his address at an 1839 dinner celebrating his management of Covent Garden Theatre, brief though it was, there was no need to name the god he served. From the outset of his reluctant management, Macready had described his endeavor as a sacrifice to the immortal Shakespeare. Much of the press surrounding his management, whether libels or panegyrics—and no paper published more panegyrics to Macready than the *Examiner*—centered on whether Macready was a true priest or a charlatan. By 1843, when he had completed his second and last stint as manager of a London patent theatre, there was little need for debate. Macready had been consecrated as the high priest of the Shakespeare religion. The period witnessed a jump not only in Macready's status and reputation, but the growth and dissemination of Shakespeare idolatry and the emergence of a new appreciation of the fitness of Shakespeare's plays for performance—or rather the stage's fitness for Shakespeare. These popular understandings of player and playwright were mutually constructed; Macready reinvented both himself and British theatre through his contributions to the reinvention of Shakespeare.

In this chapter I wish to examine this process of mutual construction during the period framed by Macready's management of the patent theatres, roughly 1837 to 1843. I will conclude by examining the consolidation of Macready's image during his farewell engagement at the Haymarket from October 1850 to February 1851, during which time he was active in efforts to raise funds for the purchase of Shakespeare's birthplace. I will examine how Macready's management was represented in reviews and popular iconography, lauded through gifts of plate and statuary, and celebrated in massive public dinners. Macready branded himself the principal defender of Shakespeare against an increasingly crass entertainment industry. This project took on a particularly nationalistic tenor during his final years on stage, which followed the bloody Astor Place Riot (1849) in New York City when partisans of the American actor, Edwin Forrest, attempted to disrupt Macready's performance of *Macbeth.*

Macready was widely regarded as England's principal tragedian from Edmund Kean's death in 1833 until retirement in 1851. Nonetheless, Macready famously abhorred his profession and entered it with great reluctance by his own account. He was born in 1793 and educated at Rugby. In 1809 the financial difficulties of his father, a provincial theatre manager, required the sixteen-year-old to leave school and help manage the theatre. So began what Macready would later describe as 'a descent from that equality in which I had felt myself to stand with those of family and fortune whom our education had made companions.'[1] Macready's professional acting debut came a year and a half later, on June 9th 1810, when he performed Romeo in Birmingham. Six years of provincial performing followed before Macready's London debut as Orestes in *The Distressed Mother* at Covent Garden.[2] He joined the Drury Lane company in 1824, where he alternated leading roles with Edmund Kean. That same year he married Catherine Atkins. His increasing fame led to his first American tour in 1826, followed by tours in 1843 and 1848. The last tour ended with the infamous Astor Place Riot.

His greatest fame came from his management of London's two patent theatres: Covent Garden (1837–39) and Drury Lane (1841–43). These managements were marked by lavish Shakespeare productions that restored much of Shakespeare's text and removed interpolations. During this time, Macready produced and appeared in seventeen of Shakespeare's plays: *The Winter's Tale, Hamlet, Othello, Macbeth, King Henry V, King Lear, Julius Caesar, Coriolanus, Romeo and Juliet, As You Like It, Henry VIII, Cymbeline, The Tempest, The Merchant of Venice, The Two Gentlemen of Verona, King John* and *Much Ado About Nothing.* In addition to his 'defense' of Shakespeare, Macready championed the work of several contemporary playwrights, most notably James Sheridan Knowles and Edward Bulwer-Lytton. He also staged the first performances of Byron's *Sardanapalus* (Drury Lane 1833), *Werner* (Covent Garden 1837), *The Two Foscari* (Covent Garden 1838) and *Marino Faliero* (Drury Lane 1842). He died in 1873 at the age of eighty.

Whether acting in Shakespeare or contemporary verse drama, Macready invariably positioned his performances as attempts to restore the dignity of a debased national stage. He failed, but it was a false project to begin with. Arguably, British theatre had been an elite form only during the brief period of the Restoration and it had never been respectable. (It would take the negative examples of music hall, film and—finally—television, combined with national subsidies and corporate giving, to transform theatre into a truly elite art, one attracting a coterie rather than a mass audience.) However, Macready's failure in no way diminishes the enormity of the cultural shift in which he participated. He successfully responded to Romantic era objections to theatricality, situating stage representation as a necessary complement to—rather than a distraction from—dramatic poetry. His stage restorations inspired the publication of popular and purer editions of Shakespeare, such as the pictorial editions of Charles Knight (a member of Macready's circle). Even if Macready could not stem the tide of animal plays and melodrama, he did help to make the theatre an appropriate site of Victorian leisure. Described by his contemporaries as the 'Eminent Tragedian' and the 'Last of the Romans,' Macready successfully played the role of the gentleman and through this performance the theatre became a gentleman's resort—or rather, 'the shrine of our country's greatest genius.'

Of course Shakespeare's divinity had been proposed as early as 1769 when David Garrick, in his Shakespeare Jubilee, had referred to the poet, redirecting and paraphrasing Juliet's words, as 'the god of our idolatry.' Like his contemporaries, Garrick performed his own adaptations of Shakespeare, as well as those by Nahum Tate and Colley Cibber, rather than the original plays. Yet by Macready's own account, looking from the vantage of his 1851 farewell benefit, the principal success of his management of the patent houses had been 'assurances that the corrupt editions and unseemly presentations of past days will never be restored, but that the purity of the great poet's text will henceforth be held on our English Stage in the reverence it should command.'[3]

Macready could rightly claim responsibility for the stage's new reverence for Shakespeare. As manager of Covent Garden and Drury Lane he performed the 'original' Shakespearean texts, replacing Tate's *King Lear* (absent from the stage throughout the period of George IV's insanity), Shadwell's operatic version of *The Tempest*, John Philip Kemble's altered *Julius Caesar*, and the various acting versions of *As You Like It*. His 1821 production of *Richard III* restored Margaret, Hastings, and Clarence (absent from Cibber) and much of Shakespeare's text, though Richard did not remain in Macready's repertoire. Macready returned *Coriolanus* to the repertoire, a play that had been performed intermittently since the retirement in 1817 of John Philip Kemble, the last actor to successfully play the role.[4] Macready consistently asserted that his use of scenic spectacle was in service to the playwright's intent. During his management, fidelity became an important measure of Shakespeare production. The original text was restored to an unprecedented degree, and the actor labored to embody the perfection formed in the mind of the genius playwright. Bardolatry had entered a new phase.

Bardolatry and the Actor's Status at Mid Century

Macready surpassed past actors in the vehemence of his idolatry and in his assertion that Shakespeare's plays were perfect for production as written (albeit with some pruning). In these respects, he shared much with the critic and historian Thomas Carlyle, who accorded Shakespeare's work messianic power and described Shakespeare as a 'hero' and a 'speaker,' whose 'great soul had to crush itself into that [the Globe playhouse] and no other mold.'[5] As such, Macready and Carlyle stand as extensions of Romantic era bardolatry even as they contradict the Romantic fascination with a personalized Shakespeare whose works thwart public performance. In 1840, squarely between Macready's two periods of management, Carlyle delivered six lectures to London audiences entitled 'On Heroes, Hero Worship and the Heroic in History.' The third lecture—on the hero as poet—asserted that all of Europe was coming to the conclusion that Shakespeare was 'the chief of all Poets'. As such he was also a prophet, for poet and prophet 'have penetrated both of them into the sacred mystery of the Universe.'[6] Revealing the preacher he might have become had he not lost his faith during his studies at the University of Edinburgh, Carlyle declaimed:

> But call it worship, call it what you will, is it not a right glorious thing, and set of things, this that Shakespeare has brought us? For myself, I feel that there is actually a kind of sacredness in the fact of such a man being sent into this Earth. Is he not an eye to us all; a blessed heaven-sent Bringer of Light?[7]

In implicitly likening Shakespeare to Christ, Carlyle wrested Shakespeare from the closet making him simultaneously a man of the world and otherworldly. Shakespeare's voice was necessarily shaped by the contours of the

Globe theatre, and therein lay his immortality, as a 'speaker or singer' like Aeschylus and Homer before him.[8] While Carlyle never discussed theatrical performance, it is clear that his Shakespeare demanded a stage no less than Napoleon or Cromwell—men who, in the historian's mind, commanded not through the content of their words but through delivery and actions.[9]

Carlyle was a great fan of Macready's acting, and the two developed a friendship at the same time that the historian developed his ideas on heroes and hero worship. Carlyle was a member of Macready's tight intellectual circle, which included Robert Browning, Charles Dickens, John Forster and Bulwer-Lytton. During his management of Covent Garden Macready provided complimentary tickets to leading figures in literature, art and science, and included Carlyle on that list. Carlyle recorded the impression that Macready's performance made on him during the actor-manager's first season at Covent Garden in a thank-you note dated October 12th 1837. In that note, Carlyle marveled at 'a touch of wild sincerity' in Macready's performances and described them as 'extremely striking.' The performances renewed Carlyle's respect for English drama and for the possibilities for performance suggested by Macready's restoration project: 'I wondered at the Drama, wondered at your Herculean task.'[10] In another letter, Carlyle noted that he attended Macready's Shakespeare productions about once a week.[11] Carlyle's likening of poet and prophet came after his immersion in the new theatrical culture that Macready had forged.

The press, searching for new superlatives with which to describe Macready's Shakespeare restorations, echoed Carlyle's suggestion that the bard might be divine. Discussing the excitement in the audience on the opening night of Macready's 1841 management of Drury Lane, the *Era* thrilled that Macready had driven the moneychangers from the temple:

> There was not one among the excited thousands that thronged the walls of 'Old Drury' on Monday night, that did not vividly feel that the master mind had evoked and banished the old obscenities—that a new altar had been raised, and the era of a new worship had commenced. The offerings of abominations will be no longer seen where the Muses had ministered. The pure of mind, and the poetic of heart, may now listen uncontaminated and fearless to the prophetic revealings—for the poet is the true prophet . . .[12]

While the enthusiasm might seem excessive to the modern reader, it is important to note how disheartening it was for British theatregoers that the previous manager of England's unofficial national theatre had been forced to resort to musical concerts before going bankrupt; that the manager before that had been caught absconding with the house receipts before being dragged back to England to stand trial; that by 1839 Covent Garden had resorted to displaying tightrope dancers and lion-tamers; and that the presence of prostitutes at both patent theatres prevented attendance by many respectable people. In such a context, Shakespeare may have seemed as removed from popular entertainment as a religious prophet, and Macready's sanctifying restoration of Shakespeare was indeed akin to raising an altar on sullied ground.

While the veneration of Shakespeare articulated by Carlyle, Macready, and the popular press culminated a process that had been substantially furthered by Romantic critics, the idea that words (whether those of Shakespeare or Cromwell) gained their force through performance directly contradicted much Romantic thought. Charles Lamb provided the most famous Romantic anti-theatrical critique when he wrote in 1811 that 'the plays of Shakespeare are less calculated for performance on a stage than those of almost any other dramatist whatever.'[13] For Lamb, Shakespeare's words are not about the display of passions but a means of tracing 'the inner structure and workings of mind in a character.'[14] As pure abstraction, this tracing resists embodiment. Performance might excite but:

> When the novelty is past, we find to our cost that, instead of realising an idea, we have only materialised and brought down a fine vision to the standard of flesh and blood. We have let go a dream, in quest of an unattainable substance.[15]

Far from serving Shakespeare, restoring his texts to the stage would only further degrade the bard and harm the public. Readers would be denied 'that delightful sensation of freshness' that one encounters when turning to 'those plays of Shakespeare which have escaped being performed, and to those passages in the acting plays of the same writer which have happily been left out in the performance.'[16]

Even a theatrephile like William Hazlitt felt ambivalent when watching Shakespeare's plays in performance, especially *Hamlet.* For Hazlitt, the character was less a figure in a play whose existence might be imagined than an almost mystical manifestation of a universal mind. In *Characters of Shakespear's Plays* (1817) he explained that:

> Hamlet is a name; his speeches and sayings but the idle coinage of the poet's brain. What then, are they not real? They are as real as our own thoughts. Their reality is in the reader's mind. It is *we* who are Hamlet.[17]

Not surprisingly then, Hazlitt concluded that 'we do not like to see our author's plays acted, and least of all, Hamlet' and that 'no play suffers so much in being transferred to the stage.'[18] The plays of 'our' Shakespeare exist only as reverberations of our memories and experiences, and the character Hamlet in particular is as familiar and as hard to describe 'as our own faces.'[19] Hazlitt ended by critiquing the two major Hamlets of the Romantic period, John Philip Kemble and Edmund Kean, both of whom, in his estimation, failed to become the universal reader.

In such criticism, the actor is an interloper robbing Shakespeare of his power and encroaching on his fame. Lamb's essay begins with his 'scandalized' discovery that a monument to Garrick stands in Westminster Abbey, introducing 'theatrical airs and gestures into a place set apart to remind us of the saddest realities.'[20] (In Henry Webber's sculpture, Garrick holds aside stage curtains, as if taking a bow. Below him are seated the figures of Tragedy and Comedy.) Lamb is particularly aghast to discover that inscribed under this 'harlequin figure' are lines that rate Garrick's performances as an act of creation comparable to Shakespeare's writing. In Lamb's mind, this is like rating a bookseller gifted at reciting 'Paradise Lost' as Milton's equal.[21] Both clown and shopkeeper are equally distant from the author. In this respect Lamb was generous; many of his contemporaries and most of Macready's placed actors well below shopkeepers on the social ladder.

The low social position of his profession was a constant irritant to Macready and he labored to elevate the actor to the status of a gentleman. Macready's diaries and *Reminiscences* are filled with musings on the indignities he suffered as a result. He complained of learning 'that an ignorant officer could refuse satisfaction of a gentleman on the ground that his appellant was a player,' leaving the reader to speculate on the circumstances that prompted the observation.[22] More mundanely, Macready bristled at a landlady in Bath who, in 1835, noted that she had not been informed of her lodger's less than respectable occupation:

> My blood rose at this impertinence, and I was foolish enough to be so angry as to observe that there was no person in Bath, whether titled or not, that could claim a higher character and that I would relieve her of the inconvenience of such an intimate.[23]

His indignity at social prejudice against actors was matched by his own disdain for his fellow thespians. He frequently complained of the ungentlemanly behavior of politicians and lords, but he saved his worst invectives for actors. He refused to fraternize with them, and on reading the obituary of

Charles Mathews, Macready simply noted in his diary that the comedian was 'not so dishonourable as [the tragedian and theatre manager Charles] Kemble, nor so penurious as [the comedian John] Liston, but he was not a high-souled man, nor what I distinguish as a gentleman.'[24] When informed by his prompter at Covent Garden that the actors in his company, who risked part of their salaries to join Macready in his venture, also hoped to share in any potential surplus, the actor-manager fumed: 'I see the impracticability of the attempt to raise them from the condition of serfs; they have not the nobleness to be really free; they will not even with example make a sacrifice to be so.'[25] In Macready's mind, both tradition and practice barred actors from the ranks of gentlemen and only through considerable effort would he avoid the taint of his profession. As he states simply at the start of his *Reminiscences*: 'In other callings the profession confers dignity on the initiated; on the stage the player must contribute respect to the exercise of his art.'[26]

Service to Shakespeare was a principal means by which Macready gained gentlemanly status, but it was undoubtedly a sincere service. His diaries recount constant study and struggle to understand fully his Shakespearean roles and how those roles functioned within the play. He was a prominent member of the Shakespeare Society from its founding in 1840. A year earlier, he was feted by the Shakespeare Club (which preceded the Society) and there he expressed his respect for all who honored the playwright. At that meeting, after Dickens toasted him, the actor responded with his characteristic assertion that all praise should be reserved for Shakespeare. Macready wrote in his diary for March 30th 1839:

> In reply I said, 'That in expressing the peculiar gratification of such a compliment from a society met to do honour to Shakespeare, I disclaimed all credit beyond what was due for faithful service to him, transferring from the priest to the object of their adoration the honour they offered. I had no claim for originating or creating; I had merely removed and restored to its sublime simplicity the text of Shakespeare.'[27]

If Lamb's invective against acting Shakespeare's plays was inspired by the scandalous idea that an actor could join that poet's ranks, then Macready seemed intent on deflecting similar critiques. He did not create, he asserted, but simply restored a sublime simplicity (a somewhat tenuous argument, we shall see, given his lavish productions). To give the actor greater praise would be to make a priest into a false god. The trope of Shakespearean actor as priest was one that he would repeat throughout his career.

Macready was considerably less circumspect in his response to Romantic era critics of Shakespeare. His diary entry for August 20th 1833 ends:

> Read the last act of *Anthony and Cleopatra*, and Hazlitt's observations on that play and *Lear*. What conceited trash that man has thought to pass upon the public, and how willing many of them receive the counterfeit as sterling.[28]

While one can only guess at the precise nature of Macready's objection, it is worth noting that Hazlitt concluded his analysis of Lear in *Characters of Shakespear's Plays* with an extended quotation from Lamb that begins 'The Lear of Shakespeare cannot be acted.' The problem, as Lamb explained, was that in reading the play we can grasp the greatness of Lear but that on stage 'we see nothing but corporal infirmities and weakness.' When we read, 'we see not Lear, but we are Lear.' Macready devoted his career to disproving the assertion that spectacle interrupted sympathetic engagement with the mind of the character. Lamb (via Hazlitt) asserted that: 'the contemptible machinery with which they mimic the storm which he goes out in, is not more inadequate to represent the horrors of the real elements than any actor be to represent Lear.'[29] Macready responded with better machinery and better actors.

Macready's Acting Style

It is commonly asserted among theatre historians that Macready was responsible for instilling a heightened degree of professionalism among nineteenth-century actors, requiring that his fellow performers act during rehearsals (rather than 'saving it for performance'); that they be well acquainted with his planned stage business; and that they group themselves in such a way as to give maximum effect to that stage business. Macready himself was known for relentlessly studying the plays in which he performed and imagining a role as a coherent and evolving character rather than as a sequence of 'points'. He demanded historically accurate scene painting and costuming, and—as noted—restored Shakespeare's own words to a stage long dominated by adaptations. Macready's detractors asserted that he was effective only in modern plays, and it is true that he was particularly lauded for his performances in Bulwer-Lytton's *Richelieu* and Knowles' *Virginius*, that he championed the work of Thomas Noon Talfourd, Robert Browning, Knowles, and Bulwer-Lytton, and that he offered the first productions of four plays by Byron. Yet the idea that he was successful only in Romantic drama is belied by the tremendous enthusiasm that met his frequent and varied Shakespeare revivals. During his lifetime, one of his former actors, George Vandenhoff, penned a description that modern commentators have largely repeated: 'Macready's style was an amalgam of John Kemble and Edmund Kean. He tried to blend the classic art of the one with the impulsive intensity of the other.'[30]

Theatre historian Alan Downer credited Macready with introducing 'the domestic style of acting' to England.[31] There was indeed a touch of the Victorian gentleman in all Macready's creations. To his critics, such choices stood out as strange idiosyncrasies or diminished a play's tragic potential. Reviewing Macready in the 1816 revival of Robert Jephson's verse drama *Julia; or, The Italian Lover*, Hazlitt complained that: 'Mr. Macready sometimes, to express uneasiness and agitation composes his cravat, as he would in a drawing-room. This is, we think, neither graceful nor natural in extraordinary situations.'[32] The most notorious of these domestic touches came on Hamlet's line 'I must be idle,' just before the play-within-the-play, when Macready would 'wave his handkerchief fantastically, and assume an air of exaggerated jauntiness.'[33] It was in response to this bit of stage business that Edwin Forrest famously hissed his British rival. A related device was the 'Macready pause,' which some modern historians attribute to a desire to render blank verse more conversational.[34]

While these devices can all be described as domestications of tragedy, they can also be seen as creating opportunities for the actor to represent thought. In this respect, Macready's acting stems from a central Romantic assumption: the greatest drama depicts a mind in action. (Four decades later, Henry Irving would strive for an identical effect with Hamlet.) The same quality was ascribed to Macready's leading lady, Helena Faucit. Henry Morley complained that as Imogen in *Cymbeline*, Faucit was too careful 'to make every gesture an embodiment of thought.'[35] This effort to depict the evolving processes of thought also accounts for Vandenhoff's sardonic reference to Macready's 'extra-syllabification of utterance.'[36] By drawing out phrases, Macready expressed the temporality of thought. In other words, Macready inserted opportunities to represent externally the inner life of his characters.

Macready's diaries present a running commentary on his success or failure at becoming absorbed by his characters, which he considered central to great acting. He complains of a 'want of abstraction' in his soliloquies as Iago. After rehearsing Hamlet he found himself speaking and acting 'with an abandonment and a reality that surprise me' and speculated that such 'power of identification' is most readily available to those who spent their earliest years on the stage. On still another occasion he contrasts a failed and a successful performance—'I was labouring to play Macbeth; on Monday I *was* Macbeth.'[37] It was said that before entering as Shylock, he would work himself into an actual rage, cursing *sotto voce* and violently shaking a ladder affixed to a backstage wall.[38]

Such deep identification with his characters helps to account for the intense and extemporaneous choices that sometimes enlivened the performances of an actor known to rehearse his roles fanatically, at least by the standards of the day. Faucit recounts such a moment in her oft-cited description of the first time she appeared as Hermione opposite Macready's Leontes in the celebrated revival of *The Winter's Tale* which opened the 1837 Covent Garden season. In the statue scene, the actress explains, Macready exhibited an 'uncontrollable rapture' for which she 'was not, and could not be' prepared. She describes the actor's complete identification with his character; at her approach, he was 'absorbed in wonder.' On touching her and with the cry that accompanied his line 'Oh, she's warm!', Macready 'was Leontes's very self.' As the statue come to life, Faucit wore a veil. It unexpectedly fell and her hair, which came unbound and fell to her shoulders, was 'reverently kissed and caressed.' Overwhelmed by the unexpected intensity, Faucit cried out hysericallyand Macready momentarily came out of character, whispering to calm her. Faucit explains: 'It was the finest burst of passionate, speechless emotion I ever saw, or could have conceived.' Even later, when she was better prepared for his reactions, the actress felt that 'the intensity of Mr. Macready's passion was so real, that I never could help being moved by it, and feeling much exhausted afterwards.'[39] Macready's long diary entry on that busy opening night includes only one line on his performance: 'Acted Leontes artist-like but not, until the last act, very effectively.'[40]

In appearing to lose himself in the role, to be 'Leontes's very self,' Macready allowed his spectators to share in the character's rapid and harrowing emotional changes. When audiences are moved by the intensity of a passion (to paraphrase Faucit) rather than disturbed by a display, they avoid the pitfall Lamb ascribed to theatre; they avoid being left outside to cringe before Lear's agedness. Macready's empathic acting allowed spectators to identify with an internal passion. Similarly, Macready's efforts to display the thought that produces speech enabled spectators to trace the invisible workings of the mind and share in the 'coinage of the poet's brain.' This quality of absorption, pioneered by Siddons and furthered by subsequent actors like Macready, facilitated the imaginative engagement with the mind of the character and, through character, the author. For such an overdetermined author as Shakespeare, at his return to a stage debased by animal acts and melodrama, it is not surprising that Macready's revivals became the object of great debate.

Bunn versus Macready

In some ways Macready was pushed into the role as Shakespeare's defender by his deep disdain for the journalist-turned-theatre manager Alfred Bunn. Bunn gained control of both Covent Garden and Drury Lane from 1833 to 1835, retaining control of the latter until 1839. (He again managed Drury Lane from 1843 to 1850, during which time he went bankrupt.) One of his few defenders in the theatre industry, the antiquarian and playwright J. R. Planché, recorded that

> . . . in health and prosperity [Bunn] was imperious and occasionally unjust, and sadly addicted to that common fault of theatrical managers, the using up of his performers. What natural talent he possessed was uncultivated; his language and manners were coarse, and his taste deplorable. His management was sheer gambling of the most reckless description, in no one instance that I can remember terminating prosperously, whatever might have been the success of certain productions in the course of it.[41]

He was precisely the sort of ungentlemanly figure to infuriate Macready, who performed under his management at Drury Lane from 1833 to 1836. Bunn's strategy was to cater to the public appetite for spectacle while retaining enough legitimate drama to placate his critics. This was nothing new. When Macready testified before Bulwer-Lytton's parliamentary Select Committee on Dramatic Literature in 1832 he acknowledged that during the two years of his then current engagement at Drury Lane, *Macbeth* had been given six times, *Richard III* five times, and *Hamlet* but once.[42] However, Bunn's constant 'puffing' of the bills and his questionable tactics at attracting a house (as when he falsely announced that a production of Byron's *Sardanapalus* would feature Charlotte Mardyn, a former actress widely thought to have been the poet's lover) deeply offended Macready, and he grew absolutely irate when the manager pressed him into roles he disdained.

The dispute came to a head in 1836 when Bunn announced in the bills that on April 29th Macready would appear in the first half of Cibber's *Richard III* (acts one through three), followed by two operatic spectacles: the first act of *Chevy Chase* and *The Jewess.* Macready deemed this a gross affront to his dignity as an actor, but ultimately agreed to perform rather than forfeit his salary. After exiting the stage on the 29th, and still in costume, Macready passed Bunn's office and impulsively burst in and attacked the manager—a gross violation of the actor's own insistence on gentlemanly behavior. News of the fight quickly circulated. Rather than hindering his career, the event seems to have propelled Macready forward, allowing him to negotiate a favorable contract for the remainder of the season. Macready was aware that his star was rising, and effectively named his terms for this engagement. Ironically, Macready benefited from loutish behavior far exceeding that which he condemned in other actors. While his diaries initially record great self-reproach, he seems to have gotten over his guilt quickly. One senses that the tragedian protested too much when he recorded that on refusing an earlier Covent Garden offer, he explained that 'he did not wish to trade upon, or raise my terms on, this unfortunate occurrence, but . . .'[43]

Immediately after the fight, however, Macready was convinced that it had permanently destroyed his reputation. He recounted that he was sickened to see, on May 1st, that the placards of the *Age* carried the announcement: 'Great Fight. B—nn and M—y.' However, the papers were generally sympathetic to Macready. The *Morning Chronicle* began its account of the event by noting Bunn's insistence that Macready appear in an afterpiece, and that 'last night Mr. B got up *the first three acts of Richard the Third.* Mr. M. was bound by his contract to [act] Richard, although the very best parts of the character are contained in the fourth and fifth. Mr. M was, of course annoyed at this . . .'[44] The most partisan account, echoed in regional newspapers, appeared in *Jackson's Oxford Journal,* which described Bunn's actions as an insult to both Macready and Shakespeare:

> There has been a terrible squabble between the Lessee of Drury Lane and Macready, in consequence of the former degrading latter in his profession—these managers are as imperious as an Autocrat, and pay little regard to feelings of men of talent and education as most arbitrary despot—Macready had submitted to repeated professional indignities, but 'curtailing *Richard* of his fair proportions' and mutilating Shakespeare by playing only the three first acts was too much for *human nature,* and

> after opprobrious epithets of 'scoundrel' and 'rascal' to *great* Lessee, he gave the *little* man a sound licking.[45]

As one would suspect, Macready's close friend at the *Examiner*, John Forster, rushed to his defense. On May 1st, the *Examiner* cast the fight as the product of Bunn's sustained attack on the drama generally and Macready personally. The article began by alluding to the partially performed *Richard III* as the 'singular annoyance practiced against Mr. Macready by the manager of Drury Lane,' and announced that it was apparently only the most recent of Bunn's transgressions, all intended to goad Macready into breaking his contract with Drury Lane:

> It would appear that Mr. Macready has been struggling during the entire season with attempted insults and injuries of a more serious description than this, and that during the last three weeks especially, every possible means have been resorted to that could have a tendency to drive him out of the theatre.[46]

The article goes on to refer to the attack as an 'intemperate personal chastisement of Mr. Bunn.' According to Forster, the truncated Shakespeare production was just the most recent sortie in an ongoing campaign to drive Drury Lane's leading Shakespearean actor out of the national theatre.

In the battle for popular opinion, Macready the esteemed actor held a distinct advantage against Bunn the despotic profit-hungry manager. However, as an actor, Macready was no freer from taint than his adversary. The fact that he had attacked Bunn dressed as the villainous Richard III (including a hump on his back and a lump on his leg, according to court records[47]) cut both ways. His costume suggested the attack was unpremeditated and associated the actor with the mutilated work of the national poet, but at the cost of likening Macready to a known assassin. At least that is how one illustrator saw matters. One print has Macready in costume striking a corpulent Bunn while shouting 'Down, down to h—l and say I sent thee hither.' The line is Richard's from *Henry VI, Part 3*. While there is a certain benefit to Shakespeare's defender being depicted speaking Shakespeare's words, the fact that in the quoted scene Richard assassinates the unarmed and imprisoned King Henry VI hardly speaks of Victorian fair play. Moreover, in the scene, Henry greets his assassin with the question, 'What scene of death hath Roscius now to act?' Inveterately false Richard proffers new justifications for each of his transgressions, and so is aptly compared to an actor—hardly the image of the profession that Macready sought to project.

If there were any question as to how audiences would receive Macready following the fight, they were laid to rest after his first appearance at the rival playhouse Covent Garden. A report from the *Morning Post* (reprinted in the *Examiner*) described his reception in enthusiastic detail:

> We have never heard within the walls of any theatre more enthusiastic, loud, and long continued applause, than that which greeted Mr. Macready last night when he appeared upon the scene in the character of Macbeth. The audience which was numerous, and decidedly the most respectable we have witnessed this season, rose *en masse* when Macready crossed the bridge, and began a storm of cheering which lasted until long after he had advanced to the footlights. The waving of hats and handkerchiefs, the successive peals of 'Hurrah,' the prolonged cries of 'Bravo,' and the incessant stamping, were most animated. Reiterated exclamations of 'One cheer more' became the signal for renewed approbations. Exhausted at length apparently by the vocal acclamations, a clapping of hands were resorted to, which was also maintained with immense vigour for some time, and nearly ten minutes elapsed before the tragedy was allowed to proceed.[48]

The correspondent was embarrassed to admit that this enthusiasm was generated by the fact that Macready had struck his manager, but hastened to note that 'there is no actor who has enjoyed a higher reputation in the relations of private life than Mr. Macready' and that his 'high literary attainments' and 'habits' have assured him 'considerable regard and esteem.' The correspondent's assessment of Macready's performance was equally marked by superlatives, and began with the assertion that 'to our minds, he has never acted with a more just perception of the beauties of Shakespeare.' Fresh from his battle to defend the Bard, the actor emerged with a renewed understanding of the poet's genius.

The following season Macready contracted to perform at Covent Garden for £40 a week for twenty-two weeks, with a half clear benefit—a substantial increase over the already considerable £30 a week he had earned at Drury Lane. According to William Archer's estimation, during the 1836–37 season, Macready performed Othello fourteen times, King John fourteen times, Brutus thirteen times, Macbeth seven times, Leontes twice, and Hamlet once for a total of fifty-one Shakespearean performances. By contrast, during his last season with Bunn he performed in Shakespeare on only twenty-five occasions, including the abridged *Richard III.*[49] During the two-and-a-half months that Forrest appeared at Drury Lane, Macready performed an exclusively Shakespearean repertoire on the nights that his American rival acted.[50] The contrasts between Macready and Bunn were doubtless salient to a public that had begun to identify Macready with the defense of the Bard.

Covent Garden Management, 1837–39

Covent Garden's 1836–37 season, which featured Charles Kemble's farewell performances, was well received by critics and audiences, but did little to revive the fortunes of a theatre that had been losing money. When the management failed at the end of the 1837 season, Macready saw his opportunity. On several occasions, his diaries record his interest in managing a London theatre, even though his one previous experience co-managing theatres in Bath and Bristol for a short winter season in 1835 left him swearing off the 'hateful profession.'[51] Nonetheless, he had become convinced that it had fallen to him to protect English theatre from speculators like Bunn.

This was the storyline carried in the *Examiner*, which announced Macready's leasing of Covent Garden as a selfless endeavor to save that theatre, the drama, and—by extension—the nation. The paper described Macready as 'the only resource that can now save that theatre, and with it, for a time, the English drama itself from utter destruction.' Far from trespassing on the fame of great dramatists, the actor was their humble servant; Macready had 'stepped in, at every personal sacrifice, to rescue the noble art to which his life has been devoted.' This project was in fact one of national preservation, for in devoting his life to the art of theatre, the actor was also devoted to an art 'with which the greatest glories of our language and history are associated eternally.'[52] While the idea of the actor rescuing the drama dates back to Garrick, there is a marked shift in the tone here. The Westminster Abbey memorial to Garrick describes that actor and Shakespeare as 'twin stars' that 'earth irradiate with a beam divine' (an inscription that particularly provoked Lamb's ire). By contrast, it is not Macready's own luminosity or stage presence that will save the great works of English drama, rather it is his commitment to producing with appropriate resources those works as they were written.

The *Examiner* article ends with a quotation from Macready's preface to the published acting version of Beaumont and Fletcher's *The Maid's Tragedy* (published as *The Bridal*), which Macready had brought to the Haymarket earlier that summer to much acclaim. In citing Macready's preface, the *Examiner* effectively reminded readers that Macready had been responsible for restoring a great English drama to the stage, drawing attention to his role in preparing that text for production. Those who had read Macready's preface would know that he had discussed the play's stage history in some detail and explained that the acting version differed from the original principally in the removal of 'offensive situations and language' that were 'neither essential to the delineation of character, nor conducive even to an effect of contrast.—They are in fact disfigurements of a splendid picture.'[53] The preface then notes where the dramatist Knowles had provided additional scenes necessitated by the deletions. Whether or not Macready actually had respected the original play—and no modern reader would come to that conclusion—he clearly asserted that his approach to the text had been genuinely dramaturgical, such that he omitted only that which was neither essential to character nor supported effect. The play was already a 'splendid picture' and only its disfigurements were removed. This was a noted contrast to the language of earlier adaptors, as when Tate famously described Shakespeare's *King Lear* as a 'Heap of Jewels, unstrung and unpolisht.' The *Examiner* piece concluded by quoting from Macready's preface: according to the actor, the success that greeted his revival of Beaumont and Fletcher afforded a 'promise of success in the appropriation of our stage to its legitimate and nobler purposes.' A harbinger, the *Examiner* would seem to suggest, of Macready's upcoming Covent Garden season.

That season was eagerly awaited by those who longed to see great English dramatic authors, and Shakespeare in particular, given their proper due. Letters to the *Morning Post* and the *Morning Chronicle* offered suggestions for Macready's coming management. According to one writer, Shakespeare's 'immortal tragedies' were currently performed in a 'slovenly fashion' whereas great expense was devoted to trifles:

> What must foreigners think of us to see one of [Shakespeare's] plays succeeded by a concoction of nonsensical dialogues badly translated from some trashy French *drama*, but at the same time allied with the most gorgeous splendour which the scenic art can exhibit, and in which all the taste and research of a first-rate antiquary appear to have been exerted in order to provide correct and beautiful costumes?[54]

Then as an example of the misuse of the stage's resources, the writer cited two musical spectacles: *The Jewess* and *Fair Rosamond.* Both were successful productions that Bunn had mounted at Drury Lane, and the former was the very play that had been crammed onto the bill with the first act of *Chevy Chase* and the first three acts of *Richard III* on the night Macready had struck his manager. Bunn's misuse of the theatre's resources—his lavish attention to un-English operatic spectacle and his shoddy Shakespeare production—had shamed the nation in the eyes of foreigners.

Macready publicized his management as a service to the nation in advance of his opening. The week before, he posted a pre-season announcement explaining that 'the decline of the drama as a branch of English literature is a matter of public notoriety' and then delineating a project of 'improving the conditions of that great national theatre' and advancing 'the drama as a branch of national literature and art.' This would be accomplished first and foremost through 'fidelity' coupled with 'appropriateness.' Just as importantly, these great works would have the full benefit of all of the recourses of the stage, promising 'superior execution of the several means of scenic illusion.' No longer would new settings and stage technology be reserved for musical spectacle. Macready made good on his promise, devoting 118 nights to Shakespeare, 144 nights to other legitimate plays and only seventy-nine nights to opera and pantomime.[55] This constituted a near reversal of the policy of recent managers, and Macready devoted as much care and expense to Shakespeare productions as he did to opera and pantomime. From the outset of his management Macready had realized the necessity of including opera in the Covent Garden season. As he explained in the pre-season announcement, 'English Opera has become an essential part of the amusements of a metropolitan audience.' Even here, Macready noted that he had procured the aid of 'native' musical talents, careful not to compromise the theatre's national character.[56]

Not surprisingly, Macready opened his season with Shakespeare. His choice, *The Winter's Tale,* had been restored to the stage by John Philip Kemble in 1811. (Since the mid-eighteenth century, audiences regularly encountered two adaptations, both titled *Florizel and Perdita,* which presented the last two acts independently of the rest of the play.[57]) Kemble's version, which Macready followed, adhered closely to the First Folio text, only omitting passages likely to offend (such as Leontes' speculation that many men's wives have been 'sluiced in's absence/ And his pond fish'd by his next neighbour.'[58]) Macready first performed Leontes in 1823 at Drury Lane when he played the role twelve times, but following that season he performed the role only an additional seven times before his Covent Garden management.[59] The play offered clear advantages: it was a tested Shakespearean revival, its infrequent performance made it something of a novelty, and Leontes would seem an ideal role for an actor whose performance style featured sudden emotional shifts, pathos and domestic tenderness. However, the role never became a staple of Macready's repertoire—notwithstanding historians' frequent citation of Helena Faucit's description of his powerful performance.

Reviews for the opening night are striking for the space given to subjects other than the performance—principally, repairs to the house, Macready's pre-season announcement and the enthusiasm of the audience. It was only well after the season was underway that the *Morning Chronicle* could look back on the production as demonstrating 'that entire harmony and adaptation of scenic effect, costume, and arrangement' that marked the initial productions of the season.[60] Apparently, before he could restore the drama, Macready needed to restore the physical theatre, and both *The Times* and the *Literary Gazette* gave extended attention to the fact that the theatre had been cleaned and painted. As *The Times* explained, 'ladies may now enter the boxes without any apprehension of their dresses being soiled by filth, or torn by projecting nails.' *The Times* elided the sorry condition of the house with the sorry state of the drama, which 'could scarcely be reduced to a lower state than that in which it is at present.' However, the paper clearly considered it a quixotic project to attempt to change public taste: if audiences craved pantomime and operatic spectacle, 'there is no possibility of resistance in such a matter.' The audience seems not to have shared such reservations. The *Literary Gazette* asserted that 'the house, which was full to the ceiling, rose to a man; and we never, to our knowledge, heard such a tumult of applause as welcomed Mr. Macready and the legitimate drama.' The *Examiner* noted that cheers frequently interrupted Macready's address and that 'the name of Shakespeare at the end of the address called forth the loudest cheer of all, as if the Genius which is the greatest glory of our nation had once more [a] fond home.' Even *The Times* begrudgingly acknowledged that 'it is scarcely necessary to say, that Mr. Macready was loudly and enthusiastically cheered on his entrance.'[61]

The Times' skepticism towards attempts to restore legitimate drama to the English stage led to a more striking complaint—*The Winter's Tale* is bad theatre and thus a poor choice for an opening night. According to that paper, while the play contains 'passages full of nature, passion, and the highest poetical feelings,' it is, nonetheless, 'one of Shakespeare's least attractive productions, as an acting drama.' The review then provides two reasons for confining the play to the closet: the statue scene is the only dramatic scene and Leontes' jealousy is shocking and unrealistic. Such an assertion, in the end, was far more damaging to Macready than

The Times' tepid response to his acting, for the idea that Shakespeare should be read but not seen contradicted the central premise of the actor-manager's project. In making its case that the theatre, as a business, must privilege illegitimate fare because that is what sells tickets, the newspaper found no less an authority than Samuel Johnson and repeated the well-known passage from the prologue that he had composed for Garrick's inaugural production as Drury Lane's manager in 1747. In short: 'The Drama's laws the Drama's Patrons give, / And we who live to please must please to live!'

The assertion was a clear challenge to those who championed Macready's reforms and a victory for his enemies. Bunn quoted the same lines in his own Drury Lane address, asserting that the fact that Shakespeare's plays had produced nightly losses, and that plays such as *The Jewess* had run over 100 nights, demonstrated that in his programming 'public pleasure and private enterprise have been equally consulted.' Reporting on the address, the *Examiner* described Bunn's position as an example of 'rare impudence and ignorance.' According to the *Examiner*, illegitimate fare and all the other ills of the patent theatres were the result of 'sordid adventuring speculators' who were interested in the theatre only as an investment, 'while the good has been the work of those more interested in the theatres themselves, not merely as a matter of profit, but of honour and fame.'[62] The paper placed Bunn squarely among the speculators whereas Macready represented a much-needed return of a manager interested in the good of the theatre and for whom the greatest remuneration was the respect of his audience.

Even as Bunn claimed that box-office takings were the sole measure of good management and public service, he attempted to present himself as a defender of the Bard. Bunn opened his 1837 season with a musical version of *The Merry Wives of Windsor* (though he also managed to include on the bill a new Planché melodrama starring the French dancer, Madame Celeste, as 'the dumb boy,' as well as overtures from Weber's *Oberon* and Harold's *Zampa*). More significantly, Bunn contracted Charles Kean (son of the famous actor Edmund Kean) for forty-three nights of Shakespeare, and puffed the young actor considerably through contacts in the press.

Bunn's efforts to promote the young actor as Macready's Shakespearean rival culminated in a dinner held in Charles Kean's honor at Drury Lane on March 30th 1838. The evening's speakers celebrated Kean's excellent acting and his service to English drama, although he had not yet established a reputation as a tragedian. However, that did not stop Bunn from presenting his actor as the true savior of the drama. In his address, Bunn explained that:

> He [Bunn] had been accused by certain persons of having neglected the legitimate drama. That accusation was unfounded. He was too well aware of the excellencies of Shakespeare to exhibit any representations in the place of his plays whilst he had proper persons to represent the characters the immortal bard had depicted. He knew that whilst the stream of time had swept away the works of other dramatists, the adamant of Shakespeare remained untouched (applause). As soon as he had found an adequate representative of the characters of the immortal bard, he had produced him on the stage of Drury-lane theatre (applause)—and the public and responded to the appeal he had made to their judgment by the manner in which they had received the gentleman to congratulate whom they were that day assembled.[63]

A contrasting opinion of the actor appeared the following week in the *Morning Chronicle* when Kean closed his engagement at Drury Lane as Shylock. The reviewer explained that 'Mr. C. Kean's previous performances had convinced us of his utter want of intellect to render his physical powers of execution subservient to the harmonious illustration of dramatic character; but they had not prepared us for so thorough a failure as that of his Shylock.'[64] Macready had an equally low opinion of Kean's acting (and Kean's character) and was particularly incensed to read of Bunn's assertion that Macready's own poor acting at Drury Lane had been the reason the manager had provided meager support for Shakespeare productions. In his diary, Macready provided a succinct assessment of Bunn's argument: 'It is well that such a wretch should talk thus; truth even in degrees would misbecome him.'[65]

Macready's next revivals, *Hamlet* and *Othello*, received little attention in the daily press (though both were lauded in the *Examiner*), and it was not until *Macbeth* that he would have a Shakespearean hit. His Hamlet would seem to have been a highly original interpretation, and over the course of that season Macready refined an 'elastic lightness of manner' that divided his critics and incensed Edwin Forrest. Kemble had already restored much of the play, displacing Garrick's radical adaptation with its substantially abridged fifth act. One probably has to be skeptical of the *Examiner*'s description of Macready's production as an 'absolute restoration.'[66] However, whether or not Macready performed every line of the play (in whatever version one took to be authoritative) he was understood to have achieved complete fidelity.

His principal innovation was performing Hamlet as an irreverent student, demonstrating 'the quiet smile on the lips and the humorous comment of the eye' when confiding with Horatio or his student companions.[67] *Othello* won particular praise for the attention and care in its mounting, evidence that Macready was true to his word that the full resources of the theatre would be devoted to Shakespeare production. The *Examiner* described the scene in the Venetian council chamber as a facsimile of the High Council Hall as painted by Tintoretto, replete with scores of actors playing the Council of Forty, the Council of Ten, the Doge and their secretaries and messengers.[68] When the play was remounted a year later, the *Morning Chronicle* reprised a familiar nationalistic trope with the assertion that this scene in itself would be the best means to 'impress a foreigner . . . with the noblest idea of our national theatre.'[69] Neither production elicited the enthusiasm that greeted *Macbeth.* Even the normally hostile *John Bull* conceded that '[t]he poetry of the drama is now for the first time put into motion.'[70] While *The Times* described Macready's Macbeth as inconsistent, it praised the production for a strong ensemble in which lead actors condescended to play small parts (previously unheard of in English theatres), even performing the choral interludes taken from compositions by Locke and Purcell. Macready, apparently, valued opera when it was in service to Shakespeare and composed by old English masters.

The patterns of criticism that greeted these four Shakespearean productions—heightened (but not absolute) regard for textual authenticity, respect for a disciplined ensemble that included lead actors, praise (sometimes begrudged) for accurate costuming and scene painting and enthusiasm for English music—were repeated throughout Macready's Covent Garden management. The *Morning Chronicle* commended a charity performance of *Julius Caesar* for 'the reality of the Roman populace as they thronged around the rostrum,' with each supernumerary demonstrating 'individuality of garb and manner.' According to that paper, Macready's willingness to take the role of Friar Lawrence in *Romeo and Juliet* gave that character its 'true position in the play,' demonstrating that part of Shakespeare's genius was to make small roles integral to the drama as a whole. However, this would have been revealed more perfectly 'if the original text were restored.'[71] Like his contemporaries, Macready used Garrick's adaptation in which Juliet awakes before Romeo's death and the lovers then exchange seventy lines of interpolated dialogue before their tragic deaths. (London audiences would have to wait until 1846 to see a restored *Romeo and Juliet*—though one pruned of indecencies—in Samuel Phelps's production at Sadler's Wells.) *As You Like It* won praise for its scenic painting of 'pretty pictures of sequestered and romantic glades.'[72]

Macready's last Shakespearean revival at Covent Garden, *Henry V*, demonstrated both his commitment to restoration and his anxiety that the uncut text might require a little help from scene painters. He restored the choruses but then illustrated them with moving panoramas by Clarkson Stanfield; apparently this cockpit *could* hold the vasty fields of France (which ensured that those specific lines were omitted in performance). Macready struck a nearly apologetic note in his playbill when he explained that the panoramas serve to 'render more palpable those portions of the story which have not the advantage of action' but 'are still requisite to the Drama's completeness.'[73] *John Bull* mocked the visual aid, particularly the choice to accompany the chorus's metaphorical description of the 'warlike Harry' with 'famine, sword, and fire' crouching at his heels with an illustration of 'a figure in armour with three furies clinging to his feet.' According to the paper, the theatre had been reduced to a 'raree-show'—a peep show inside a box.[74] However, the *Morning Chronicle* praised this image, along with the depictions of 'the voyage of the English fleet from Southampton, and the commencement of the siege of Harfleur; the hostile camps in the night before the battle of Agincourt, and the triumphant entry of Henry into London.' That paper enthused: 'We confess our inability to criticize, or even record, in detail, a series of theatrical effects, to which every art connected with the drama furnished its contributions, while the master-mind combined them all, in one harmonized and intense impression.'[75] *The Times* was ambivalent. Its review began with the observation that 'excessive pageantry is no sign of the revival of the drama' but concluded that as such pageantry goes, the production merited 'unqualified praise' and that one scarcely knows 'whether to most admire the care, taste, and research displayed in the design, or the beauty of the execution.'[76]

The restoration that gave Macready the most pause was the one that earned him the greatest praise. His sixth Shakespearean revival, *King Lear*, did away with Tate's adaptation, with its happy ending and marriage between Cordelia and Edgar, which had held the stage since 1681. Romantic critics had already stressed the importance of the Fool. Coleridge, for example, had asserted that far from merely providing comic relief, 'the contrast of the Fool wonderfully heightens the colouring of some of the most painful situations.'[77] However, Macready was nervous before the production, writing in his diary that: 'Like many such terrible contrasts in poetry and painting, in acting it will fail of effect; it will either weary and annoy or distract the spectator. I have no hope of it, and think that at the last we shall be obliged to dispense with it.'[78] Despite his apprehensions, the inclusion of the Fool was highly acclaimed. *John Bull* asserted that the presence of the Fool in the storm scene revealed the full pathos of Lear's reduced state.[79] *The Times* applauded the restoration, declaring that the Fool 'is not a mere jester, like many of the clowns, simply introduced to relieve tragedy with his jokes, but he actually stands forth a moral personage.'[80] The most detailed study of the character's importance came from the *Examiner*, which argued that the Fool acts as a surrogate to Cordelia in Lear's mind. After detailing the King's attentiveness to his Fool and distress at his absence, the journal explains:

> Can there be a doubt, after this, that his love for the *Fool* is associated with *Cordelia*, who had been kind to the poor boy, and for the loss of whom he pines away? And are we not even then prepared for the sublime pathos of the close, when *Lear*, bending over the dead body of all he had left to love upon the earth, connects with her the memory of that other gentle, faithful, and loving being who had passed from his side—unites, in that moment of final agony, the two hearts that had been broken in his service—and exclaims—'And my poor fool is hanged!'[81]

The connection may have been suggested by the choice to cast a woman, Priscilla Horton, as the Fool. Whether or not audiences shared the *Examiner*'s subtle analysis they apparently approved the restoration: *King Lear* played to full houses. Part of its attraction was undoubtedly the medieval scene painting, which was nearly as widely praised as the restored text. *John Bull* described the setting: 'The castles are heavy, somber and solid; their halls are adorned with trophies of the chase and instruments of war; druid circles rise in spectral loneliness on the heath; and the "dreadful pother" of the elements is kept up with a verisimilitude which beggars all that we have hitherto seen attempted.'[82]

For pure spectacle, the crowning achievements of Macready's Covent Garden management were his productions of *Coriolanus* in the first season and the *Tempest* in the second. These productions demonstrated the complicated relation of theatrical spectacle and textual authenticity, even as the press responses revealed a growing consensus that Shakespeare wrote—first and foremost—great acting plays and that contemporary scenic technology was a valuable means of exploring the poet's mind. Over the course of the season, attention to the degrees of textual fidelity grew increasingly sharp, with the *Morning Chronicle* announcing that in Macready's *Coriolanus* 'the genuine text was scrupulously preserved,' except for 'a few words in the last scene and some needful curtailments.' This was, in the mind of the reviewer, much more than simple antiquarian hunger for authenticity, but a rebuke to the playwrights who had tampered with these works of genius and to 'the obstinate tastelessness of successive managers who insulted the public by adhering to corrupt versions, as better adapted for theatrical effect.'[83] Managers, in their ignorance, pandered to an audience onto which they projected their own tastelessness. Actors, however, understood that Shakespeare's texts were great acting plays. Taking up the production in a second review, the *Morning Chronicle* explained that Macready restored the text because he understood that its perfection was in its whole, and that this perfection was both poetic and theatrical:

> Into all his Shakespeare revivals, eminently in *Coriolanus*, Mr. Macready has infused the very soul of Shakespeare. It is not merely that the text is restored; not merely that the painting and costume are faithful to the place and period; not merely that the grouping is ever most artistical, and the effects most genuinely dramatic; but there is beyond this rare and indeed unprecedented harmony, the pervading presence of the conception that imparts to the drama its distinctive intellectual and poetical character.[84]

Macready created a total work of art by grasping the 'soul' of his playwright and translating it into a stage picture in which every detail was planned and controlled.

Such illustration was possible because of modern scenic technology; textual restoration was simply the first step in revealing the mind of the playwright:

> The verbal restoration of these plays, although that be an unprecedented merit, is amongst the subordinate claims of the present management of Coven Garden Theatre. Mr. Macready restores, or, should we rather say, for the first time realizes, the pictorial conceptions and imaginings of Shakespeare's mind. To Shakespeare himself they could be only imaginings. But he never stinted his fancy to accommodate it to the beggarly properties of such theatres as then existed. Their poverty seemed rather to stimulate him to revel in beautiful and grand impracticabilities. They are so no longer.[85]

Far from bringing a 'fine vision to the standard of flesh and blood,' the stage realized what could previously only exist in Shakespeare's imagination.

Over two separate reviews, the *Morning Chronicle* carefully detailed the production's scenic marvels, proof that Macready had entered into Shakespeare's mind and then—through the wonders of the stage—gave pictorial reality to the wondrous images that hitherto had defied the capabilities of the stage. According to the *Examiner*, audiences saw an accurate depiction of republican Rome, one that replaced the marbled imperial anachronism of Kemble's production with 'the rude city of the rude age of the Conqueror of Corioli.' The review provided detailed descriptions of each scene, drawing attention to their beauty and historical accuracy. Both papers heaped praise on the use of supernumeraries, impressed with 'Their varied and sordid garbs, their excited looks and gestures, the miscellaneous weapons of their insurrection, and the truth of their movements to the effect of the speeches addressed to them.'[86]

The Tempest was by far the most spectacular of Macready's productions, though here the tremendous marshalling of stage machinery, elaborate costuming, and dioramic scenes could not be said to serve the cause of historical accuracy. It is a tenuous argument to assert that historically accurate scene painting and costumes automatically reveal the poet's conception. Shakespeare's actors, because they did not strive for historical accuracy, looked to the past for universals rather than idiosyncratic manners. Moreover, the Romantic idea persisted that the plays worked principally as a spur to the imagination. As *The Times* explained in its review of *The Tempest,* because no stage was broad enough to embrace the reality of 'armies, mobs, battles, &c,' it was better to 'at once admit the impossibility of faithful representation, and merely to give such visible effects as are calculated to act as stepping-stones to the imagination rather than attempt to substitute its operations.' Such a critique, *The Times* admitted, did not apply to the *Tempest,* which had more in common with the spectacular masques of the Stuart court than Shakespeare's English chronicle plays.

While the *Examiner* crowed that audiences were finally spared the Dryden and Davenant 'adulteration' with its 'nauseous' and 'disgusting' changes, *The Times* noted that the 'announcement that the piece was to be taken from the text of Shakespeare must be received with some qualification' because the entire opening scene at sea was cut and replaced with a view of ships in the distance followed by a onstage shipwreck. (The *Examiner* marveled that 'the hugest vessel that we ever beheld on the stage laboured in a genuine and most tremendous gulf of water.') *The Times* gave uncharacteristically detailed descriptions of elaborate wing and groove transformation scenes, magic appearances accomplished with transparencies and flying machinery. Commenting on such spectacles, the *Morning Chronicle* reprised its earlier argument that the plays were essentially unfinished until Macready and Victorian stage technology had realized the poet's suppressed intention: 'The conception was Shakespeare's, the theatrical realization was reserved for Macready.'[87] All that remained to ensure success was a healthy inclusion of incidental music, and Macready again turned to the old English masters, with music taken from Purcell, Linley and Arne.

Macready announced on April 8th 1839 that his management would terminate at the end of the season, and then began his final series of Shakespeare revivals, culminating with the new production of *Henry V*. The last of these reprised revivals was *The Tempest*. The decision to end with the *Tempest* was likely motivated by a desire to ensure a large house at the end of the season, *The Tempest* and *Coriolanus* being the most popular shows of his management. However, it is tempting to imagine that Macready was likening the close of his management to the end of the playwright's career. In 1838, Thomas Campbell first suggested that in *The Tempest* Shakespeare represented his own retirement from theatre, an idea premised on the assumptions that the play was the last he wrote and that it could be read for clues to the dramatist's life. According to Campbell 'Shakespeare, as if conscious that it would be his last, and as if inspired to typify himself, has made its hero a natural, a dignified, and benevolent magician.'[88] Whether or not Macready was familiar with Campbell's Shakespeare edition, published the previous year, the idea of Prospero as autobiographical creation resonates through the *Morning Chronicle* review, which finds in the play a fitting 'farewell' to the past two seasons:

> Again and again did the imaginary associations of previous events in the life of Prospero transfer themselves to the real magician of these scenes; and as the wand was broken, all the glorious exhibitions that have made the last two years an era in dramatic history, the splendours of *Lear, Macbeth, Othello, Coriolanus,* seemed to be 'melted into air, into thin air.'[89]

With the termination of Macready's management, the London stage had lost its Prospero. The review laments the loss of so many splendid productions of Shakespeare and leaves the reader wondering if such spirits ever will be summoned again.

With the end of Macready's project, even critics who had been skeptical rose to praise him. Reviewing the actor's final performance as manager of Covent Garden, the *Sunday Times* expressed amazement that a man who could easily earn £6,000 a year would instead give up his income 'to better the condition of his brethren' and 'to snatch the drama from destruction when it had been squalled and danced and pranced almost to death by *soi disant* singers, meaningless dancers and piebald steeds.' The paper, referencing the fact that the previous manager of Covent Garden had resorted to casting an impressive menagerie of animals and had left the theatre filthy, compared Macready's efforts to the fifth labor of Hercules: 'he entered the Augean stable . . . and raised upon its site a Shakespeare temple.'[90] Once squalid, now sacred. His management may have failed but the theatre and its public had been saved. As Macready asserted when called back to the stage after appearing as Henry V on the final night of his management:

> It has been my recompense—and though circumstances have tended to make it my only recompense, still it is a proud one—it has been my recompense, ladies and gentlemen, in [Covent Garden's full] attendances, to read a refutation to the libel that the taste for classic drama in England is extinguished, and from them to receive a confirmation of the faith, which against doubt and despondency, I have still held in the enduring power of our dramatic poets, and, above all, of him who 'was not for a day, but for all time'—our Shakespeare.

In asserting that Shakespeare was the shared timeless lineage of the English, Macready chose well in ending his management with *Henry V* with its St. Crispin's Day speech. Outnumbered by the massive audiences for melodramas, hippodramas, and aquatic spectacles, still the Covent Garden few, that band of brothers, had gathered to defend 'our Shakespeare.'

Shakespearean Masculinity

If the Romantic period saw the consolidation of English nationalist constructions of Shakespeare, the Victorian period can be said to have witnessed English *masculine* constructions of Shakespeare.[91] Gifts, public dinners and club celebrations—all of which were reported in the press—defined a male band of Shakespeare defenders. When the artist Clarkson Stanfield refused full payment for a diorama painted for a Christmas pantomime, Macready responded to this act of friendship with the gift of a silver salver presented at a private dinner. Macready then sent notices of the gift to several London newspapers. Macready's artistic circle was in attendance at the dinner—including Robert Browning, John Forster, the playwright James Kenney, the barrister and journalist William Wallace, the artist George Cattermole and others. The salver's inscription made no reference to the fact that Stanfield had painted a diorama for a pantomime but instead thanked the artist for bringing 'the magic of his pencil and the celebrity of his name' to the 'aid of a discouraged and declining sister art.'[92] The presentation of the salver, in the presence of his artistic circle and reported in *The Times*, served as Stanfield's public induction into Macready's band of the drama's defenders. Later that year, Macready's actors—represented by a delegation of male actors in the presence of the entire company—presented him with a silver salver. The actors thanked him for the sacrifice he had made to 'champion the cause of the declining drama', all of which was reported in the *Morning Chronicle*.[93]

Although the Shakespeare Club honored Macready for his management of Covent Garden, the most lavish of such celebrations came on July 20th 1839 when over 400 men attended a public dinner celebrating Macready at the Freemasons' Tavern. The Duke of Sussex presided over an assembly of the cultural elite. While public dinners were male activities, Macready's wife (who had dined earlier) was in attendance in the ladies' gallery on the left.[94] Most of the proceedings were devoted to lauding Macready's Shakespeare revivals. However, still more interesting, according to the Duke of Sussex, was an aspect of his management impacting 'the morals of the country at large and happiness of the public':

> What was once a scene of great moral confusion, the saloon of the theatre, has been, under his management, made so innocuous to propriety, so totally changed in its features and character, that the father and husband may now walk through it without fear of having the feelings of those who are dearer to him than life itself shocked or offended.[95]

Put more simply, Macready had created a private lobby for the first tier of boxes to ensure that respectable patrons did not encounter prostitutes looking for clients.

The Duke's word choice draws attention to the gender coding implicit in the publicity surrounding Macready's management. Macready and his male cohort defended the drama, just as fathers and husbands defended those dearer than life itself from the threat of the illegitimate. The presence of Macready's wife in the gallery, watching on as a train of distinguished gentlemen praised her husband for preserving the sanctity of England's drama, daughters and wives, completes a powerful domestic staging of Victorian masculinity as channeled through Shakespeare.[96]

Drury Lane Management, 1841–43

Several weeks before the July 20th public dinner, Macready penned a very brief entry in his diary: 'Came to the conclusion that if it were ever proposed to me to undertake the management of a theatre again, I should give no answer *until I had read carefully over the diaries of the two years now past.*'[97] Whether or not he had followed his own advice and read his diaries, he was soon again running a patent theatre. In March 1841, Macready agreed to manage Drury Lane. His lease stipulated that he could close the theatre on a day's notice without paying additional rent; that his own salary be counted among the theatre's working expenses; that his improvements to the property be deducted from the rent; and that the theatre not open and that he not be charged rent until Christmas.[98]

In managing Drury Lane, Macready produced Shakespeare according to the principles he developed at Covent Garden: frequent and varied revivals; detailed historically accurate settings and costumes; the restoration of Shakespeare's texts; and careful attention to the performances of supernumeraries, especially in crowd scenes. His one departure was in his embrace of opera, though here as well he initially attempted to confine his repertoire to seventeenth- and eighteenth-century English opera. Reviewers responded enthusiastically. Macready's status as Shakespeare's true defender had solidified and he developed increasingly lavish designs to provide sufficient pictorial illustration to the plays.[99] However, most papers concluded that at no point did spectacle overwhelm poetry.

The mania for authenticated spectacle had been mocked from the moment it was first introduced on the stage. Charles Kemble's historically accurate productions in the 1820s prompted one reviewer to complain, 'We expect to next see legitimate authority produced for the dressing of Puck and authenticated wings allotted to Musterseed.'[100] While some might question when a production had slipped into such needless and obscuring detail, the *Examiner* offered a simple rule. In its review of Macready's *Macbeth,* the paper observed: 'Everything should be done of which the art of the stage is capable, to realize the intention of the dramatist; the idea of the drama. If this is lost sight of for an instant,—the greater the splendour, the greater the mistake.' The belief that a single 'idea' dictates the shape of each of Shakespeare's plays is indebted to Romantic criticism—see, for example, Coleridge's often-cited assertion that the first scenes of *Richard II* lay out the 'germ' of a 'ruling passion' that is then developed over the course of the play.[101] However, the *Examiner* departed from Romantic criticism with the assertion that stage production could 'realize the intention of the dramatist' and 'the idea of the drama.' It was a departure that Macready's earlier management had made possible.

While Macready's Covent Garden management had prompted some skeptics to express discomfort with audience enthusiasm for spectacle, such concerns were largely absent during his Drury Lane management. The previously reserved *Times* lauded Macready's production of *King John*:

> Mr. Macready has brought before the eyes of his audience an animated picture of those Gothic times which are so splendidly illustrated by the drama. The stage is thronged with the stalwart forms of the middle ages, the clang of battle sounds behind the scenes, massive fortresses bound the horizon. The grouping is admirably managed. The mailed figures now sink into stern tranquility; now, when the martial fire touches them, they rouse from their lethargy and thirst for action.[102]

It is not surprising to read that Macready devoted an entire morning to rehearsing the supernumeraries in the first two acts of the play.[103] Macready himself seems to have grown comfortable with the increased spectacle of his Drury Lane revivals, or at the very least in advertizing it. With his production of *The Two Gentlemen of Verona*, Macready provided patrons with a flyleaf noting the specific locations represented in the scene paintings and identifying the sources for the shields in the coat of arms. The approving *Era* reproduced the flyleaf in full in its review, which commended the production's 'strict adherence to the text of Shakespeare.'[104]

As before, a significant portion of Macready's cultural authority rested on his promise to restore Shakespeare's texts. In this context, considerable attention was devoted to the authenticity of Macready's acting texts, and competing papers provided competing assessments. The *Morning Chronicle* began its review of his *Cymbeline* with the announcement that the play had been 'revived in the purity of its original text.'[105] However, *The Times* complained of 'sundry minor elisions which completely pass our comprehension.'[106] Such critiques were not always justified. The *Post* complained that in *As You Like*, Macready contorted the First Lord's description of Jacques (2.1.26–63) into a speech delivered by Jacques, the very role which he himself performed. It was a common practice but not one that Macready had employed.[107] Displays of Shakespeare scholarship were becoming as common among reviewers as they were among managers. In the course of its review of *The Two Gentlemen of Verona*, *The Times* paused to contest an emendation in Charles Knight's recent edition. Knight had reassigned lines so as to effectively remove Valentine's 'gift' of his beloved Silvia to the man who had attempted her rape; however, *The Times* found textual support for the darker reading performed by Macready.[108]

The *Morning Chronicle* showed erudition in its command of stage history. The review noted the play's infrequent performance, complained that Benjamin Victor's adaptation had reigned since Garrick, provided examples of Victor's barbarous interpolations, and noted that this adaptation persisted into the last London production—that of John Philip Kemble. Among the problems with Victor's adaptation, according to the review, was that it reconciled the young men's 'incongruities' and explained their 'inconsistencies' (including Valentine's gift of Silvia).

On turning to Macready's production, the *Morning Chronicle* read staging choices in relation to Shakespeare's biography, implicitly asserting that design technology made the Victorian theatre more 'authentically' Shakespearean than past theatre. The paper anachronistically praised the production of *The Two Gentlemen of Verona* for displaying the 'lightness of a Christmas entertainment.' As the critic explained: 'Produced as it was written, it realized a piece of the poet's youth for [the audience]—the careless beauty of its romance, the riotous impulse of its . . . spirits.' The review concluded by reading Macready's design in relation to an apocryphal detail from Shakespeare's youth: 'The scenery was in true keeping with the effects of the comedy. The outlaws in their greenwood might have helped the poet at one of his exploits of deer-stealing.'[109] Design expresses the author's biography and experiences—accurately or not!—and in doing so delivers the 'true' Shakespeare—not the author's words but the author's life.

According to the *Morning Chronicle*, Macready's own veneration of Shakespeare had spread to his audience. In its review of *Cymbeline*, the paper asserted that Macready's commitment to staging a play that did not afford him a powerful role demonstrated a reverence of Shakespeare unknown to the typical 'star-mongering manager.' More importantly, that reverence was reflected in the audience:

> Indeed, it was pleasing evidence of the spirit in which the public appreciated [Macready's] views, to see how many books of Shakespeare's works in all sizes and editions, were opened in boxes and pits, and intently followed line by line by devouring critics who seemed glad to acknowledge that their favorite bard was, in this work, after so long an exclusion, restored to the stage.[110]

Shakespeare resided in the text, but that text revealed its totality in performance. It was only in the audience with book in hand that reader/viewers could experience fully their bard. Each laudatory review served as an invitation to join this community of Shakespeare conjurors, in the boxes and the pits, following texts of all sizes and editions.

While this community was expansive, it was not exactly classless. In invoking this body of Shakespeare acolytes throughout the theatre, the paper pointedly neglected to mention the presumably working class audiences in the gallery. There may even have been an element of class aspiration in the habit of bringing one's text to the show. A year earlier, *The Times* reported on the King of Prussia's attendance at *The Two Gentlemen of Verona*: 'The king, taking his seat, paid the most intense attention, making quite a study of the performance. He had a book with him, which he followed the actors line by line, and we do not think he could have missed a word of the piece.'[111] Pit and boxes copied such behavior in demonstrating their love of bard through textual study in the theatre.

In this context, it was of some concern to many of Macready's supporters that the Queen rarely attended Drury Lane.[112] Even before Macready announced that he would terminate his management, the *Era* expressed concern that without royal support he would be forced to relinquish the national theatre to purveyors of animal acts and acrobatics:

> The finest works of the greatest masters are now produced in a style of grandeur never before dreamed of; all that genius, aided by cultivation of art, can effect, Mr. Macready is effecting; and the Queen, and her Court, are bound, as a matter of national duty, if not of private inclination, to bestow their fostering patronage on so meritorious and national an effort.[113]

All the more galling was the fact that the Queen repeatedly attended Isaac van Amburgh's lion show at Drury Lane. Shortly after Macready announced he would relinquish his lease, a letter to the editor of *The Times* essentially blamed the Queen for the financial failure of his management:

> . . . one cannot help regretting—most respectfully regretting—that the highest personage in this realm, distinguished no less by her virtues than her rank, and therefore far too valuable a patroness not to exercise an immense influence, should not have found it convenient to enter Drury-lane Theatre once during the present season . . .[114]

The perpetuation of a national theatre was not simply a matter of aesthetics but of public policy. At the start of Macready's Drury Lane management, the *Examiner* had announced that a 'well-conducted theatre' was essential to 'popular cultivation and improvement,' and that in such a project Shakespeare reigned supreme.[115] With neither state support nor royal patronage, there seemed little hope for a national theatre devoted to Shakespeare, undermining the already tenuous arguments for the privilege of patents.

Macready initially supported restricting Shakespeare to the patent theatres but by 1843 he had reversed his position. In 1832 he testified in support of theatrical monopolies before Bulwer-Lytton's parliamentary Select Committee on Dramatic Literature. Macready argued that such monopolies were necessary to ensure a strong troupe at a national theatre devoted to Shakespeare. To his mind, repeal of the monopolies would disperse quality actors over a great many houses and the 'public would suffer in consequence of the efficient companies being broken up.'[116] However, by 1843 he had concluded that the monopolies in fact hindered Shakespearean performance. In his closing address from the Drury Lane theatre after his final performance, he attacked the theatrical laws that effectively gave control of the drama to the proprietors of the patent houses, 'persons utterly unacquainted with the drama, and all appertaining to the dramatic arts.' The result was that the patent theatres were now untenanted; 'the holders of their patents are themselves unable to present the glorious works of Shakespeare to an English audience, and yet are armed by the law with the power to forbid their representation elsewhere.' He concluded his comments with an emotional appeal for his own right to perform Shakespeare:

> For were I now, after all I have given and endured to maintain the drama in these theatres—were I, excluded as I am by circumstances from them, to attempt in a theatre lately licensed by the Lord Chamberlain for performance of the brutes and brute-tamers—were I to attempt there the acting of a legitimate play, 'the law, with all their might to urge it on,' would be put in force to prevent or to punish me! May I not ask for what public benefit such a law is framed? Or for what good purpose it is persisted in?[117]

As the *Examiner* commented in its report on the close of Macready's management: 'Mr Macready was the last and best friend that these patents had . . . They are doomed at last. Nothing can save them.'[118] In fact, barely two months later, Parliament abolished the patent system in the Theatres Regulation Act of 1843.

His management of Drury Lane ended with another public celebration, the presentation of a large piece of silver-plated statuary before an audience of hundreds at the Great Hall of Willis's Rooms.[119] The *Morning Chronicle* described the statuary in detail. Shakespeare stood on a pedestal, at the base of which Macready appeared 'engaged in the restoration of the original text of Shakespeare's plays, and in preparing them for the representation of them in a pure and classic form.' The three sides of the bases depicted scenes that earned Macready particular praise for his management of scenic spectacle: the Senate scene in *Othello*, the Prologue to *Henry V* and the Senate scene in *Coriolanus*. On the angles of the base appeared small images depicting three other Macready productions: *King Lear*, *Macbeth* and *The Tempest*. Macready's 'restoration' leads directly to spectacle—both literally support the bard who stands above. Presented days after Macready's emotional address from the stage of Drury Lane, and after his announcement that he would soon embark upon an American tour, the testimonial served as a spirited farewell to England's great defender of Shakespeare.

Farewell to the Stage

Macready began a series of farewell tours in 1848, performing for the last time in February 1851. First he made a third and final tour of the United States followed by his last provincial engagements and two engagements at the Haymarket. As is well known, his American tour ended in violence when a riot outside the Astor Place Opera House in New York City left twenty-two dead. The Astor Place Riot has been thoroughly discussed and my purpose here is to examine its coverage in London rather than to analyze the riot or the events leading to it.[120] However, some summary is necessary.

The riot stemmed from the rivalry between Macready and Edwin Forrest dating from the American actor's tour of Britain in 1836–37. Forrest performed for Bunn at Drury Lane in the autumn, while Macready performed at Covent Garden, during which time Macready's close friend, John Forster, published scathing reviews of the American. At first simply dismissing the actor as a failure—'Mr. Forrest attempted Lear on Friday night, and failed, we think, even more decisively than in Othello'[121]—his final review took on a decidedly anti-American tone. Writing of Forrest's Richard III, Forster asserted:

> Mr. Forrest's ideas of heroism, and of the passion of courage or despair, appear to have been gathered among the wilds of his native country . . .

> and truly, if hideous looks and furious gestures, ear-splitting shouts and stage-devouring studies, could be supposed to embody a princely dignity, a courageous gallantry, or a terrible despair, why then Mr. Forrest was Richard indeed.

The review concluded by describing Forrest's performance of Richard's battle with Richmond as 'one of the most wretched and melo-dramatic tricks of the profession.' With long black hair that 'came tumbling over his forehead, eyes, and face, with every barbarous turn and gesture,' Forrest degraded the princely Plantagenet into 'a savage newly-caught from out of the American back-woods.'[122]

Forrest reportedly believed these attacks to be motivated by Macready (though Macready visited Forrest's manager to disavow the reviews[123]) and that they were inspired by anti-American sentiment. Though most London papers issued favorable reports during Forrest's first London engagement, his return engagement in 1845 received generally unfavorable notices, which he again attributed to Macready's intervention. Forrest's anger came to a head when he watched Macready play Hamlet in Edinburgh in March 1846. When the actor twirled his handkerchief on the line 'I must be idle,' a loud hiss issued from a box. The objector's identity became common knowledge when *The Times* published a letter by Forrest in which he acknowledged hissing Macready, claiming it every man's right to hiss or applaud and describing Macready's 'fancy dance' as a 'desecration of the scene.'[124]

Forrest remounted the attack when Macready toured the United States in 1848. The 'Eminent Tragedian' was to begin in New York City, and then travel to Boston, Philadelphia, Baltimore, Washington, Richmond, Charleston, New Orleans, St. Louis and Cincinnati before returning to New York for his final engagement. At the start of Macready's Boston engagement, the *Boston Mail* accused the English actor of turning the London press against Forrest and packing his audiences with an angry claque, stressing Forrest's reputation as 'a man of the people' who had risen from poverty.[125] During Macready's engagement in Philadelphia, Forrest appeared in a rival theatre performing the same roles whenever possible. Macready's opening performance was met by an organized disturbance and Macready performed over competing hisses and cheers. At the end of the performance, he addressed the audience, disavowing any role in Forrest's poor reception in London and complaining, 'I had been hissed in a public theatre by an American actor, an act which I believe no other American would have committed, and which I was certain no European would have been guilty of.'[126] Forrest responded by repeating in the *Public Ledger* the accusation that Macready had orchestrated the opposition to Forrest's London performances.

Macready encountered little resistance during the rest of his tour (though in Cincinnati someone in the gallery threw a sheep's carcass onto the stage). However, matters came to a head on his return to New York. His first performance at the Astor Place Opera House was overwhelmed by organized protest. The *Herald* reported that shouts issuing from the gallery included: 'Three groans for the codfish aristocracy!'—'Down with the English hog!'—'Take off the Devonshire bull!' and 'Remember how Edwin Forrest was used in London!'[127] The curtain was abruptly lowered during the third act as chairs were thrown onto the stage. Macready had no intention of performing the following day, but after a committee of prominent New Yorkers petitioned the actor to perform, he agreed. That day, handbills calling on 'Workingmen' to protest the performance appeared in the city. Ten thousand or more reportedly descended onto the theatre, and as bricks rained through its windows, the mayor called out the militia. Twenty-two were killed before the crowd was dispersed. The next day Macready escaped to New Rochelle, where he boarded a train for Boston, and from there sailed back to England.

Londoners were able to follow Macready's American tour through local press reports reproduced or summarized in the London papers with a lag time of about two weeks. The riot, of course, produced a flurry of articles and letters but there was considerable coverage before that. The *Daily News*, the *Era*, the *Morning Chronicle* and of course the *Examiner* fed Londoners daily doses of Macready's favorable notices in United States papers. Taken as a whole, these reports reassured Londoners that Macready had been recognized as the true interpreter of Shakespeare. Following such coverage, reports of disturbances no doubt seemed a senseless affront.

English press accounts of the protests at the Philadelphia theatre and the Astor Place Riot emphasize Macready's calm composure. *The Times* carried two reports of the disturbances when Macready performed in Philadelphia. In both, Macready emerges as a marvel of restraint, demonstrating 'the most gentlemanly forbearance' in the face of gross insults.[128] The *Examiner* announced that '[u]nder unexampled provocation he remained firm and unmoved, and met the grossest assault on his character and person with the utmost forbearance and dignity.'[129] For *The Times*, Macready's high-minded behavior was a heightened example of English manners, and Forrest's charge that Macready conspired to turn critics and audiences against the American was a slur on English national character, not simply an attack on Macready as a private individual:

> If Forrest could establish his charges of inhospitality, persecution, subordination, and Heaven knows what, against Mr. Macready, he would drive that gentleman from every stage in this country, as well as from the Opera House in New York. We in England know no such practice . . . Mr Forrest has mistaken not so much Mr. Macready as the dramatic and literary society of this country when he imagines an organized attempt to deprecate his merits emanating from any man high in British estimation.[130]

The attack on Macready had become an attack on British literary society.

Ultimately, for *The Times* this was not simply a contrast between English forbearance and American ruffianism; it was a contrast between a constitutional monarchy and a republic. The paper began its initial report on the Astor Place Riot by noting that the news followed almost immediately on the report that the parliament building in Montréal had been burnt by an angry mob. As disturbing as it was to learn that a 'bankrupt faction had burnt the Parliament House of our principal colony . . . and had grossly insulted Her Majesty's representative [Lord Elgin]' that news was nonetheless soon overshadowed by 'a more marvelous and more painful affair,' mob violence against an English actor. From here the paper remarked on the similarity between the events in New York and the revolutions and civil war that had rocked Europe a year earlier. The wandering account evidenced more anxiety than cogency, but finally found its grounding in an analysis of the class conflict that disproportionately affects republics. The riot could not be attributed simply to theatrical partisanship or national chauvinism:

> Unfortunately there is a class question in the affair; and nowhere are class questions so terrible as in Republics . . . The Opera house, with its evening dress, and no admission under a dollar, always unpopular, was an additional crime in Mr. Macready . . . When we read of a heavy piece of wood and four chairs being hurled on the stage on the previous Monday, we are forced to suspect something more than a theatrical squabble. On the fatal night the mob was proceeding to the actual destruction of the theatre. This was the work of a 'social' democracy pulling down everything to its own level.

The attack on Macready is much more disconcerting than the recent events in Montréal because Macready so deeply embodies a stereotype of Englishness: urbanity, scholarship, and immersion in the mind of Shakespeare. 'Social' democracies, intent on relentless leveling, can make no room for genius, cannot countenance Shakespeare except in grotesque ranting form. England, with its long traditions of balancing rights and privileges, had produced the institutions that delivered Shakespeare's genius in a fullness that had been impossible in any past age. Except that that was not the case. As Macready had complained, unable to produce Shakespeare, the patentees had succeeded only in preventing others from doing so. The privilege of the patents had failed to protect Shakespeare and it was as yet unclear how the bard would survive in this new age of theatrical leveling.

Macready returned to England more popular than before. *The Times* reported his departure from Boston and his donation of £1,000 to the families of the riot victims, his progress past Halifax, and his arrival in Liverpool on June 4th—in a steamer that also carried Allan MacNab, Member of the Provincial Parliament of Canada. Macready began his final provincial engagements in Birmingham on June 26th. The actor was surprised by the enthusiasm his appearance generated. He recorded in his diary that the Birmingham audience,

> gave me a reception such as I have never witnessed out of London, and *very, very, rarely even there.* They stood up all through the house, waving hats and handkerchiefs, till I was anxious to proceed. I thought to myself: 'Will I not act for you!' The stillness—the rigid stillness that followed—every word ringing on the ear—was really awful.[131]

The announcement of Macready's final performances, combined with the news of his noble patience before the violent animus of American ruffians, generated great box-office. After a highly successful provincial tour he returned to London for his final two engagements at the Haymarket during which he performed primarily Shakespearean roles: Macbeth, Lear, Hamlet, Othello, Henry IV, Wolsey, King John, Shylock, Brutus, Cassius, Benedick and (for the first time in London) Richard II. This was followed by a final benefit at Drury Lane.

Macready's status as a British hero in the Anglo-American culture wars is referenced in several of these reviews. Not surprisingly, on his first performance in London, the reviewer noted that:

> The outrages committed against Mr. Macready during his second [*sic*] visit to America, the perils to which he had been exposed, and the dignity and courage with which he sustained those perils, were fresh in the minds

> of the whole audience, and they seemed resolved that the honours they bestowed should stand in marked contrast to the indignities offered on the other side of the Atlantic.[132]

Subsequent reviews similarly recalled these indignities in describing the enthusiasm of Macready's audience. Later that month, *The Times* remarked that the audience for his *King Lear* was 'as numerous and excited as that which greeted Mr. Macready . . . when he made his first appearance since his return from America.'[133] Even a year later *The Times* would begin its review of his *Macbeth* by noting that '[a] crowded pit rose as Mr Macready entered, and greeted him with an enthusiasm which called to mind the hearty bursts that welcomed him on his two [*sic*] several returns from America.'[134] When finally settling down to discuss the productions, the reviews do not so much discover new features as remind readers of familiar excellencies that will soon pass from view.

At the same time that Macready was winding down his career, he was active in raising funds to pay for the purchase of Shakespeare's birthplace. In 1847, two private committees had purchased the house for the nation, but the sponsoring committees were forced to take out a bank loan when they failed to raise sufficient funds.[135] On Tuesday November 12th 1850, Macready read *Hamlet* at Rugby, his old school, at the request of the head boys who wished to contribute to the funds for Shakespeare's House. The school, head scholars, and principal families of the town witnessed the event. It was recorded in the *Examiner*, which also memorialized the reading in a poem (one of a half dozen or so poems lauding Macready and published in the final year of his career). Similar readings followed at Oxford, Cambridge and Eton.[136] It is evidence of the continued prejudice against actors that on November 18th Macready recorded that the Vice-Chancellor of Oxford had agreed to the reading 'with great reluctance and under compulsion' and, later, that it appeared that he had managed to prevent the reading, 'which he dared not openly refuse,' through a 'trick.'[137]

Macready acted publicly for the last time on February 26th 1851, taking the role of Macbeth at Drury Lane for his benefit performance. *The Times* reported that the crowds surrounding the theatre were so thick that police had to create a cordon so that ticket holders could approach the theatre.[138] On more than one occasion, audiences had to wait for Macready to address them after the performance; he would change out of his theatrical costume preferring to greet his audience as a gentleman rather than an actor. He did the same on that night, returning to the stage in a simple black suit.

On this occasion, however, he had an additional reason for changing out of costume. As George Henry Lewes wrote in his account of the farewell performance:

> Some little time was suffered to elapse wherein we recovered from the excitement, and were ready again to burst forth as Macready the Man, dressed in his plain black, came forward to bid 'Farewell, a long farewell to all his greatness.' As he stood there, calm but sad, waiting till the thunderous reverberations of applause should be hushed, there was one little thing which brought the tears into my eyes, viz., the crepe hat-band and black studs, that seemed to me more mournful and more touching than all his vast display of sympathy: it made me forget the paint and tinsel, the artifice and glare of an actor's life, to remember how thoroughly that actor was a man—one of us, sharer of sorrows we all have known or all must know![139]

On February 24th 1850, between his two Haymarket engagements, Macready's first-born child, Christina, died of tuberculosis, his second child to die of that disease. (Within three years tuberculosis would also claim both his wife and his youngest son, Walter.) As was customary, a year later Macready still donned mourning crepe and black studs.

For Lewes, the sudden intrusion of Macready's personal sorrows onto the stage reversed the gestalt. Macready had made a career of giving over his own domesticity to his characters, allowing them to live as familiar Victorians. He incorporated physical choices that seemed drawn not only from everyday life but from his own person. The *Spectator* noted that Macready's strongest effects were the product of 'little familiar touches—say an ironical expression of contempt, which belongs exclusively to his own manner, and almost to his own physique.'[140] For some, such choices were jarringly mundane. Westland Marston found fault with one of Macready's most 'applauded transitions' in the last act of *Macbeth*: he switched suddenly from 'impetuous command' to an 'ultra-colloquial' voice when asking about the health of his wife.[141] Such familiar solicitations for an ill wife might threaten to transform Macbeth into a domestic drama. However, in Lewes's account it is not that Macready's own sorrow made Macbeth our living contemporary (whether or not that is desirable). Rather, Macbeth's fall clarified the tragic scope of Macready's life, and all of our lives. In that moment, Lewes comes to understand the audience's adoration.

A final outpouring of public approval came on March 1st when upwards of 600 men packed the Hall of Commerce for a dinner honoring Macready.

The speeches given at the six-hour event were recorded in several papers, the *Examiner*'s coverage (not surprisingly) being the most complete. That evening provided a condensed form of the picture of Macready that had been evolving in the popular press over the past several years. First, his greatness emanated from performances that provided clear revelations of Shakespeare's meaning. Bulwer-Lytton, taking the chair, asserted that Macready's farewell performance 'conveyed a more exact notion of what Shakespeare designed than I can recollect to have read in the most profound of the German critics.' Second, Macready had ended the scandal of prostitutes arranging trysts in the general saloon: 'For the first time since the reign of Charles II a father might have taken his daughters to a public theatre with as much safety from all that could shock decorum as if he had taken them to the house of a friend.' Most importantly, Macready had always maintained a gentlemanly decorum. Given Macready's disdain for those high-born who did not merit the privileges they enjoyed, Bulwer-Lytton's final compliment may have most impressed the actor: 'The great may have sought in him the accomplished gentleman, but he has never stooped his bold front as an Englishman to court any patronage meaner than the public, or to sue for the smiles with which fashion humiliates the genius it condescends to flatter.'[142]

Bulwer-Lytton's speech presents Macready as defender of Shakespeare, female innocence and English liberty in the face of inherited privilege. He was, in short, the summation of the middle-class Victorian male. In fact, it was his willingness to bend in deference to women and literature that in part defined this masculine liberty. This idea was underscored in the speeches and banter at the Hall of Commerce. Breaking with tradition, the organizers had intended to provide seats for ladies to be admitted for the dessert course at a reduced fee, but had to abandon the plan soon after announcing the Hall of Commerce venue. The organizing committee was 'besieged by applicants, and in a short time the list of applicants amounted to 1,400,' making room for women an impossibility, according to *The Times*.[143] However, seats for about a dozen women were apparently set in a recess behind the chair.[144] Macready's wife was not among the select, but she was present in Thackeray's toast, which imagined her buying up the next day's papers 'to read every word that is said in praise of her husband' and 'every name of every distinguished man here who has met to do him honour.' Macready replied that his wife was in fact 'home by her hearth,' but that she was 'still in spirit here' telling him to thank the toaster, and 'like a dutiful husband, I obey her orders.'[145]

Macready, as an English gentleman, would never stoop for patronage baser than that of the public. However, this English liberty was contingent on his voluntary obeisance before the idols of both his theatre and his hearth (neither of whom, of course, could be present to question the sincerity of his service). Subservience to Shakespeare had become as much a cliché as subservience to one's wife, but it was through such clichés that Macready asserted his respectability and rightful prominence in society. As an actor, Macready could never take respectability or prominence for granted. In his own speech, Macready alluded to the tenuous status of the actor. Thanking the speakers, he noted that 'my position in society is determined by the stamp which your approbation has set upon my humble efforts' However, that did not leave him coveting traditional distinctions; 'without undervaluing the accident of birth or titular distinction,' he would not exchange their good opinion 'for any favor of advancement that the more privileged in station could receive.'[146]

Formal public honors would await later actors who lavished even greater resources on Shakespeare. Though Irving would be knighted in 1895, the example in Macready's plain view was that of Charles Kean. Kean already enjoyed tremendous royal patronage, a fact that further confirmed Macready in his low opinion of both that actor and the Queen. Kean's biography in some ways resembled Macready's—both were public school students who entered their family's disreputable profession in response to their fathers' financial difficulties and then went on to raise the status of the actor through historically detailed Shakespeare productions. Looking back from retirement, Macready saw a resemblance with a tinge of horror. On reading a review of Kean's 1856 revival of *The Winter's Tale*, he worried aloud to Helena Faucit (now Lady Martin) that he might in some way be responsible for what he saw as a frivolous trend in the theatre:

> 'Do you know,' said he, 'why I take it so much to heart? It is because I feel myself in some measure responsible. I, in my endeavor to give Shakespeare all his attributes, to enrich his poetry with scenes worthy of its interpretation, to give his tragedies their due magnificence, and to his comedies their entire brilliancy, have set an example which is accompanied with great peril, for the public is willing to have the magnificence without the tragedy, and the poet is swallowed up in display. When I read such a description as this of the production of a great drama, I am touched with a feeling something like remorse. Is it possible, I ask myself. Did *I* hold the torch? Did *I* point out the path?'[147]

Did Macready point the way to detailed engagement with the complexities of some of the world's richest plays, or did he demonstrate the power of scene-painting and machinery to fill a house?

Both ways of reading Macready's legacy were on view in the year of his retirement. In 1851, Charles Knight dedicated his famous Pictorial Edition of Shakespeare to Macready. Knight explained that when he had started his project twelve years earlier, the actor had just begun his management of Covent Garden, 'presenting, at one of our then national theatres, the text of Shakespeare, not deformed by presumptuous innovations, and not vulgarized by stage conventionalities.'[148] That same year, Macready could be seen in wax effigy at Madame Tussaud's dressed as Coriolanus 'in the most splendid Roman costume ever seen in the country.'[149] William Charles Macready, Shakespeare scholar or Shakespearean popular attraction? It is more or less the question that Macready himself posed to Helena Faucit. These two testaments to Macready's cultural influence—an eight-volume Shakespeare anthology and a waxwork—point out the false dichotomy of Macready's anxious question, 'Did *I* point out the path?' The popularization of Shakespeare was an industrial project—whether the goal was to sell books or tickets to an exhibition. Religious imagery notwithstanding, every industry seeks to maximize profits and the Shakespeare industry proved no exception. Such was Macready's legacy.

Chapter 2

Edwin Booth: What They Also Saw When They Saw Booth's Hamlet

Gary Jay Williams

Dedicated to Charles H. Shattuck, 1910–92.

Say, if you like, along with Ben Jonson, that Shakespeare was not for an age but for all time. However, among the special gifts of the significant Shakespearean actors has been their genius for registering a conversation between Shakespeare and their own times. I do not mean to assign actors any singular, heroic agency. I speak, rather, of transactions between performer and audience that often occur in a cultural sea change when the individual actor embodies—not without the actor's canny management of it—a sensibility whose encounter with Shakespeare audiences are keen to track. Alexander Pope went three times to see David Garrick's first major outing as Richard III. William Hazlitt went three times to Edmund Kean's Shylock. Young Walt Whitman was swept away by Junius Brutus Booth (1796–1852). Booth embodied Richard III with an aggressive individuality that helped Whitman find his song of himself: 'His genius was to me one of the grandest revelations of my life, a lesson of artistic expression.'[1] The conventional terms that we commonly use for acting, such as 'impersonation' or 'interpretation,' especially in the wake of psychological realism and Stanislavskian actor training, hardly seem adequate to describe transactions of this kind. When Junius's son, Edwin Booth, played Hamlet in 1864–65, Americans turned out in record numbers for his unprecedented 100 consecutive performances. Time after time, their responses were, 'Booth *is* Hamlet,' or 'He looks like Hamlet.'

In this perceived merging of Edwin Booth and Shakespeare's Hamlet lies my subject. To understand it, we need to situate Booth's performance historically with some corrective specificity. We must not dehistoricize him in well-meant efforts to appreciate him by universalizing him. Certainly we also must resist the patriarchal idealizing and romantic framing that characterize many narratives of his life. Americans experienced Booth's Hamlet amid the extraordinary circumstances of the Civil War and the assassination of President Lincoln by the actor's brother, John Wilkes Booth. Seeking to understand the impact of these events on the perception of Booth's performance, this chapter considers, among other things, the arc of actions in the closing year of the war, the theatrical nature of the assassination itself, and a civic ceremony conferring a 'Hamlet medal' on Booth. It considers Walt Whitman's platform readings on the meaning of Lincoln's death and suggests why Americans found compelling the embodied performances by Whitman, the aging national poet, and Booth, the nation's preeminent performer of Shakespeare's Hamlet. It also tracks the ways in which a circle of journalists and handlers close to Booth played a role in the formation and public perception of Booth's Hamlet.

Coming to Booth today, one meets at the door the late Charles H. Shattuck, whose book-length 'reconstruction,' *The Hamlet of Edwin Booth* (1969) is one of the fullest studies of a single actor in a single role ever done. Shattuck was a gifted writer, with a deep knowledge of nineteenth-century theatre practices, astute in theatrical judgment, and firmly planted in his era. His studies of nineteenth-century English and American staging of Shakespeare's plays helped open the way for scholars of my generation to study Shakespeare in performance in the American academy, where formalism had long prevailed.[2] Formalism treated drama as a literary construct, much as Aristotle had treated tragedy, focusing on how it achieved universally recognized effects proper to its perfected, 'natural,' generic form, quite apart from performance. A play's performance was regarded, when considered at all, as suspect: a temporal contamination of the literary text. Shattuck's works helped validate the study of the theatrical lives of Shakespeare's plays. Since then, there have been many profound developments in historiography in general and in theatre history in particular. It has become a given of a systematic theatre historiography that Shakespeare performed is always Shakespeare culturally mediated, and the cultural formations inscribed on any performance invite the historian's scrutiny, whether they have to do with, say, gender constructions in the nineteenth century or postmodern insights into the construction of narratives in the late twentieth. In all cases, we would understand what cultural values are being reinforced (or critiqued) under the sign of Shakespeare and how the actor's embodied performance is in play in this.[3] Few studies of Edwin Booth, however, have reflected such lines of inquiry.[4] Thus it is that my sub-title points to the problems and limits of earlier approaches to the 'reconstruction' of performances and to the need to situate Booth's Hamlet historically and culturally.

The premise of the very first line of Shattuck's preface to his study of Booth's Hamlet would block the path of part of my main argument: 'When the curtain rises on a play, we care nothing for the private lives of actors, but only for their art.'[5] Shattuck was understandably discontent with the little attention the Booth biographies paid to the creative work of the actor in performance. But, of course, the embodied actor is never a thing apart from his art. And spectators in a theatre bring a good deal of information with them, constituted culturally as they are. At a personal level, they may know something about the actor, including other roles he has played, about the fictive identity of Hamlet, or about how other actors have done the role. As we will see, cognitive studies have shown empirically that our minds are always busy merging information and concepts and creating new blends. Spectators are not wholly passive receptors. Booth's Hamlet would not be the first time in theatre history that audiences have experienced the persona of the always-embodied actor together with the fiction of the role. Young Walt Whitman, as mentioned earlier, who loved the masculine environment of the Bowery Theatre in the mid-1830s, was admiring the expansive energies of Junius Brutus Booth himself as Booth performed Richard III. ('Performed' would seem to be a more useful term than 'impersonated.') Contemporaries of Edmund Kean watching him perform King Lear saw the sufferings of the prematurely aging actor and those of his Lear as one.[6] Sarah Bernhardt did not wholly disappear into her Camille or her Hamlet, nor does anyone seem to have wanted her to. Her many self-representations in various media fascinated the public. In Richard Burton's Hamlet (Old Vic 1953 and Broadway 1964), the Welsh actor's virility, rich voice and command of Shakespeare's language, and his 1964 marriage to Elizabeth Taylor were all aspects of a fresh persona, well known to the public through the media. In the Broadway production, the taped voice of John Gielgud as the ghost of Hamlet's father (seen only as a shadow) provided a ghosting of Gielgud's own Hamlet from the 1930s alongside the Hamlet of Burton, the new contender. In recent years, scholars have been exploring the issues of the persona of the actor, 'doubleness,' and 'presence' in live performances.[7]

Shattuck's interest in the 'art' of the actor is in some part a symptom of a historiographical problem: the tension between his ostensible historical project and his universalizing and essentializing one. That is to say, Shattuck wanted his readers to appreciate a Booth whose impersonation of Hamlet transcended Booth's era and was, as far as possible, congenial to the sensibilities of Shattuck and his readers. Shattuck took his main bearings from a manuscript journal of Charles Clarke, in which the young man recorded (based on seeing eight performances and studying reviews) a 60,000-word account of Booth's 1870 performance, including line readings and stage business, together with the strong impressions Booth made on him.[8] Shattuck finds Clarke's sensibility admirable, and for Shattuck's purposes, the journal is ideal in its private, close focus on Booth's performance as an ostensibly self-enclosed, high art event.[9] Inside of Shattuck's reconstructive process of discerning line readings, stage business and scenic details from Clarke's account, the promptbooks and reviews, Booth's Hamlet often seems to exist in an eternal present. Shattuck smartly marks some historical differences (e.g., the elaborate pictorial scenery and the pruning from the text of anything bawdy or indecorous). However, these matters are read as almost harmless accidentals. When Shattuck is working his way toward the 1870 Hamlet at Booth's new theatre, through the long-run Hamlet of 1864–65, he gives but a sentence or two to the assassination of President Lincoln by Edwin's younger brother in 1865, although it affected the public perception of Edwin and his Hamlet thereafter, as we shall see.[10] For Shattuck, even this national tragedy at the end of the Civil War was to be dealt with as something apart from Booth's 'art.'

Shattuck issued the usual cautions in his preface (Booth's 'was not the Hamlet for all ages . . .'). But within the next few sentences, we hear a mix of other notes: 'Yet Booth's art, framed in Victorian plush and ormolu, would be precious to us if we could see it again, beautiful in itself, a lesson in high dedication, a reliving of things long gone.'[11] He continues, saying of the well-known Sarony photograph of Booth in the role in 1870: '. . . and as we memorize its features we want to exclaim, as his father did when Booth was a boy, he "looks like Hamlet."'[12] This was, of course, to assume that there was, and ought to be, a cultural consensus about what Hamlet should look like and mean, and about a golden past to be recovered.

Shattuck's project, a reflection of traditional liberal humanism, is understandable for theatre history studies at the time. The cultural ground barely had been seeded for inquiries such as those into Victorian patriarchy, gender construction, textual instability, or the visual language of empire in the British scenic world for Shakespeare. The systematic study of Shakespeare's plays in performance was in the position of seeking a place at the high table of scholars devoted to the paragon of canonical literature. However, aspiring to that meant, paradoxically, underplaying the profoundly temporal, culturally contingent nature of the theatre. One strategy in the new field was to compile for a given play a line-by-line variorum of actors' line readings and stage business from across four centuries—a kind of conversation among bodiless angels. Some critiques of these earlier theatre history practices are available elsewhere, so my comments here will suffice to bring us to a preliminary view of some of the cultural coordinates of Booth's Hamlet.[13]

The perception, 'Booth *is* Hamlet,' derived in some part from Booth's appealing physical appearance in the role, captured not only in performance but, at the height of his success, in the new photography and media technology (see Figure 1): the slight, lithe, young man in the black Elizabethan tunic, with the casual tumble of black curly hair around the handsome, sensuous face, with the dark, melancholy eyes: all-in-all an image more poetic than patrician, more Etruscan than Northern European. A new genteel class had taken a proprietary interest in Edwin as a new Booth for their more refined era, and with him and in him they found an image of a poeticized, suffering prince.[14] This audience knew, too, that they

Figure 1 Edwin Booth as Hamlet. An 1886 rotogravure reproduction of the original 1870 photograph by Napoleon Sarony. Courtesy of Gary Jay Williams and Josephine S. Williams.

were watching an old order pass and a new generation rise in this son of the legendary Booth. When Whitman offered his often-quoted comparison of the father and son, it was grounded in Whitman's sensibility formed in that earlier era:, 'Edwin had everything but guts. . . . His father had more power and less finish.'[15]

In addition, when Booth began his long-run *Hamlet* in New York in 1864, the war-weary North was just emerging from some of the darker hours of the Civil War. Booth himself was mourning the recent death of his young wife. Within weeks of the end of the run came Lincoln's assassination by John Wilkes Booth. Ultimately, that tragedy would add a national dimension to the perception of Booth's Hamlet. As Booth played the role over the years, many other circumstances in his personal life came into play in a cumulative process that added layers to his persona. So, 'Booth *is* Hamlet' beckons us on like the ghost in the play, signaling a number of intersections of actor and culture, role and performance. I provide below an overview of highlights of his career and then trace in key stages of his life developments in the formation/perception of his Hamlet.

Overview of Booth's Career

Over the three decades from the early 1860s to the late 1880s, Edwin Booth (1833–93) became widely respected as America's finest Shakespearean actor. Hamlet was his signature role for much of that span. Booth rose among many good American actors in the 1860s, in part with the help of the legend of his father, and he then achieved and held a special place, both by virtue of his talent and historical circumstances.

Booth came to be admired especially for his intelligent, lucid delivery of Shakespeare's language, deliberate and well phrased in his mellow, velvet, well-modulated baritone voice. He had a compelling stage presence and created theatrically effective moments in his major roles. His mature style represented a departure from the grand, Romantic tradition of fire-breathing actors—from Edmund Kean through his own father to Charlotte Cushman toward a more refined, relatively natural (but never naturalistic) style. He offered an idealized nobleness or a neo-romantic emotional intensity in relatively temperate registers; in them, American audiences from the mid-1860s through the early 1880s found both a welcome, genteel refinement and relative immediacy. Booth's persona and his style were rooted in a mid-nineteenth-century sensibility and a traditional, conservative view of art as having a high, ennobling purpose.

To describe him as a transitional figure as some have is to misrepresent him. He had no interest in the coming modern realism. Alongside Henry Irving, when they alternated the roles of Othello and Iago in London in 1881, Booth's style looked traditional to critics—what one called 'the old classical school.'[16] Irving himself praised Booth politely as 'a magnificent reader.'[17]

His Hamlet was often described as a melancholic, poetic prince, graceful, with a self-possessed quietude and intelligence, thrust into a tragic responsibility beyond his bearing. From the assassination of Lincoln at the end of the Civil War to the end of Booth's long career, American audiences saw his suffering Hamlet as inseparable from the actor himself. Booth's Richard III, long a staple in his repertoire, probably offered more traces of the theatrical intensity of the older tradition than did his performances in other Shakespearean roles. He also played Shylock, Othello, Benedick, Macbeth, Richard II, Romeo and, in *Julius Caesar*, Cassius, Brutus and Antony. His Shylock (which impressed Lincoln) seems to have been an unsympathetic villain. 'I believe you hold a different estimate of the character,' he once wrote to critic William Winter, 'but I have searched in vain for the slightest hint of anything resembling dignity or worthiness in the part.'[18] His avowed strategy with Iago was to appear to be sincere, not to play the villain overtly.[19] However, there were mixed responses to it. When Booth played Iago to Irving's Othello, critic Mowbray Morris found him to be 'seeming [to be] careless to what goes on . . . yet ever watching his prey with sly, sleepless vigilance.'[20] But Ellen Terry (Desdemona) found Booth's Iago 'deadly commonplace . . . the villain in all the scenes,' and given to ornate, polished effects.[21] Booth's range included the sentimental, as with his Lear (although he got rid of Nahum Tate's version of the play), but sentimentality coupled with the woes of patriarchal figures had a large Victorian audience.[22] Late in his career, he had Hamlet die with the suggestion of a smile as he looked upon the image of the king, his father, in the locket he wore, held up to his eyes by Horatio.[23] In the roles of Shakespeare's lovers, Booth was never comfortable and had little success.

The most admired among his performances in melodramas was the Cardinal in Edward Bulwer-Lytton's *Richelieu*. Written for William Charles Macready, it is a melodrama laboring heavily to be a high poetic drama, full of patriarchal fantasy and fustian to our sensibilities but popular with Victorians for decades. In a baroque plot, the wily Cardinal, now aging and the object of conspiracies, schemes to protect his young female ward from court predators. Booth liked to light a flame with it, mounted it when he felt like 'acting,' and played it across his entire career, perhaps more than any other role save Hamlet. Many thought him at his best in this non-Shakespearean role, opinions that need remembering in any quest for the historical Booth. John Collier, portrait painter of the famous, depicted Booth in a key moment late in the play when the old Cardinal summons up his last remaining powers as a priest of the Church of Rome to protect his young ward:

> Set but a foot within that holy ground
> And on that head—yea though it wore a crown—
> I launch the curse of Rome![24]

Reproductions of the painting and many photographs of Booth in the role were published widely. Among his other impressive roles in melodrama were Sir Giles Overreach in Massinger's *A New Way to Pay Old Debts,* and the deformed jester, Bertuccio, in *The Fool's Revenge.*

Booth made two Edison wax cylinder recordings in 1890 of two Shakespearean set speeches: Othello's story for the Senate of wooing Desdemona and Hamlet's soliloquy, 'To be or not to be.' Only the first survives and is available.[25] The crackling surface noise overwhelms the words at times, but there is enough for one to discern Booth's mellifluous voice, his clear, deliberative delivery (perhaps intensified by the need to make the recording understandable), with its intelligent phrasing and the tonic notes of the idealizing nobility. A recording of Booth delivering a passage from *Richelieu* or *Richard III* might have given us a welcome piece of the rest of him. Booth's biographer Robert Lockridge once suggested that there were always two Booths.[26]

Booth remained, by virtue of his sensibility and background, untouched by the rapidly developing modernist ideas whirling around him, such as those of Marx and Darwin. Their suggestion of the absence in the universe of 'a divinity that shapes our ends' could not have been further from the old world ideals that Booth invoked from the beginning to the end of his career. He suffered many personal tragedies, but it was not in his sensibility to see the human condition with the despair of America's first modernist playwright to come, Eugene O'Neill (1888–1953). Booth was nearer the generation of Eugene's father, Romantic actor James O'Neill, whose Othello Booth admired.[27]

Booth assumed the mission of the high-minded theatre manager, producing Shakespeare's plays in a campaign for art, beauty and respectability. From 1863 to 1867 he co-managed the Winter Garden Theatre in New York, the venue for his long-running *Hamlet* of 1864–65 and other Shakespearean plays. When that theatre burned in 1867, destroying all his scenic and costume stock, Booth rose again, wooing financial supporters for the erection of a lavish, million-dollar theatre in his name. The structure, to be devoted to the highest art in drama, acting and scenic art, was the work of the star architect of the day, James Renwick, designer of the city's St. Patrick's Cathedral. In his new theatre, Booth mounted eight of Shakespeare's plays between 1869 and 1872, taking his cue from Charles Kean's historically researched and romantically pictorial scenery: *Romeo and Juliet, Othello, Hamlet, Julius Caesar, Macbeth, Much Ado About Nothing, The Winter's Tale* and *Richard III.* Members of his casts in these years included Lawrence Barrett, E. L. Davenport, J. W. Wallack, Jr., Emma Waller and Fanny Morant. Audiences expected Booth to be there as the star, however, and so did Booth. He also acted with major international stars of his day, including Cushman, Tommaso Salvini, Irving, Terry and Helen Modjeska. A tour of Germany in 1883 won him laurels from his German peers.

Booth was little inclined to daily oversight of productions and rehearsals, and had little heart for hard business. The expensive enterprise came to disaster during the financial panic of 1873–74, and Booth went into bankruptcy. His reputation and endurance were such that by touring he subsequently paid off his debts and earned another fortune. In an eight-week stand in San Francisco in the late 1870s, he reportedly grossed an unprecedented $96,000.[28] Out of his wealth, he was known to be generous. He was beloved within the profession for giving financial help to struggling fellow actors. His resilience was remarkable by modern standards. In his 1876–77 engagement at the Lyceum Theatre in New York, for example, Booth gave sixty-nine performances over sixty-seven days, performing fifteen different roles.[29]

He became quite careful in the management of his image and talent, availing himself of knowledgeable supporters and pursuing respectability hungrily. He demanded that both his first and second wives, Mary Devlin and Mary McVicker, with whom he had acted, give up their stage careers entirely so that their status as suspect women of the theatre profession would not taint his own reputation. He was devastated by the dishonor that Lincoln's assassination brought to the family name, and worked to redeem it. Booth's own theatre was as lavish a temple to dramatic literature, Shakespeare in particular, as America had ever had.[30] He put his productions into respectable print in promptbook-based editions of fifteen plays in his repertoire, edited by William Winter, the critic who idolized him. In addition, he achieved a respectability among scholars that must have gratified him, for he had had little formal education. Horace Howard Furness took the unprecedented step of asking him—an actor—to provide notes for his variorum editions of *Othello* (1886) and *The Merchant of Venice*

(1888), which Booth did. In his last years, Booth, together with others, including Mark Twain, founded The Players, a gentlemen's club modeled on London's Garrick Club. In his address at its opening, Booth said he wanted it to bring members of the acting profession 'in communion with gentlemen in other arts and professions, whose appreciation of the value of the drama as an aid to intellectual culture must inspire the humblest players with a reverence for his vocation . . . which too many regard as merely a means to the gratification of vanity and selfishness.'[31] It, too, formed part of his long quest for respectability for his profession. He hung a full-length portrait of his father over the fireplace in the Great Hall. He resided on the third floor until his death at age fifty-nine in June 1893. Located on Gramercy Park in Manhattan, it survives today and includes a research library. The current Booth Theatre on West 45th Street was built in Booth's honor in 1913 by producers Winthrop Ames and Lee Shubert; Ames's father had been dedicated to preserving Booth's legacy.

His life, and the lives of his father and younger brother, John Wilkes Booth, have drawn and continue to draw biographers (see the bibliography). Eleanor Ruggles's once popular *Prince of Players* (1953), romantic and skillfully dramatic, was quickly taken up by Twentieth Century Fox as the basis for its 1955 film of that title, starring Richard Burton as Edwin and Raymond Massey as his father. The Booths have been the subject of several plays, none with staying power, including Milton Geiger's *Edwin Booth* (1958), starring Jose Ferrer and Austin Pendleton's *Booth* (1994). Several actors have created one-person shows on Edwin, including Gary Sloan, John Ammerman and Rodney Lee Rogers.

Being the Son of Junius Brutus Booth

To prepare the ground for considering the performance and public perception of Booth's Hamlet, I begin with the influence of his father on his formation as an actor. I will then follow his career, tracking especially the threads of his creation and management of his image of Hamlet with the assistance of Adam Badeau, Mary Devlin, and several key journalists and social elites.

His father, the English-born actor, Junius Brutus Booth, had emigrated to the United States in 1821 and had built his reputation there by the time Edwin was born twelve years later. The family home and Junius's beloved retreat was near Bel Air, Maryland, about twenty-five miles northeast of Baltimore, on a farm deep in the woods. Edwin was the seventh of ten children of Junius and Mary Ann (Holmes) Booth (1802–58). Of the six who lived to maturity, three had careers in the theatre—Junius Jr. (1821–83), Edwin and John Wilkes (1838–65). The youngest, Joseph Adrian (1840–1902), dabbled in it. Asia (1835–88) married actor John Sleeper Clarke, a school friend of Edwin's, who later co-managed the Winter Garden Theatre with him and was its leading light comedy actor. Asia wrote loyal but valuable biographies of her father, Edwin, and John Wilkes. By the 1840s, the family was living on the farm in the summers and in Baltimore in the winters, supported by the income from Junius's tours.

Junius had established a reputation as an actor of prodigious talent and emotional intensity in London. In 1817, not yet twenty-one, he had astounded audiences at Covent Garden in the role of Richard III, winning favorable comparisons to Edmund Kean, the Romantic starburst of the era, then at the height of his career at Drury Lane. In the competition with Kean, Junius showed power sufficient to stimulate the great actor to even greater heights, and audiences loved the rivalry between the star and the new contender. Kean and his claque made sure the threat was defused, however, shrewdly manipulating the green young actor out of position. But Junius had further successes over the next three seasons, including an impressive King Lear at Covent Garden.[32]

If Junius at some point in these years had considered seeking his fortune in the United States, he soon had a compelling, personal motive. He wanted to take up a new life with Mary Ann Holmes, an attractive Covent Garden flower girl with whom he was in love.[33] In doing so, Junius was fleeing an unhappy marriage, deserting his first wife of six years, Adelaide Delannoy Booth (1792–1858) and their two-year old son, Richard Junius Booth (1819–68). In 1821, Junius and a pregnant Mary Ann sailed for Norfolk, Virginia, where Junius began to build his career in America. For years, Junius kept Adelaide and Richard in the dark about his Maryland family, although providing his English family with regular financial support. After Adelaide's discovery of the Maryland family and the subsequent public acrimony, Junius and Adelaide were finally divorced in 1851. Shortly thereafter, Junius and Mary Ann were married in Baltimore, probably for both legal reasons and respectability.[34]

For the three decades from 1821 to 1851, Junius was a touring star in major American cities, bringing the romantic style of acting Shakespeare across the country long after Edmund Kean had come and gone.[35] He was afflicted by periods of temporary mental aberrations, and he drank heavily at times. Both were visible to the public, and the press carried stories of the 'mad tragedian.' Like George Cooke and Kean before him, Junius's tour de force was Richard III. His repertoire consistently included Shylock, Hamlet, Iago, Othello, Macbeth, Lear and melodramatic staples such as Sir Giles Overreach and Sir Edward Mortimer in *The Iron Chest.* Out of his theatrical formation in London and his work with actors such as Charles Kemble, John Duruset and even, on one occasion, Sarah Siddons, Booth had an intelligent command of Shakespeare's language in the classical tradition—Edwin bore his influence in this—and he could sustain a characterization throughout a performance. These attributes he brought alongside the big ship of his Romantic intensity, and it was for this combination that at least one American critic preferred him to Kean and Kean's flashes of lightning.[36] Junius's voice was deep and massive but capable of flexibility and melody. In an exuberant volume of posthumous praise, his friend Thomas Gould provided many examples, at one point describing Booth's delivery of the opening lines of Hamlet's 'To be or not to be' soliloquy 'in a voice like the mystic murmur of a river running under ground.'[37] An independent spirit with limitless energy, he was well matched to the dynamics of the young nation, as was his close, younger friend, Edwin Forrest (1806–72), for whom he named his son, Edwin.[38] The elder Booth's fame and republican political views drew him into the company of Sam Houston and Andrew Jackson on a few occasions.[39]

With the peaks of fame, there were also, increasingly, the valleys of Junius's drunkenness and his legendary psychological breakdowns. During one episode he was found naked in a stable yard in the snow at midnight, declaiming lines from *King Lear.* He once appeared at a church service in his full costume for Cardinal Richelieu, from the Bulwer-Lytton melodrama. He sometimes suddenly disappeared before advertized performances, driving theatre managers to despair. He would recover from his aberrational periods within a few days and return to normal. However, he experienced serious breakdowns in the years after three of the couple's then six children died in a cholera epidemic in February 1833. These were devastating to Mary Ann as well.[40] Junius attempted suicide twice in the next few years. Still, through the last year of his life, he was earning wide respect for his powers. At age fifty-five in 1851, in a run at the National Theatre in New York that was like that of many of his tour stops, he played Lear, Richard III, Giles Overreach, Macbeth and Iago across five evenings. Although he was playing with an inept company on this occasion, a critic for the *Spirit of the Times* said of him what many critics before had: 'Mr. Booth is undoubtedly the best tragedian in this country at the present day, and in the world, to our knowledge.'[41]

An earnest appreciation of his powers, together with the tales of his madness, was written by Thomas Ford in 1846, *The Actor; Or, A Peep behind the Curtain. Being Passages in the Lives of Booth and Some of his Contemporaries.*[42] Ford justifies his coverage of Booth's madness (widely known in any case) by taking the standard Romantic view that it was inseparable from the actor's genius for representing the passions. In genius 'is the great and insatiable craving of the soul which this world cannot satisfy.' When Edwin came to write an essay on his father in 1886, he defended him in much the same way.[43]

From 1847 to 1852, Edwin, beginning at age fourteen, served as dresser and caretaker of his unstable parent on tours, a difficult, sometimes painful vigil for him, according to his sister, Asia. Edwin's painful vigils were not the whole of his relationship to his father, however. His father had a capacious if flawed mind, and an intellectual curiosity that roamed restlessly from farming to theology.[44] Junius had received a classical education and showed an early interest in painting and sculpture (as Edwin later would).[45] Junius shared his own father's passionate admiration for the emerging new republic, and ultimately he brought his widowed father, a lawyer, to live with the family in Maryland.[46] Junius was well read and valued his books. When theatre manager Thomas Hamblin once visited him on the Maryland farm, which Asia Clarke describes in romantic, Wordsworthian terms, Hamblin asked Junius how he managed to bear the solitude. Junius replied, pointing to his books, 'Look—there are Shelley, and Byron, and Wordsworth; here are "rare" Ben Jonson, Beaumont and Fletcher, and Shakespeare and Milton. . . . These are my companions.'[47] Junius was proficient enough in French to give two successful performances of Oreste in Racine's *Andromaque*, performing with a French cast for a largely Francophone New Orleans audience in 1828.[48]

Junius and Mary Ann arranged for their children to have some formal education. Junius read to the family and took the children to the occasional respectable theatre performance in Baltimore, one of which was of Byron's gloomy patriarchal tragedy *Werner*, with Macready. Edwin, however, almost certainly received less formal schooling than his brothers.[49] Winter reported that Edwin's education was 'fitful and superficial,' because he was taken out of school to accompany his father.[50] He attended a neighborhood school in Baltimore and he took violin and banjo lessons. He acquired no languages then (nor later in life), nor did his intelligence run so restively to the speculative as did his father's. He was sent to study at intervals with a Mr. Kearney who encouraged dramatic representations among his teenage boys. On one occasion at this school, Edwin and his friend John Sleeper Clarke enacted the quarrel scene between Brutus and Cassius in *Julius Caesar.* Junius slipped into the back of the schoolroom to watch.[51] In his early teens, Edwin was focusing his energies on performing, organizing a little group that gave some basement performances for pennies and then, at a brave fourteen, persuading the manager of Baltimore's Holliday Theatre to cast him. For that, he was not prepared, and it all came to embarrassment.[52]

It was at this point that the duty of minding his erratic father during his tours fell to Edwin, after his older brother's stint in this capacity. Edwin proved to be an effective, firm caretaker, probably drawing on a part of his temperament derived from his mother. Mary Ann often nursed Junius back to health after his breakdowns. She managed their homes for three decades and cared for their children and her alcoholic and aging father-in-law. She was required to be the steady-burning lamp for the family.[53]

As to his theatre training, Edwin wrote that his father discouraged his children from following his profession and that he 'never gave me instruction, professional advice or encouragement in any form.'[54] However, a rather different picture emerges if we look closely at his years with his father—even granting that Junius was an intimidating, authoritarian figure who could be quite self-absorbed. During the five years when Edwin traveled the circuits with his father, he would have watched him repeatedly perform some twenty roles in as many plays, nine of them Shakespearean.[55] 'Watched' may not be quite accurate, for Junius reportedly restricted Edwin to the dressing room, where he listened and learned the plays by ear and by heart.[56] He spent more time with his father's plays than the schoolbooks he brought with him. In time, Edwin was performing in them. His first role on the tours came on September 10th, 1849 at the Boston Museum. The stage manager assigned him the part of Tressel in Colley Cibber's version of *Richard III*, with his father in the title role. When Edwin came to his father's dressing room in costume before the performance, Asia Clarke tells us, his father grilled him:

Junius: Who was Tressel?
Edwin: A messenger from the field of Tewksbury.
Junius: What was his mission?
Edwin: To bear the news of the defeat of the king's party.
Junius: How did he make the journey?
Edwin: On horseback.
Junius: Where are your spurs?

Edwin glanced quickly down, and said he had not thought of them.

Junius: Here, take mine.[57]

Every actor who has earned his spurs would recognize the fundamentals being taught here (and probably even the catechetical style).

The teenage Edwin also played Laertes to his father's Hamlet, Macduff to his Macbeth, Cassius to his Iago, Gratiano to his Shylock and Edgar to his Lear. Junius was now in his early fifties, and these pairings would not meet any modern ideal of ensemble acting, but in the touring star system in nineteenth-century America, that was not the game. And trials by fire that these would have been for young Edwin, he was apprenticed to a genius. There was a great deal to be learned from his father's command of language, his intellectual comprehension, his dramatic imagination, and his emotional power. He observed his father's absorbing preparations for his performances. 'If Shylock was to be his part at night, he was Jew all day,' Edwin remembered.[58] The roles in his father's repertoire became Edwin's own first ground. When in the summer of 1850, Edwin and Clarke, his future brother-in-law, decided to give some dramatic readings at the Court House in Bel Air, the selections came from Junius's repertoire. Edwin also did a solo piece from *Richelieu*, a role Junius seldom performed, believing himself too short for it at about 5'3".

In 1851 in New York, Junius, pretending to be ill, thrust his protesting eighteen-year-old son into the role of Richard III at the National Theatre. Edwin won prolonged applause, no doubt offering some semblances of his father in the role. He was years away from finding his own voice. The manager led him before the curtain, introducing him proudly as 'the worthy scion of a noble stock,' and adding *sotto voce*, 'I'll wager they don't know what that means.'[59] However, that audience and those to come knew Edwin was the son.

In the summer of 1852, Junius decided to try the West at the urging of Junius, Jr., then managing a theatre in San Francisco. Edwin accompanied his father for what was to be the last time. The three Booths played together in San Francisco and Sacramento. For his benefit on the final night in Sacramento, Edwin played Jaffier to his father's Pierre in *Venice Preserv'd*. Asia Clarke records an exchange with his father that night that Edwin would remember after his father's death as having contained a pledge:

> Arrayed in black for his part of Jaffier, Edwin perceived his father seated on the steps of his dressing room, who at his approach observed, 'You look like Hamlet; why did you not act Hamlet for your benefit?' Edwin carelessly replied, 'If I ever have another, I will.'[60]

Junius decided to return to the East, advising Edwin to remain and perfect himself in his profession. Enroute home on a steamboat on the Mississippi River after an engagement in New Orleans, Junius was afflicted with an infection that swiftly took his life. Edwin was stunned; the large genius and difficult love of his father would be a haunting presence for the rest of his life. At the time, he was not ready for responsible adulthood nor was he prepared to develop his gifts carefully. Over the next four years, he managed to win work in Gold Rush mining towns in Nevada, returning to work in San Francisco under his brother's management. He then toured Australia as the leading man with Laura Keene's company, playing Shylock to her Portia, but the tour was unsuccessful, for which Keene blamed Edwin's acting. In these years, he also began spending himself in sexual debauchery and alcoholism. 'Before I was eighteen I was a drunkard, at twenty a libertine,' he later recalled in a remorseful letter to a friend. 'I was allowed to roam at large, and at an early age in a wild and almost barbarous country where boys became old men in vice very speedily,' he wrote, ascribing his faults to the 'wilds of California and the still less refined society of Australia.'[61] Returning East did not cure him.[62] It would be ten years later, with the death in 1863 of his first wife, Mary Devlin, his 'angel' who had sought to inspire poetic idealism in him, that Edwin finally would modify his drinking habits. His remorse about these years would contribute to his long quest thereafter for respectability.

Becoming Booth's Hamlet

He returned to the East Coast at twenty-three in 1856 to try to build his career. Boston was his target, but when his agent could not place him there immediately, he toured for six months, from Baltimore's Front Street Theatre through theatres in the South and the Midwest. For two weeks in February, Edwin then played the grand new Boston Theatre, with a capacity of 3000, then the country's largest, with a deep bow-front stage, stacked with four plush boxes at either side. Critics, interested in the promise of Junius's son, found him better suited to his repertoire of fiery roles than to Hamlet. They saw in him traits of his father, some admirable ('the fire, the vigor, the strong intellectuality . . .') and some annoying (the 'peculiar nasal twang.'). The critic for the *Traveller* acknowledged the technical skills that he had acquired: 'He has the charming and accurate modulations of voice . . . the magnetic sympathizing quality in his tones. They charm you, without telling you the secret of their charm.'[63] Shattuck reports that a group of Cambridge citizens and Harvard professors, together with fifty-one students, were impressed enough with his Hamlet (of which he gave only one performance) to petition for an extension.[64] That was not possible, but this response from a genteel elite suggests that in this role Edwin was striking some notes in a different, quieter key than his father's. Edwin's acting soon would undergo much more refinement in that direction.

Booth tried New York after Boston. William Burton booked him for his New Theatre, advertizing him as the 'Son of the Great Tragedian' and 'Hope of the Living Drama,' epithets that distressed Booth.[65] The genial, English-born Burton, a Shakespeare bibliophile, had earned some stature. He had staged relatively refined Shakespearean revivals at his old theatre on Chambers Street but now was struggling to sustain his new theatre against the competition and amid a general economic crisis. However, the occasion proved a crucial one in Booth's career. Here he was seen by Adam Badeau, a twenty-five year old arts and culture critic, who became his influential mentor.[66] Winter, then early in his career as a critic, wrote sympathetically of Booth bearing the burden of his father here.[67]

Booth opened with *Richard III* and followed with the melodramas and *Hamlet*. He has great promise and 'the true fire of genius,' wrote the *Herald*'s critic, but 'Art has done little to mature him,' he added. 'His elocution is often faulty, his attitudes strained and unnatural.' He is described as being of the 'old school.' But then again, 'in particular scenes, however, he is truly great.'[68]

For Badeau, the faults came from inexperience. In one of his columns for the *Sunday Times*, published under the name 'the Vagabond,' he wrote of seeing genius in Booth, 'the unmistakable fire, the electric spark, the god-like spark, which mankind has agreed to worship.' To experience that one touch of genius, an audience member might wait for an entire act, but then 'it is transcendent, it goes straight home, it compensates.'[69] In Booth, Badeau found an actor 'who has made me know what tragedy is.'[70] Among his other virtues, he told his readers, were Booth's youth and beauty, his mobile face, his musical voice, and his 'impulsive, soulful nature.'[71] Badeau offered himself as a mentor and, in effect, a handler who could facilitate the circulation of notices of Booth in the press and arrange some important introductions.[72] Booth welcomed the intercessions.

Badeau took Booth to art galleries and provided him books on theatre history. They corresponded frequently on theatrical matters, with Badeau urging Booth on to new heights of poetic idealism and beseeching him to stop drinking and smoking, and to avoid venereal disease.[73] Badeau seems to have taken special care in his curatorship of Booth's Hamlet.

He introduced Booth to William Hazlitt's picture of Hamlet as the 'young and princely novice,' the 'gentleman and scholar' on whose brow should sit 'a pensive air of sadness,' whose passion is to think, not act.[74] Another reference point was Goethe's famous Romantic image of Hamlet as the thoughtful man with a 'tender soul,' whom fate asks to undertake a great action. Goethe describes him as having 'a lovely pure, noble and most moral nature, without the strength of nerve which forms a hero, [which] sinks beneath a burden which it cannot bear and cannot cast away . . .'[75] Badeau in later years wrote of having worked closely with Booth in rehearsals and practice sessions, but one doubts the effect of this on Booth, who as Badeau knew, worked intuitively, never in the abstract.[76]

Badeau saw in Booth no less than a symbol of a new kind of American art for a new American age. 'The spirit of God had moved on the waters,' he writes in a 'Vagabond' essay.[77] Badeau nearly worshipped Booth over the next few years, sometimes competing for his time and affection with Mary Devlin, whom Booth was soon to marry. (Badeau even sometimes addressed Booth in letters as 'Prince,' which Booth disliked).[78] In several of Badeau's letters to Booth there are indications that he was sexually attracted to Booth, and Lisa Merrill believes the men were sexually intimate, based on Badeau's 'Vagabond' essay, 'A Night with the Booths.' The relationship, she believes, influenced the images of the young, beautiful, soulful Booth as Hamlet that Badeau so successfully circulated. Both Ginger Strand and Merrill have shown a similarly close relationship between critic James Oakley and Edwin Forrest, from which issued, of course, a different kind of branding.[79]

Booth soon found another source of personal devotion and support of his art in these critical years from the rising young actor, Mary ('Mollie') Devlin (1840–63). In Richmond in 1856, she had played opposite Booth, and their paths had crossed since. In June of 1858, she played Juliet to Charlotte Cushman's Romeo.[80] They became engaged in 1859, at which point Booth, apparently now cautious about marrying a woman whose virtue, as a member of the theatre profession, would be suspect—his own promiscuity notwithstanding—required that Mary forsake the stage. Further, he sequestered Mary for a year in a residence in Hoboken, New Jersey, providing tutors in French and music, and enlisted Badeau (her competitor), to oversee her while he went on the road. It is some indication of how anxious Edwin Booth was for respectability and the lengths to which he would go in managing his image. Sadly, Mary submitted to the tyranny: 'You need never tell me, Edwin,' she wrote to him, 'what your motive is for having me seclude myself this one year—I know . . . that it is for me, for *me* alone, that your bounty gives so much.'[81] She promised she would not 'mix again with the world until I am your wife.'[82] Mary was devoted to help him become 'everything that the world has predicted.' 'If my love is selfish, you will never be great—a part of you belongs to the world. I *must* remember this . . .'[83] Often in her letters, she refers to herself playfully but devotedly as his 'daughter,' and later Edwina, their daughter, wrote that Mary often called Edwin her 'Hamlet.'[84] They were married in Boston on July 7th, 1860. Cushman wrote to her young lover, Emma Crow: '*Edwin Booth is not a gentleman.*' Gentlemen did not 'descend into being "Masters" merely for the sake of . . . showing their power over a weak woman.'[85]

Mary Devlin now saw Edwin as called to the highest purposes of dramatic art and in her letters urged him to rise to this. Like Badeau, she offered guidance, infused with idealized devotion. She wrote to him of Goethe's idea of Hamlet. She delved into the aesthetics of French critic Victor Cousins, who celebrated a Platonic ideal of beauty as the intelligible, sensible form of Truth. Art should bring us to our highest good.[86] Speaking of the decline of drama into the immoral and commonplace, Mary told Edwin that the day would come when 'Tragedy will have its sway! you are held as its only true representative in this day—and you can, if you *will*, change the perverted taste of the public, by your truth—and sublimity and you *must study* for this!'[87]

Mary also reinforced him as he worked at what had become the key practical development in his style: 'The conversational, colloquial school you desire to adopt is the only true one, Edwin, for the present day; but, as you reasonably add, "too much is dangerous." ' In support of this, Mary cited the example of Matilda Heron, an actor whose once moderate 'naturalness' had deteriorated, Mary believed, into the commonplace.[88] Mary commended Edwin in the same letter for improvements he had made in the part of Richelieu; so his moderations apparently were extending at least somewhat to his melodramatic roles. After Mary's death three years into their marriage, Booth would cling dearly to the idealism that she had represented.[89] Devlin and Badeau were both important partners in the education and refinement of Edwin Booth, and in the management of his image. The public perception of Booth also was to be deeply affected by events yet to come.

By the early 1860s Booth was rising to prominence. In Boston in September 1860, critics praised his Hamlet, now apparently showing fruits of the Badeau-Devlin coaching. Critics spoke of his 'natural grace' and the 'delicacy and refinement of his conception.'[90] Neither his Richard III nor his Macbeth generated the same interest. Booth then moved to New York, where Forrest reigned but gradually outdrew him, his Richelieu being the biggest attraction. Still he was regarded as 'a fine copy' of his father and as better in melodrama than in *Hamlet*.[91] His other Shakespearean roles now included Iago and Othello. In Philadelphia he starred in *Macbeth* opposite Cushman. She told the slightly built, relatively genteel Booth, 'Your rehearsal is very interesting—but Macbeth was the grandfather of all the Bowery ruffians.'[92]

For 1861–62, Booth set his eye on his first engagement in London, at the Haymarket Theatre, leaving the United States as the Civil War was beginning. He was not received with any special enthusiasm, except as Richelieu, in London, Manchester, or Liverpool. England's economy had a great stake in cotton imports from the southern states, and that was where its sympathies lay. Mary Devlin's letters home record the antipathy she and Edwin felt.[93] Their daughter, Edwina (Mary had hoped for a son) was born in Fulham, west London, in December. According to one anecdote, Edwin put an American flag on his wife's bed so that Edwina would be born under it.[94] In any case, Edwin and John Wilkes, born in the border slave state of Maryland, itself a house divided, were already on opposite sides of the war.

On their return to New York, the Booths came into the elite and influential New York literary salon of Richard Henry Stoddard, poet and literary editor, and his wife, Elizabeth Drew Stoddard, a novelist and short story writer. In this circle were Thomas Bailey Aldrich, poet and later editor of the *Atlantic Monthly*, and a close friend of Winter; and Lilian Woolman—Mrs. Thomas Bailey Aldrich. There Booth met Bayard Taylor, the journalist and travel writer, and Launt Thompson, a sculptor who would soon do a bust of Booth as Hamlet. In this circle were also E. C. Stedman, poet, critic, member of the Board of the New York Stock Exchange, and editor of Edgar Allan Poe's works; James Lorimer Graham, art connoisseur, Century Club member, and eventually American consul-general in Italy; and Parke Godwin and George William Curtis, associate editors at *Putnam's* magazine.[95] The journalists among them promoted Booth in feature essays in the decade to come. Curtis in *Harper's Magazine,* Taylor in the *Spirit of the Times,* and Stedman in the *Atlantic Monthly* would instruct their readers in the development of Booth's new, post-Edwin Forrest, high-culture Hamlet. As we shall see, their essays are registers of the sensibilities to which Booth was then appealing.

Booth was welcomed back in both New York and Boston in the fall of 1862 by large audiences. In his Hamlet, with which he opened in New York, a *Herald* critic found freshness and originality but a lack of 'force.' But he added, 'It has merits of its own that will recommend it to people of cultivated taste.'[96] Booth also played Shylock, Petruchio, Richard III and Romeo. He remained for seven weeks, half of it performing in melodramas.

By the time Booth moved to Boston in November, his wife had become afflicted with tuberculosis. Booth rented a home in Dorchester and put her under a doctor's care but she declined rapidly. Some account of her death and his behavior at the time are necessary, for both had lasting impact on him. In February Edwin returned to New York to perform. Aldrich and Thompson became close chaperones, trying to keep him sober, monitoring Edwin much as Edwin had his father.[97] However, they were not wholly successful. Mrs. Stoddard even wrote to Mary to come to New York, sick or well, to intervene because Booth was so drunk at one performance that the management considered ringing down the curtain before the play was half over.[98] If the cause was Edwin's anxiety about his wife, his drinking—and not even she had been able to save him from his history of alcoholism—was not helpful.[99] On February 18th and 19th he received two letters from Mary's physician reassuring him that she was gaining strength and urging him (possibly at Mary's request) not to be anxious. Drunk in his dressing room during his performance of Richard III on February 20th, Edwin ignored telegrams imploring him to come home immediately because of Mary's declining condition. When the stage manager finally read one to him, the last train to Boston had gone. His wife was dead by the time he arrived home the next day. The *Herald* on the 23rd asked the public to understand that the cause of his recent poor performances had been his wife's illness and then blamed the theatre's management for continuing to feature him. But Edwin's drinking was his own failing, with sad consequences for Mary Devlin. And it haunted him.[100]

He buried her in Mount St. Auburn Cemetery in Cambridge and plunged himself into sorrow over his wife's death and remorse about his drinking, to an extent that his friends worried for his sanity. Mrs. Aldrich remembered: 'Much of the time he was as Hamlet—with the "antic disposition" of variable moods of black despair, hysterical laughter, and tears.' He sought out a spiritualist for séances and poured out his grief in self-indulgent letters to friends. Writing to Badeau, now in the Union Army and recently wounded, he spoke of death, asking that if Badeau were to die, 'if you do go, *come back to me,* and assure me of the reality of what perplexes us all so often. None need the conviction more than I.'[101] Booth's loss was, of course, widely known, and some would see the effects in his Hamlet. Mrs. Stoddard wrote a poem on his wife's death, published in the *New York Post* (March 4, 1863) and a then well-known poet, Dr. Thomas W. Parsons, composed two four-stanza poems for her, one of which was intended for a tablet for her grave.[102] Booth absorbed himself in his two-year-old daughter, Edwina, and seems to have brought his drinking under some control.[103]

Over the next eighteen months, leading up to his 100-night *Hamlet* of 1864–65, Booth devoted himself assiduously to refining his performance. He took not only inspiration but also some guidance from the marble image of his Hamlet that Launt Thompson had sculpted in the summer of 1863, a classical bust of a pensive, troubled Hamlet, somewhat more mature and tempered, which was where his performance was headed.[104] He even had the bust displayed in Boston theatre lobbies and art shop windows.[105] Seeing him perform the role in the fall of 1863, the *Herald* critic credited him for working toward filling in 'what had been but a sketch of a great picture,' yet still found inconsistencies: 'He puts in quite as many bad touches as good, quite as many faults as beauties.' Among the faults were 'his tendency to overact, to gesticulate too much, to twist his body into unnatural shapes.' He had a choice to make: if Booth would become the greatest actor in the country, 'he must now act for the intellectual, and not for the gallery portion of his audiences.'[106]

In the spring Booth enjoyed sensational success with his performance in *The Fool's Revenge,* his revision of Tom Taylor's version of Victor Hugo's *Le Roi s'amuse.* Booth played the deformed jester, Bertuccio, who must demean himself in a dance for the amusement of cruel courtiers. His wife had thought the piece beneath the art ideals at which Edwin should aim, but the melodrama became another staple in his repertoire thereafter.[107] Booth's judgment about what would draw at the box office—he always knew his own power as a star figured in the equation—proved correct. This success, together with his recent profitable acquisition and operation of the Walnut Street Theatre in Philadelphia (co-managed with Clarke, his brother-in-law), probably helped give him the bankroll and the confidence with which to enter into the management of the Winter Garden in the summer of 1864 with Clarke and William Stuart.

Booth also continued to refine his Hamlet. Seeing it in May 1864, Bayard Taylor in the *Spirit of the Times,* instructed his readers to attend to the process:

> You see it today, and pronounce it perfection; go next week, and you find that he has gilded refined gold, shaded a little here, touched with sharper color a point here, evoked a new meaning from some apparently meaningless phrase, and all with that reverent regard for the author which all true Shakespearean actors must ever feel.[108]

Booth now immersed himself in plans for a full-dress production of *Hamlet* as the major event of the fall season at the Winter Garden Theatre, with sets featuring Norman architecture. In this, he imitated Charles Kean's mid-century historical pictorialism, a practice Booth followed throughout the rest of his career. For his own performance, Booth by now had arrived at a firmer hold on the Hamlet he had been developing, and American audiences were apparently ready for it. Between the first night of this famous *Hamlet* on November 26th 1864 through to its closing on March 22nd 1865, a critical consensus emerged that Booth had attained new heights in the art that put him in the ranks of Garrick and the elder Kean. Even the *Herald* critic was now fully persuaded. Booth 'gave to the very life the picture of a reflective, sensitive, gentle, generous nature, tormented, borne down, and made miserable by an occasion and by requisitions to which it is not equal.' This sounds much like the criticism of Hazlitt and Goethe in which Adam Badeau and Mary Devlin had educated Booth. The *Herald* stressed Booth's lucidity: 'The performance of Hamlet by Mr. Booth is a continual elucidation of Shakespeare.' Now, 'there are no inconsistencies, no mysteries no knotty or incomprehensible points in the part . . . All is as clear daylight.' The *Times* thought Booth now had no living equal in the part, with each new performance revealing 'fresh traces of intellectual command, persistent study and emotional sensibility.' The *Albion* spoke of the 'spiritual ideal' of Shakespeare's genius having been realized.[109]

The reviewers gave few explicit performance details, for their chief interest was in describing their overall impression of Booth, as we shall see. Like later critics, they were struck by how he played Hamlet's first encounter with his father's ghost. Badeau described it better than most when he first saw Booth address the ghost: 'I'll call thee Hamlet, / King, father, royal Dane (1.4.26).'

> Booth portrays him awed, of course, at the tremendous visitation, but still more imbued with a filial and yearning tenderness. The tones of his voice, especially when he falls on his knees to the ghost, and cries out 'Father!' The expression of his face, and above all, of his eye, embody this new and exquisite conception, and seem to me more affecting even than the fright of Garrick could have been, which Fielding says made all spectators also fear. Booth makes them share, instead, his tenderness.[110]

The cry of filial yearning on 'father' originated with John Philip Kemble more than half a century earlier, although Booth fell to his knees on it. Kemble did so on the ghost's exit, while Booth then fell prostrate to the floor. At some point in Booth's career, for the closet scene, in which Hamlet confronts his mother with a picture of his father, Booth wore in his locket the image of his own father ('Look here upon this picture . . .' [3.4.52]).[111]

More than any single moment, it was the image of Booth ('Mr. Booth looks the ideal Hamlet') together with the consistency of the emotional tone of his performance that George William Curtis stressed in his long, end-of-season editorial essay in *Harper's*. Booth's image was not in the familiar visual tradition of Thomas Lawrence's 1802 painting of Kemble as Hamlet, imperious and 'preternaturally tall' in a long black cloak, trimmed in fur, a skull in hand and wearing both the Order of the Garter and the Danish Order of the Elephant pendant on a ribbon around his neck.[112] Booth's Hamlet, Curtis wrote, was 'princely,' of 'greater fitness,' given 'his small, lithe form, with the mobility and intellectual sadness of his face, and his large melancholy eyes that satisfy the most fastidious imagination that this is Hamlet as he lived in Shakespeare's world.'[113] This image of Booth's 1864–65 Hamlet would have been very much like that in the 1870 Sarony photograph. Writing with some humor to Badeau about all the production preparations, Booth said: 'I shall be called upon to be genteel and gentle, or rather pale and polite, about the 27th of November.'[114] Booth was well aware by now, of course, of what his handlers and the 'cultivated' and 'intellectual' audiences expected of him, and of what he could do effectively. The other point that Curtis developed at length was 'the pervasive sense of the mind of a true gentleman sadly strained and jarred,' a mind 'conscious of its power to master the mystery of life,' but overwhelmed by the burden that confronts him. 'Throughout the play the mind is borne on in a mournful reverie.'[115]

Mrs. Aldrich, recalling her impression of that performance, wrote not of Shakespeare's imagined world but of Booth's real one:

> The profound sorrow of Mrs. Booth's death had deepened the introspective expression of Mr. Booth's face, and made his body seem still frailer. In playing 'Hamlet' this year he used no make-up save his inky coat and sable weeds, nor did he need to, looking Hamlet's self. His kinship with Shakespeare revealed itself more and more with every utterance of Shakespeare's verse.[116]

In both responses one senses that in the public perception, the body and persona of Edwin Booth were as if laminated onto the character of Hamlet, his performance already more than an impersonation.

On March 22nd 1865 Booth undertook his record one hundredth consecutive performance as Hamlet. Of the long run, Booth confessed privately that he had been 'heartily sick and wearied of the monotonous work' and felt it was 'seriously affecting my acting.' When he asked for a change of the bill, manager William Stuart, wild with the success, pushed him to continue, saying, 'No, not at all, my dear boy! Keep it up, keep it up! If it goes a year, keep it up!'[117]

Here we need to take a step back to get some perspective on Booth's Hamlet in 1864–65 within the context of the Civil War and try to understand how this might have affected audience perceptions. The losses of life on both sides were already of a magnitude still hard to grasp today, much less to imagine what they meant for the still-young nation. Earlier in the year, the war's casualties had loomed large in the public mind, and Lincoln himself had been politically embattled. The late summer battles in 1864 had resulted in disastrous consequences for the armies of Grant and Sherman—100,000 men killed or wounded in Grant's armies alone in six weeks of incessant fighting with Lee's forces in Virginia, including the siege of Petersburg. Northern newspapers, controlled by the War Department, had carried stories of Grant victories, but in Washington, D.C., the hospitals were filling rapidly. Lincoln said the war might go on for three more years and called for 500,000 more soldiers from northern states.[118] But the nation was war weary. It had been three years since the battle at Antietam and two years since Gettysburg, where over 51,000 had died. Washington itself was again under threat from a few contingents of Confederate troops on the outskirts of the capital. In April, a haggard Lincoln had written a letter to a Kentucky newspaper editor explaining his shift to the policy of emancipation for slaves. 'I claim not to have controlled events, but confess plainly that events have controlled me. Now, at the end of three years' struggle, the nation's condition is not what either party, or any man devised, or expected. God alone can explain it.'[119] Lincoln, who deeply believed that the actions of individuals were predetermined and shaped by an unknowable divine purpose, had long been fond of citing Hamlet's lines to that effect: 'There's a divinity that shapes our ends, / Rough hew them how we will—' (5.2.10–11).[120]

Then in early September came the fall of Atlanta to General Sherman's army and the prospect of the war's end. Lincoln was re-elected on November 8th. (Booth voted for him, the first time he had cast a ballot.[121]) The President delivered his famous second inaugural address on March 4th 1865 ('With malice toward none . . .'). We can understand, I think, why audiences at the Winter Garden that fall and winter were keenly susceptible to Booth's suffering, intelligent prince, a young man tormented that he has been called upon to set the world right. They may have found appropriate the tone of 'mournful reverie' of his performance as their nation was moving into the final stage of the war—albeit with little sense yet of how the nation might reconstruct itself.

Richmond fell on April 3rd. Six days later, on Palm Sunday, the Civil War officially ended with Lee's surrender to Grant at Appomattox. Over 640,000 soldiers had died and over a million injured. Northern cities celebrated with the ringing of church bells, the firing of cannons, processions, marching bands and the singing of hymns. Outside the New York Stock Exchange, hundreds of men removed their hats and sang 'Praise God from Whom All Blessings Flow.' Hundreds of freedmen gathered on the lawn of Lee's home in Arlington to sing 'Year of the Jubilee,' and Lincoln gave a speech to crowds gathered outside the Executive Mansion. Cartoonist Thomas Nast later created a Palm Sunday print showing in adjoining frames Christ the Redeemer entering Jerusalem and Grant and Lee meeting at Appomattox. On the evening of April 13th, there was 'a grand illumination' of the capital, with gaslight, candles in windows and fireworks overhead.[122]

The next night, April 14th, John Wilkes Booth shot and killed Abraham Lincoln as he and his wife watched Laura Keene's company perform *Our American Cousin* from their box at Ford's Theatre in the capital. The effect on the nation was dramatic and profound. In the coming weeks, the public followed accounts of Lincoln's funeral, the frenzied manhunt for and capture of John Wilkes Booth and his closest accomplices. The name of Booth was now a national anathema. Edwin assumed the assassination meant the end of his career (as it did for Laura Keene), but as we shall see, it would actually lend him tragic stature in the public eye, especially to his suffering Hamlet.

John Wilkes Booth had long been sympathetic to the Southern cause and popular as an actor in the South. Since Lincoln's re-election, this Booth had been brooding over killing or kidnapping the President and had recruited conspirators. He had been at Ford's Theatre early enough on April 14th to learn that the President would be attending the play that night and to make his plans. Well known at Ford's, where he often had played, he easily gained access to the President's box and shot Lincoln in the back of the head with a derringer. With a Bowie knife he nearly mortally wounded Major Henry Rathbone, one of the Lincolns' companions, who tried to capture him. Booth then vaulted over the box balustrade to the stage twelve feet below. The flag draped on the front of the box supposedly caught one of Booth's spurs, forcing him to land on one leg, breaking it. On stage, he raised his bloody dagger and shouted to the audience, as if performing one of his melodramatic roles, *Sic semper tyrannis* (the Virginia state motto). He then crossed the stage and exited to make his escape on horseback toward southern Maryland.[123]

The assassination was, of course, a highly theatrical performance of vengeance, and John Wilkes Booth intended it that way—to an extent that one wonders if, in his mind, there was much distinction between theatre and reality. In a pocket diary he kept while being pursued, Booth entered what amounted to a dramaturgical defense of his actions. While fleeing he had read accounts in both Northern and Southern newspapers deploring the assassination, and in his diary he wrote of being 'in despair' and saw himself as misunderstood. He saw himself as a hero out of a romantic drama. 'Why,' he asked, was he being 'hunted like a dog' for 'doing what Brutus [in *Julius Caesar*] was honored for, what made [William] Tell a hero.' Like them, he had rid his nation of a tyrant.[124] (One of his earlier plans was, if possible, even more theatrical and bizarre. It involved kidnapping Lincoln in the theatre, lowering him, trussed, from his box to the stage in full view of the audience, and then delivering him to the Confederacy.)[125]

The public was shocked to learn the next day that Booth also had dispatched two co-conspirators, George A. Atzerodt and Lewis Paine, to kill Vice-President Andrew Johnson (Atzerodt got cold feet) and Secretary of State William Seward (Paine nearly succeeded). The drama of the events rippled through public sensibilities like aftershocks, generating theatrical framings everywhere. The War Department at one point issued a poster offering large rewards for information leading to the arrest of Booth and his two accomplices, with a dramatic exhortation signed by Edwin M. Stanton: 'Let the stain of innocent blood be removed from the land by the arrest and punishment of the murderers. . . . Every man should consider his own conscience charged with this solemn duty, and rest neither night nor day until it be accomplished.'[126]

Between Palm Sunday and Good Friday, the nation went from hymns of jubilation to the dead march of muffled drums. Cities were soon hung in black crepe. In New York, an anonymous diarist walked for miles down Broadway and many tributary streets sketching memorials to the martyred president that had been erected spontaneously in storefronts—including poems, portraits, wreathes and busts. His twenty-six pages of sketches provide a touching record of the impact of Lincoln's death on the general public. One page includes a tribute erected on behalf of actors, their profession having been stained, of course: 'All actors mourn the deep damnation of

FIGURE 2 Page from an anonymous sketchbook of makeshift tributes to the assassinated Abraham Lincoln, April 1865. By permission of Brown University Library.

his taking off' (Figure 2). It borrows an apt phrase from *Macbeth* in which Macbeth, reconsidering his plan to kill Duncan, refers to the outrage that would follow because the king was such a virtuous man.[127] Other pages include further quotations from Shakespearean plays familiar to the public. In Washington, Lincoln's body was taken from the Executive Mansion to the Capitol in a solemn procession to lie in state. On April 21st, a train bearing his remains began a two-week journey toward the late President's hometown of Springfield, Illinois, with stops in many cities, including New York, Albany, Cleveland, Chicago and Springfield for mourners to pay tribute—eleven-and-a-half million of them.

On April 26th, Booth the assassin was tracked down by soldiers and shot and killed in a burning tobacco barn in northern Virginia. Artists created color prints of this theatrical climax.[128] The drama of the capture and trials of the conspirators occupied the public's attention through early July when four of John Wilkes Booth's collaborators were hanged. Photographs of the execution by Alexander Gardner, who had photographed Lincoln many times, were widely published.

After his success in New York, Booth had taken *Hamlet* to Boston, where it opened in the Boston Theatre on March 24th. Horrified at the news on April 15th, he obtained a release from his contract from manager Henry C. Jarrett and wrote to thank him, speaking of being 'oppressed by a private woe beyond words' over his brother's crime and Lincoln's death. Booth wrote in grief to Badeau of all his previous attempts to establish an honorable name for his family, mourning also for 'all the beautiful plans I had for the future—all blasted now . . .' and worried over how difficult this would be for his mother. Edwin would receive death threats, but he also had many sympathetic supporters, such as the Governor of Massachusetts, John A. Andrew, and his influential friend from the Stoddard circle, James Lorimer Graham.[129] His friends circled protectively around him once again, fearful about his drinking.

On April 25th both the *New York Times* and the *Chicago Tribune* carried a remarkable story about Booth, previously unknown to the public. It obviously was placed in the papers to help rehabilitate his name. About a month before, he had saved the life of a young man in the Jersey City train station. In the jostling crowd, the man had stepped into the wrong car, and, as he attempted to get off, he slipped and fell between the platform edge and the now moving train. Booth, just behind him, yanked him back up onto the platform by his collar. Booth did not know it at the time, but the young man was Robert Todd Lincoln, the President's son. He recognized Booth from having seen him on the stage and thanked him by name.[130] The *Tribune* writer thought it appropriate amid the nation's grief to recall this story when 'a man so stricken and overburdened with woe as Mr. Booth is spoken of,' for 'the Union has had no stronger or more generous supporter . . . From the commencement he has been earnestly and actively solicitous for the triumph of arms and the welfare of our soldiers.' (Booth performed in a benefit in 1863 to raise funds for the Sanitary Commission, a government agency that promoted clean and healthy conditions in Union Army camps.) The young Lincoln, whom Booth did not know, was at the time on his way from Harvard to join General Grant's staff. Badeau was now Grant's secretary, and when the young Lincoln reached Washington he told him the story of the rescue, knowing that Badeau and Booth were friends.

In turn Badeau wrote to Booth to tell him whom he had saved.[131] It is likely that it was Badeau who placed with the newspapers the timely story of the patriotic Booth brother who recently had saved the life of the dead President's son.

Booth withdrew from the stage for the remainder of the year, by which time his supporters had encouraged him to plan his return, although the *Herald* tried to whip up indignation at the thought of it.[132] He returned with *Hamlet* on January 4th 1866. An audience of friends and supporters welcomed him at his first appearance in the court scene with five minutes of standing applause, waving handkerchiefs, tears and nine rounds of cheers to which Booth responded with many bows. At the close of the first act he was called before the curtain to receive bouquets.[133] His mother was in the audience. Such scenes would be repeated many times both in the four-week run and in subsequent performances across the country.[134] Booth's career was not only re-established, but thereafter his Hamlet took on a national resonance.

In May, E. C. Stedman wrote in the *Atlantic* at great length and with some labor of Booth's latest Hamlet. Interested only in its 'art spirit', he never mentions the circumstances of the assassination, any more than he would have related the performance to the Civil War. He devotes over a 1000 words to the theme that external beauty is the expression of the soul and then describes Booth's image at length—the black searching eyes, the harmonious grace of the symmetrical body.[135] In his experience of the performance, Hamlet *is* Booth. '. . . [I]n the princely superiority of [the play's] chief figure, there can be little *acting* in the conventional sense. . . . The player must be himself. This necessity, we think, goes far toward Booth's special fitness for the part.' In Booth's Richelieu, by comparison, Stedman says, all is *acting*: 'from first to last [we] have nothing to recall [Booth] to our minds,' he wrote, with admiration at the 'transformation.'[136] But in his Hamlet, 'we see and think of Booth.' Stedman's recollection of seeing and thinking of Booth as he watched him perform Hamlet is an account of the process neuroscience has identified as 'conceptual blending'. Our minds, unconsciously seeking to construct knowledge from our experiences of the world, are always projecting information and structures from 'input spaces' (what Stedman knows of Booth and what he knows of Hamlet) into a blended space (Booth/Hamlet). In the theatre, we commonly create the actor/character blend, sometimes seeing the actor in the foreground, sometimes the character, and sometimes we oscillate between.[137] For Stedman, Hamlet seems to be Booth more than Booth seems to be Hamlet.

Responses to this same 1866 performance by Boston friends of Booth offer another example. Annie Fields wrote in her journal in early January:

> ... [W]e went to see Booth upon the occasion of his reappearance. The unmoved sadness of the young man and the unceasing plaudits of the house, half filled with his friends, were impressive and made it an occasion not to be forgotten.[138]

She and her husband saw his Hamlet again in Boston in September and invited him to tea with friends. In a journal entry she wrote, 'He seems deeply saddened. I hear he passes every Sunday morning at the grave of his wife at Mount Auburn.' That night, she and her husband 'lay long awake, thinking over poor Booth and his strange fortune. Hamlet indeed!' This is more than a comparison. Husband and wife have come to this point having done what cognitive scientists Giles Fauconnier and Mark Turner call 'running the blend.' Booth and Hamlet have become a single, new entity.

In January 1867, a committee of preeminent New Yorkers, including the Governor, presented Booth with a medal commemorating his record run of *Hamlet* in 1864–65. The commendation, delivered by a noted judge, also praised his efforts 'to raise the standard of the drama' and spoke of the medal as a token also of their respect for him 'as a man.' From the perspective of this chapter, the ceremony can be read as a performance setting the civic seal on the perception of Booth and Hamlet as virtually one new entity. For the occasion the Winter Garden stage was set as a generic drawing room, Winter remembered, 'and entering that room, the presentation committee met Booth, *in the dress of Hamlet*—the united bands of several theatres playing, meanwhile, the Danish National Hymn (emphasis added).'[139] The medal's design included the crown of Denmark and beneath it the head of Booth as Hamlet. Among the thirty-seven committee members meeting Booth onstage in his costume were the journalists and artists who had helped articulate and disseminate the Booth/Hamlet image: Curtis, Taylor, Thomson (the sculptor of the bust of Booth's Hamlet) and illustrator W. J. Hennessey.[140]

Booth's Hamlet of 1870, brought out in his lavish new theatre, with elaborated versions of the Winter Garden sets in Norman architecture, was now seen as rich, matured and definitive.[141] In his journal of Booth's performance, Charles Clarke described the tragedy as that of 'a man of first class intellect and second class will,' who is baffled by the burden of having to kill the king and, having done the deed, feels bewildered and appalled. Young Clarke found it an exhilarating tragedy of morality and wrote of 'all that Booth had done to put an edge upon my sensibility; and instruct my emotions and inform my imagination.' Clarke wants to reach up and cry, 'Oh Booth! Booth! as if his identity and power were somewhere just overhead and I was looking up toward them as to some source of mental health and light!'[142] It was at this time that Booth posed for the iconic Sarony photograph of him as Hamlet.

At this point, it will suffice to review in brief the many later events in Booth's life that added layers to his legend. His success was accompanied by well-timed biographies of his father that would have given the public new lenses through which to see him. In 1866 and 1868, respectively, biographies of Edwin's father by Asia Booth Clarke and Thomas Gould were published, circulating the legends of Junius's acting and the stories of young Edwin's painful role as his father's caretaker. Among the ordeals in the years after the assassination were the destruction by fire of the Winter Garden Theatre and the financial failure of Booth's theatre and his bankruptcy. In 1869 he married the nineteen year-old Chicago actor, Mary McVicker, and they lost an infant child in 1870, which may have contributed to her years of mental illness. She died of tuberculosis in 1881. Booth's reputation was shadowed for a time by an acrimonious feud with the McVicker family and charges and refutations in the press that Booth had been a cruel husband, a drunkard and a profligate. In 1879, while Booth was playing Richard II in Chicago, he was shot at twice and narrowly missed by a young man named Mark Gray. Captured, Gray offered only incoherent reasons for his attempt to kill Booth, which made police and physicians doubt his sanity.[143] These and other events led Booth's biographers to see him as a man of strange and tragic fortunes, 'the darling of misfortune' and 'a child of tragedy.' Asia Booth Clarke began her brother's biography, published in the United States in 1882, with the story of his birth within a protective caul, but under a shower of meteors. Actor Clara Morris once described him as 'Saint Edwin of many sorrows.'[144]

The most salient of the sorrows that the public knew about him was, of course, his brother's assassination of Lincoln. The trauma of that and the Civil War remained open wounds for the nation throughout the remainder of Booth's career. One barometer of this is the struggle of Walt Whitman who, aging and in some disillusionment, tried to make sense of the American agony. He had seen the war's results as a volunteer at the bedsides of wounded, dying soldiers and mourned Lincoln's death in two famous poems. In the last dozen years of his life, though partially paralyzed from a stroke, the poet took to the public platform to perform his vision of the meaning of Lincoln's assassination.[145] He described John Wilkes Booth in a highly dramatic narrative, with theatrical flourishes ('. . . those basilisk eyes . . .'). He then painted Lincoln as the Redeemer President whose death had unified the nation at the end of the war as no other action could have done. He cast it all as a monumental American tragedy, Greek in scale, wanting only its American playwright. Tragedy of such a terrible scale and the martyrdom of the President were to be understood, he believed, in light of the 'vast revolutionary arc' of the United States, straining toward 'nationality' and toward its destiny of transforming the petty scale of European civilization. 'What else on earth are we for?' if not that, Whitman asked Americans.[146] He performed his vision of American exceptionalism in many platform appearances to mesmerized audiences. He sometimes concluded by reading from his *When Lilacs Last in the Dooryard Bloomed.* Perhaps for spectators, the aging poet's performance, his embodied expression of this vision out of his own history, allowed them to imagine the possibility of redemptive meaning arising from the suffering of a tragic era. It is useful to set Whitman's performance alongside Booth's Hamlet.

Booth played Hamlet through his fifties, during his partnership tour with Lawrence Barrett in 1886–87, and in a faint, sad final performance at the Brooklyn Academy of Music in 1891. As he aged, Booth, once the beautiful, wounded boy, transformed into what the young novelist and essayist, Hamlin Garland, described as 'the passive, suffering center.'[147] New York critic John Ranken Towse, recalling Booth with the advantage of some perspective in 1916, observed succinctly: 'To his public, he was endeared by his misfortunes and his talents.'[148] Considered from our historical perspective today, the appeal of both Whitman and Booth might be said to lie in what they performed and embodied for their audiences—Whitman, the aging national poet striving for his vision of American singularity, and the suffering Booth, persevering with his gentrified, intelligent performance of Shakespeare's Hamlet, wrapped in old world ideals.

With Charles Shattuck, we want to know Booth's Hamlet. However, we must seek it not just in the promptbooks and reviews but in the transaction between Booth and his historical audiences who often experienced it as more than an impersonation, situated as it was within their experience of the Civil War and their awareness of Booth's sufferings of his own house divided (amidst all the other calamities in his life). This was a large part of the reason that for them Booth was Hamlet. This, too, is what they saw when they saw Booth's Hamlet.

Chapter 3

Ellen Terry

Gail Marshall

The story of Ellen Terry's life and career has been told many times and from many perspectives. Arguably the most popular and best known nineteenth-century English actress, she has been the subject of popular theatre biographies, a determining figure in nineteenth-century theatre histories, the quarry of art historians writing on G. F. Watts and Edward Godwin, and the subject of her own family's competing memories and agendas. She is also the subject of her own extensive writings: three *New Review* articles in 1891, characteristically entitled 'Stray Memories'; her 1908 autobiography, *The Story of My Life*, and its later heavily edited version, *Ellen Terry's Memoirs* (1933); and two posthumous publications: *Ellen Terry and Bernard Shaw: A Correspondence* (1931) and her *Four Lectures on Shakespeare* (1932). They chronicle a life spent in the theatre, from her earliest days to the years when she and Henry Irving ruled the Lyceum and delighted prestigious audiences with melodrama, comedy and Shakespeare.

The texts published after Terry's death in 1928 were largely the responsibility of Terry's literary secretary Christopher St John (née Christabel Marshall) and of Terry's daughter and St John's lover, Edy Craig. These two women, like Terry herself, were concerned to create an appropriate legacy for Terry, and one which would protect her memory from the competing effigy being created by Terry's son, Edward Gordon Craig—whose *Ellen Terry and Her Secret Self* (1932) threatened to submerge the acclaimed actress within the mother-figure whom he both professed to adore and sought to protect against her 'redoubtable adversary, her other self . . . Ellen Terry.'[1] Gordon Craig was battling for control of his mother's memory with St John and his sister, but also with Bernard Shaw, whose correspondence with Terry had shown the public a woman capable of the great charm for which she had been most famed, and which she reluctantly acknowledged as the vehicle of her successes; but it showed also an actress of creative distinction and accomplished professional judgment. Terry's legacy is, then, a vexed one, troubled by questions that cannot be answered about her personal and professional lives, and subject to multiple reconstructions: not only by those who knew and wished to claim her, but also by those subsequent commentators and critics for whom she came to represent—as the dead theatre actress peculiarly can—myriad forms of desirability and fascination.

So potent was her fame and popularity, and so evanescent their grounds, that her own writings accrue extraordinary significance. Within those writings, of course, Terry is visibly constructing her own legacy and re-constructing the contours of a life often lived at the edge of the respectability that the damehood conferred upon her in 1925 seemed officially to bestow, rather than necessarily to recognize. In a strategy far from uncommon in theatrical autobiographies, *The Story of My Life* glances over those episodes which might have attracted most prurient curiosity, in particular her relationships with Watts and Godwin. Her short-lived marriage to Watts in 1864 attracted attention primarily because of the thirty-year age gap between bride and groom, and is announced inconsequentially in her autobiography thus: 'In the middle of the run of "The American Cousin" I left the stage and married. Mary Meredith was the part, and I played it vilely.'[2] Her recollections of her ten-month marriage are taken up with regrets for what was lost, and memories of those great men, such as Tennyson, to whom her marriage exposed her. Terry's relationship with Godwin is similarly inconspicuously incorporated into her text:

> I left the stage for six years, without the slightest idea of ever going back. I left it without regret. And I was very happy, leading a quiet, domestic life in the heart of the country. When my two children were born, I thought of the stage less than ever. They absorbed all my time, all my interest, all my love.[3]

The children are produced immaculately out of the country air, with no mention of Godwin at this stage, though Terry had earlier credited him with teaching her a respect for beautiful things when they first met at his Bristol home.[4] Terry's second and third husbands—Charles Wardell and James Carew—receive even more minimal attention, and her relationship with Henry Irving is recalled primarily, perhaps even defiantly, in professional terms. Rumors of an amorous relationship between the actors persisted throughout their time at the Lyceum and still intrigue critics today. Terry seems determined to resist the impulse of readers to embroil her memory within a string of romantic relationships, and one of the ways in which she does this is to insist, instead, on an alternative means of self-definition—through Shakespeare.

Throughout her adult life, Terry was fond of annotating photographs with Beatrice's line from *Much Ado About Nothing*, 'There was a star danced and under that was I born' (3.1.315–316). She thus establishes a Shakespearean genealogy that she maintains throughout her autobiography, writing that 'it was a happy chance that made me a native of Warwickshire, Shakespeare's own county.'[5] She and St John were making an obvious and strategic decision to position the actress in the most familiar guise of her career—a Shakespearean actress—and in a mode that would also speak to and promote the career that Terry had newly taken up as a lecturer on Shakespearean topics. The structure of *The Story of My Life* further lends itself to a concentration on Terry's work in Shakespeare, with half of the book's seven chapters concentrating on the twenty years she spent with Irving at the Lyceum, a venue that had been popularly perceived as a primarily Shakespearean space. There are many reasons for seeing Terry and St John's decision as perfectly natural in the circumstances, and it is one that history has endorsed—through its recognition of John Singer Sargent's 1884 portrait of Ellen Terry as Lady Macbeth as her best known image and, in 2009, making Terry (but *not* Irving) one of the thirteen members of the Shakespeare Hall of Fame at the newly renovated Memorial Theatre in Stratford-upon-Avon.[6]

I now want to examine the politics of Terry's positioning herself so deliberately as a primarily Shakespearean actress in a career that spanned popular theatre, high comedy, Ibsen and Shaw. None of those elements is, of course, ignored in her wide-ranging and engaging text; but its emphasis is on Shakespeare and either the parts that Terry acted or the parts (such as Rosalind) that she was not allowed to play by Irving, or so her self-mythologizing would have it. The private and public stories of Terry's self-identification as primarily Shakespearean, the terms of her positioning, are worth examining in the context of the reviews and books that have followed a lead so enthusiastically given by the actress.

Terry is not, of course, the only nineteenth-century actress to invite or create that identification, and indeed in *The Story of My Life*, Sarah Siddons' marriage at Coventry is another happy omen; happy both because Terry is thus linked with a great actress and, more specifically, because of that earlier actress's links with Shakespeare. Helena Faucit (1817–98) and Fanny Kemble (1809–93), Siddons's niece, share Terry's anxiety to be determined by their work in Shakespeare. Both were early-nineteenth-century actresses from theatrical families, who made their professional debut as Juliet in performances subsequently committed to paper in extensive autobiographical writings that implicitly recognize and trade on the social and cultural credibility conferred on the actress by her voluntary identification with Shakespeare; and which, in Kemble's case particularly, emphasize the financial rewards of playing that role.[7]

The part of Juliet has an uncomfortably admonitory function for young girls, as it simultaneously produces on stage a vision of virginal attractiveness condoned by the authority and standing of Shakespeare, and which at the end of the play confers the ultimate punishment of death. Theatrically and commercially, an attractive young actress is prominently seen on stage in a context containing that vision within suitably corrective, perhaps coercive, structures that contain and determine appropriate femininity. The example of Juliet provides a particularly cogent instance of how Shakespeare can not only enable women's presence on stage in such a way as to prohibit any of the suggestions of impropriety that dogged, and continue to dog, the actress, but can also allow them to accrue a weight of respectability through that very appearance on stage. The work of Helena Faucit, her own writings on her acting, and her husband's hagiographic biography all persuasively reiterate that function. Even Faucit's own name testifies to her sense of the importance of Shakespeare connections: born Helen to a minor and slightly rakish theatre family, she adopted the name Helena, much to William Macready's exasperation, as being more Shakespearean.[8]

It is important to remember, though, that the relationship between Shakespeare and the actress was unquestionably a symbiotic one, which accrued benefits to both parties. Through the vehicle of crowd-pleasing actresses, Shakespeare entered the mainstream of Victorian middle-class theatregoing. Enabled partly by the efforts of Macready and Irving in particular to secure Shakespeare's own words for the theatre, and by Charles Kean's spectacular productions at the Princess's Theatre in the 1850s, the increased visibility of Shakespeare on the Victorian stage would nonetheless not have been possible without popular actresses like Terry to underpin their managers' efforts. In their turn, those actresses were able to attain a greater social and professional standing through their work in Shakespeare, and thus to participate within a major cultural movement of the nineteenth century. The Bardolatry that Bernard Shaw would later condemn in reviews and letters to Terry was an important lever in the revision of the social standing of actresses in the period.

Professional reasons go some way to explaining Terry's self-positioning in her writings, but the terms she uses when discussing Shakespeare are so intimate that it seems an explanation based on such reasons is not entirely adequate. She writes of her first Shakespearean role, Mamilius, in Charles Kean's production of *The Winter's Tale* (Princess's Theatre, 1856), that 'my heart swelled with pride when I was told what I had to do, when I realized that I had a real Shakespearean part—a possession that father had taught me to consider the pride of life!'[9] Shakespeare is a way of acknowledging her theatrical roots, and of embedding her father in particular in the narrative of her life's success. Like many other Victorian women, Shakespeare was first made known to Terry within her own family, and her autobiography duly acknowledges that debt within a narrative which otherwise speaks relatively little of the parents from whom she gradually became estranged. She goes on to cement her genealogical links with Shakespeare when she writes: 'To act for the first time in Shakespeare, in a theatre where my sister had already done something for our name, and before royalty, was surely a good beginning.'[10] For writers, readers, spectators, actresses and professional Shakespeareans such as the editor and journalist Mary Cowden Clarke, the register of family affection and personal intimacy seems as appropriate a marker of their feelings for Shakespeare as the language more usually associated with their respective careers. Uniting all these women is the understanding that Shakespeare has something to offer them personally, as women, as well as professionals engaged in a more formal relationship with him and his works.

Terry's position is rather different in that a linguistic register of affection and familiarity was also used to describe her in the numerous interviews and reviews that were written about her during her career. To the extent to which she is both user and object of such rhetoric in relation to Shakespeare, her usage of that rhetoric might signal an implicit acceptance of the ways in which such language positioned her in relation to the playwright who could engender such affection in audiences. She is both a 'charming' woman whose charm is made publicly available through Shakespeare and a woman who can transmit the charms of Shakespeare to theatrical audiences. Terry's usage of the language of affection might, however, have other less transparent connotations: that it was yet another way of diverting attention from her own romances onto the love that she professes to be strongest: her love for Shakespeare. Irving and Shakespeare vie equally for Terry's attention throughout *The Story of My Life*, with the dramatist often acting as the medium through which she and Irving most commonly met. But, tactically, the concentration on Shakespeare as the object of Terry's affections means that we are distracted from the lovers and husbands who might otherwise have threatened to supplant her professional life in the reader's eyes. During that professional life, Terry battled the tendency of reviewers to play down her professional skills in favor of paying attention to those 'charms' which were an important part of her appeal to audiences. In the strategic way in which she positions Shakespeare, she carefully turns that rhetoric against the reviewers and audiences who would dismiss her as simply charming and re-invests that language with a distinctive critical judgment which can accommodate both emotional valence and critical discrimination.

Early Shakespeare Roles

Terry's career may be divided into three uneven parts: the years before the Lyceum (1856–77), her work with Irving at the Lyceum (1878–1902), and the post-Lyceum years which saw her move into new areas of theatre and new relationships, both in and beyond Shakespeare. Before she joined Irving at the Lyceum, Terry played the following Shakespearean roles: at Charles Kean's Princess's Theatre, Mamilius (1856), Puck (1856), Arthur in *King John* (1858) and Fleance in *Macbeth* (1859); at the Queen's Theatre, Long Acre, under Alfred Wigan, Katherine in *Katherine and Petruchio* (1867); and at the Prince of Wales's Theatre, Portia in the Bancrofts' production of *The Merchant of Venice* (1875). Terry also played seasons in Bristol and Bath (1861–63) in J. H. Chute's stock company, where she took the parts of Nerissa and Hero to her sister Kate's Portia and Beatrice and also appeared as Titania to Mrs Kendal's singing fairy (probably, as Terry claims, because of Mrs Kendal's having the better voice). She makes these parts a conscious element of the narrative that she weaves around the story of how she came to be the pre-eminent actress of her day, and within those stories makes transparently clear how far her experiences in Shakespeare were responsible. Of playing Titania, for instance, she writes that it

> was the first Shakespeare part I had played since I left Charles Kean, but I think even in those early days I was more at home in Shakespeare than anything else. Mr Godwin designed my dress, and we made it at his house in Bristol. He showed me how to damp it and 'wring' it while it was wet, tying up the material as the Orientals do in their 'tie and dry' process, so that when it was dry and untied, it was all crinkled and clinging. This was the first lovely dress that I ever wore, and I learned a great deal from it.[11]

This is an interestingly constructed narrative: a particular set of Shakespeare credentials is established at the outset via mention of Charles Kean whose years at the Princess's Theatre on Oxford Street gave Terry her start in professional theatre and, more broadly, were best known for their ambitious remit to bring Shakespeare to the middle classes and to encourage them more regularly to frequent the theatre.[12] Kean was one of a string of Victorian actor-managers who sought, through association with Shakespeare, to extend the respectability of Victorian theatre and thereby achieve a degree of personal prominence and cultural centrality. Although she was only a child at the time—aged nine, she made her debut as Mamilius—Terry's association with the Keans gave her a taste of what an ambitious management could achieve through careful manipulation of the playwright. Heavily edited texts reworked Shakespeare into an essentially Victorian playwright who could speak to the interests and anxieties of a newly significant, indeed newly calibrated, section of Victorian society. The decade that saw the publication of Samuel Smiles's *Self-Help* and the first installments of Mrs Beeton's *Book of Household Management* also saw, in the Keans' tenure at the Princess's, a theatre similarly configured for the new middle classes. Terry was therefore, albeit unconsciously, present at the birth of a new phase in theatre history and the creation of new audiences. As the century progressed, she would herself become the focus of the attention of audiences for whom theatre might be a new experience, and for whom both she and Shakespeare were crucial in effecting their entry into a previously unknown set of cultural experiences.

Terry goes on to note that 'even in those early days I was more at home in Shakespeare than anything else', and in her reminiscences, we see 'home' being invoked both as a bulwark against more malicious attention—for instance, in her insistence on the simple domestic blissfulness of her time with Godwin—and as a medium between her and her actual as well as virtual audiences, for whom 'home' might ameliorate the taint of the theatre and allow the confirmation of persistent femininity in the actress. The concept of being 'at home' in Shakespeare is at the centre of a nexus of relationships which allows Terry to infiltrate the intimacies of home and family without besmirching either, and which also enables her to celebrate her own theatrical family of parents and siblings as well as the family that she went on to create for herself: her children, lovers, husbands and the Lyceum company.

It was no small thing for her to want to enter into the conventional discourse of family and domestic responsibility, given how much her own conduct deviated from it. It is curious on both sides: she was part of bohemian culture and yet she constructs herself as a bourgeoise. She clearly recognizes the importance of the domestic ideology of femininity that actresses may be seen to disrupt. The extract quoted above also introduces, in the least threatening way possible, Terry's account of her early collaboration with Godwin and the beginning of what she claims is his life-long influence on her stagecraft. Shakespeare becomes both the means of their working relationship and the guarantor of its early sanctities. The reader's hindsight and further knowledge might invest the details of Terry's clinging dress and its Eastern origins with a different interpretation, but at this stage Terry and Godwin's relationship is presented as purely professional, and effected by Shakespeare.

A Midsummer Night's Dream was not a play to which Terry returned later in her career, but as a young actress she had played Puck as well as Titania. Her Puck was well and earnestly received. The *Daily News* wrote that:

> A Miss Ellen Terry, a member of that family which seems destined to provide clever children for the stage, played Puck in an extraordinary manner. Clever children on the stage are generally repulsive; there is about them a large-headedness, a stolidity, and a preternatural gravity, which repels rather than attracts; but this little girl, who is very pretty, is all life and activity; she has a fresh, ringing little voice, a clear utterance, and when not speaking, fills up the scene with capital by-play.[13]

Terry already appears to be a true professional, a status that sets her firmly apart from the self-descriptions given of their debuts by the Shakespearean actresses Faucit and Kemble. Faucit was ever wary of the taint of the professional actress, and Kemble, though clearly from an eminent theatrical background, took pains subsequently to distance herself from being defined by that background. Terry's family is far from 'background'; rather, the stage presence of her sister Kate at this period ensures that Terry's early roles often reflected her secondary place in her family at that time. At this period, Kate was playing Juliet and Portia, amongst other roles, and it is tempting to see Ellen's later conquering of those parts as in some way a response to having seen those roles bring Kate such acclaim. She played Hero to Kate's Beatrice in *Much Ado About Nothing* in 1863. *Lloyd's Weekly Newspaper* suggested on the evidence of this role, that 'very much may be hoped for from this recent brilliant acquisition to the stage. Besides playing well generally, Miss [Ellen] Terry begins to play very prettily—with her eyes.'[14] Given that Ellen Terry was fifteen at the time, the language of this review, with its relish of alleged coquetry, is slightly disturbing, and establishes a pattern and language of personal praise that would follow Terry throughout her career.

She went on in June of that year to add Desdemona to her repertoire, a part in which she seemed to commentators to be 'a little too girlish,' though showing 'great grace, intelligence, and true feeling';[15] and to be 'pretty enough to charm the hearts of a dozen Moors,' despite lacking pathos and power.[16] Terry was clearly establishing a reputation and popularity for herself in the eyes of the public and reviewers, but her own account of this single matinee performance, which was got up for the purpose of introducing the provincial star Walter Montgomery to the London public, makes clear the terms upon which the performance was a success for the actress herself:

> An actor named Walter Montgomery was giving a matinee of 'Othello' at the Princess's (the theatre where I made my first appearance) in the June of 1863, and he wanted a Desdemona. The agents sent for me. It was Saturday, and I had to play it on Monday! But for my training, how could I have done it! At this time I knew the words and had *studied* the words—a very different thing—of every woman's part in Shakespeare.[17]

Terry's claims are not perhaps entirely credible, but hers is a narrative of the sheer hard work involved in becoming a Shakespearean actress. The work is tempered by adoration of Shakespeare, but nonetheless provides evidence of a self-conscious professionalism that would have sat awkwardly with the critics' delight in the pretty girlishness of the young actress. In a characteristic movement, Terry ends her account of this production with a self-deprecatory gesture that deflects attention from the earnestness into which Shakespeare has enticed her:

> I don't know what kind of performance I gave on that memorable afternoon, but I think it was not so bad. And Walter Montgomery's Othello? Why can't I remember something about it? I only remember that the unfortunate actor shot himself on his wedding-day![18]

She then goes on to tell more of Kate's success, of her becoming Charles Fechter's leading lady, and of the marriage in 1867 that would take her away from the stage.

During this period Terry herself married for the first time (in 1864) and left the stage for the first time, as was expected of actresses who married non-theatrical husbands, and whose married status usually reflected his social position. It is tempting to see sibling rivalry operating at this point and as a spur in later years. At the very least, it is clear that Kate Terry paved the way, or acted as a kind of exemplar, for Ellen's later career. The elder Terry daughter was particularly well known for her Shakespearean roles: *The Era* writes in 1867 of a Miss Palmer who was appearing as Juliet that 'wonderful to relate, [she] does not imitate Miss Kate Terry.'[19] Through similar means and roles, Kate achieved a more modest form of the kind of fame that Ellen would later enjoy, and even had a waltz named after her. At this period, after the break-up of Ellen's ten-month marriage to G. F. Watts, Kate represented a form of professional and romantic success that Ellen could only awkwardly attempt to emulate. Just after Kate's departure from the professional stage in October 1867, *The Era* welcomed 'the fresh and graceful style of Miss Ellen Terry' as evidence that 'Miss Kate Terry has not left the stage without supplying an efficient substitute.'[20] As this extended tribute from *The Era* makes clear, Kate's were difficult footsteps in which to tread, not least because of the apparent ease of both her theatrical and social success:

> Every one who takes the slightest interest in Theatrical matters will have observed with regret that one of the acknowledged ornaments of the stage had decided upon finally retiring from it; a resolution which was consummated last Friday and Saturday evenings, when Miss Kate Terry, in a benefit which extended over both nights, bade adieu to that Profession in the exercise of which she has won such honourable distinction. In thus abdicating the high position in her art which her industry and talents have acquired, she forfeits a future which it is given but to few actresses to look forward to, and those whose admiration for the actress is allied to a natural feeling of personal regard will, perhaps, find comfort in the reflection that Miss Terry, in abandoning her brilliant professional prospects, finds more than an equivalent in the assurance of a future of wedded happiness. Whatever difference of opinion may exist as to the extent of those powers with which no one attempts to deny she is gifted, none will be found to grudge her the advantages of a happy union. The close of Miss Terry's career has been marked by a series of efforts to take still higher ground as an *artiste*, and her late performances at the Adelphi Theatre have enabled the Metropolitan public to judge how well she has succeeded. These farewell performances at the Adelphi were but the prelude to her engagement at the Prince's Theatre, Manchester, which has terminated her professional career . . .
>
> [T]he parts which she will leave freshest in the memories of play-goers will not be those of the modern domestic drama, in which she unquestionably stands pre-eminent, but the *roles* of Julia, in *The Hunchback*; Beatrice,

in *Much Ado About Nothing*; Juliet, the fair and unfortunate daughter of the Capulets; and Pauline, in *The Lady of Lyons*. . . .

Long before her benefit came off every seat in the boxes and stalls had been secured, and the demand for seats became so pressing that it was at length decided to extend the event over the following Saturday evening, which would also be the occasion of her last appearance on the stage. The area of the stalls had to be trebled, and the prices of both stalls and boxes increased, and even then the capacity of the house was found to be too small for the eager throng of admirers who sought admittance . . .

Miss Terry appeared before the green curtain, evidently at a loss as to what remarks to offer in reply to this enthusiastic greeting. At length, after a considerable pause she found words to utter:

> What can I say? It is hardly good-bye yet, and yet to most here I suppose it has arrived at that ominous word. I cannot tell you how deep my thanks are for all the kindness I have received from friends in Manchester, who are so new to me. I feel as if I had known you all my life, and, therefore, though my words are poor, will you think 'Thank you' means a whole ocean? Believe me that I am truly and deeply grateful. And now—'Good-bye.'

Short as this speech was Miss Terry repeatedly paused, evidently at a loss for words, and the audience, rightly feeling why 'she was so poor in thanks,' filled up each pause by their hearty acclamations, and, when she had concluded, the applause was indescribable.

Between the first two acts the band played the 'Kate Terry *Valse*,' but as Mr Williams and the orchestra had been, from the commencement, consigned to the mysterious regions behind the scenes, the music was not heard to particular advantage. The afterpiece was *The Little Savage*, in which Miss Ellen Terry (Mrs Watts) appeared, and received a hearty welcome.

At the close of the performance the stage was covered with bouquets, including a wreath, with which Ellen Terry crowned her sister, Kate Terry, who was too much affected to speak; and, having retired, again appeared, led on by her sister, but was again unable to utter a word. The applause was most enthusiastic.[21]

In Kate, Ellen Terry saw an example of one who had used the legitimate stage to effect her own personal fame, popularity and reputation, and who was now being lost to the stage amidst the grief of adoring fans. Terry's own first marriage had achieved little of what she had hoped for from it.

It had lasted but ten months, after which she found herself back at home, dependent again on her parents. On stage she found herself a curiously named individual: neither Watts nor Terry, but awkwardly and parenthetically both. Reviews of Kate Terry's later career make clear how far Shakespeare was responsible for the nature and enduring quality of her reputation, and it is tempting to see Ellen's later immersion in Shakespeare, and her professed devotion to him, as a competitive response to the success of Kate's work in that area. In practical terms, Kate's departure from the stage left more room for Ellen Terry to work in Shakespeare, and to graduate eventually from Hero's supporting role to that of Beatrice, from 'The Little Savage' to Juliet. When she crowned her sister with laurels, it may have been with some relief that she shepherded her sister into married life, but also, as events showed, with a sense of how attractive that offstage life might be. The moment reflects the deep ambivalences of Terry's pull towards both stage and the perceived securities of domestic life.

By nice coincidence, just two months after her sister and rival left the stage, Terry first met and worked with Henry Irving, who would become her greatest stage partner. In 'Garrick's boiled-down version of "The Taming of the Shrew,"'[22] they took the lead roles, and failed to realize the importance of the meeting: 'I acted for the first time with Henry Irving. This ought to have been a great event in my life, but at the time it passed me by and left "no wrack behind."'[23] The brief notice in *The Times* begins by assuring readers that the part of Katherine is being played by Ellen and not by Kate, 'as has incorrectly been rumoured,' and goes on to commend what seems to have been a thoughtful and engaged performance by Terry, who 'takes a view of the character which departs from the usual routine, and which, perhaps, better than any other, accounts for that tamed condition of the shrew in the last act.' Terry's conception of Katherine's speech to Bianca after her conversion receives tributes that might have been given to Kate: 'The speech she utters [. . .] may be taken as a model of quiet elocution, so sensibly, so feelingly, and with so unequivocal an appearance of moral conviction is it delivered.' Sadly, *The Times* reviewer finds it less easy to praise Irving, finding in him the 'defects of articulation' which were an easy target for reviewers of his early years, but also suggesting, by means of a comparison with the 'gentlemanlike rollick' with which Charles Kemble had played the part, that Irving was not gentleman enough to act the role with conviction: 'when he has brought home his bride he suggests the notion rather of a brigand chief who has secured a female captive than of an honest gentleman engaged in a task of moral reform.'[24]

It might be of course that Irving found the part as distasteful as many modern critics, and was unable to see Petruchio's 'moral' actions as consonant with a gentleman's behavior, but the class implications are clear: Terry brings a degree of breeding to a stage where it is otherwise lacking. *The Times*'s comments on Terry, and other papers' views of her and of her sister, are instructive. They are both heralded as performers who literally bring class to a production; in this instance, the performance of an acceptable middle-class status that reviewers relish and which in the case of both actresses, is in large part authorized and enabled by their identification with Shakespeare and his women.

This response to the two actresses gives a particular slant to our understanding of the later Terry-Irving partnership at the Lyceum. By taking on Terry as his stage partner, Irving was recruiting not just a talented and popular actress, but someone who could give his theatre a certain cachet born perhaps of that embedded theatricality that the Terrys enjoyed from their childhood, and which Irving lacked. Identified with Shakespeare as that theatricality was by Terry and her family, it would become a lucrative acquisition for the ambitious Irving, and one which enabled him to marry his own ferocious energies to the vehicle of Terry's more assured popular and theatrical status. Before that could happen, however, Terry would make another attempt to leave the stage, in order to set up home with Edward Godwin. The relationship is constructed by Terry as an idyllic and brilliant respite from the theatre; but, given the couple's antecedents, it was also profoundly theatrical in tone.

As we have seen, she announces her departure casually, at the end of a chapter, following an offhand theatrical anecdote. In retrospect, however, and especially in the framing offered—indeed necessitated—by the genre of theatrical autobiography, that episode becomes 'A Six-Year Vacation' (the title of Terry's fourth chapter)—that is, a break from the real thing. She writes that she 'studied cookery-books instead of parts—Mrs Beeton instead of Shakespeare!,'[25] and thus makes him into the stuff of everyday life, and Mrs Beeton into the business of frivolity and respite, of holiday. This throwaway comment belies Terry's explicit understanding of this phase of her life, and places Shakespeare at the heart of her understanding of her professionalism. When Terry went back to the theatre after a wonderfully dramatic rescue by the playwright Charles Reade, who found her in a broken down cart in a Hertfordshire lane, it was not immediately to Shakespeare, but to the part of Philippa Chester in *The Wandering Heir*, a play written by Reade and inspired by the case of the 'Tichborne Claimant.' However, as Michael Holroyd suggests, Reade 'took this story and married it to an up-dated version' of *As You Like It*,[26] and it seems that the ability to play a Rosalind-like character, if not Rosalind herself, was part of the attraction for Terry. She herself notes that her role 'was a kind of Rosalind part, and Charles Reade only exaggerated pardonably when he said that I should never have any part better suited to me!'[27]

This was as near as Terry would get to playing the part of Rosalind, a role she never played at the Lyceum or anywhere else. Terry turns this omission from her repertoire into an integral part of her story, and she refers to the part throughout *The Story of My Life*. The source of her fascination with the role is suggested in her father's riposte to anyone who complimented Terry's acting in his hearing that, 'she ought to play Rosalind.'[28] It is also the vehicle for thoughts about her profession: 'The ambitious boy thinks of Hamlet, the ambitious girl of Lady Macbeth or Rosalind.'[29] Rosalind is the test of the female comedian, given the exacting pace of the role, and its combination of 'swift utterance' and 'swift thinking.'[30] Terry acknowledges freely the number of women known and unknown to her who have taken on this role, most notably Madge Kendal, Helena Faucit, Ada Rehan, Lillie Lantry, and the all-female cast, including Mary Shaw as Rosalind, whom she saw in New York. The tributes to these actresses are characteristically generous, but also occasionally barbed, and often make clear, as do letters quoted from Langtry and Rehan, that Terry felt a prior claim to the role. Of Kendal she writes that that actress had played Rosalind, and goes on, 'I never did, alas!—and [she] quite recently acted with me in "the Merry Wives of Windsor," but the best of her fame will always be associated with such plays as "The Squire," "The Ironmaster," "Lady Clancarty," and many more plays of the type.'[31] Having acknowledged Mrs Kendal's claim to a Shakespearean reputation, she then swiftly pulls back from that position to assign her instead to the realm of more ephemeral productions. Of the Rosalind of Helena Faucit, before going on to praise the 'deep and true emotion' with which she played the mock marriage scene, Terry notes that she

> never saw this distinguished actress when she was in her prime. Her Rosalind, when she came out of her retirement to play a few performances, appeared to me more like a *lecture* on Rosalind, than like Rosalind herself: a lecture all young actresses would have greatly benefited by hearing, for it was of great beauty.'[32]

There is here, as in the comments on Kendal, a deeply ambivalent quality to the praise bestowed, and a reluctance to cede the part of Rosalind to another actress.

Her final reflections on the part in *The Story of My Life* suggest that Irving was considering producing *As You Like It* in 1888, when he would have taken the part of Touchstone, because 'Touchstone is in the vital part of the play.'[33] It was not to be, however, and instead the Lyceum played *Macbeth* that year to an acclaim that, thanks in part to John Singer Sargent's portrait of Terry in the role, has become one of the most durable episodes in theatrical history. Terry's reflection on the end of that year, however, is more grating. With a confidence in her own versatility, and an age-blindness not seen on modern stages, she writes: 'Here I was in the very noonday of my life, fresh from Lady Macbeth and still young enough to play Rosalind, suddenly called upon to play a rather uninteresting mother in "The Dead Heart." '[34] She declares herself compensated for this disappointment by her son Edward Gordon Craig's success in his role in Watts Phillips' tired melodrama, but the disappointment is palpable.

What was it about Rosalind that so attracted Terry? Holroyd suggests it was the play's combination of comedy and romance, the possibility of Rosalind's testing out multiple personalities, and her touchingly happy ending with Orlando.[35] It is also, however, simply a play that would be carried by its leading lady, as twentieth-century productions starring Helen Mirren, Peggy Ashcroft, Eileen Atkins, Juliet Stevenson and Vanessa Redgrave, amongst others, have shown. Perhaps in her regret for the role, she was also regretting, or at least fundamentally calling into question, the partnership with Irving that gave her the greatest fame and highest status of her life. As a footnote to their joint career, this reflection strikes a note of somber pensiveness which Terry picks up in her lectures on Shakespeare:

> Would that I could say 'I have been Rosalind.' Would that the opportunity to play this part had come my way when I was in my prime! I reckon it one of the greatest disappointments of my life it did not! In my old age I go on studying Rosalind, rather wistfully I admit![36]

In the lectures she *could* be Rosalind, but the circumscribed setting of the lecture space was the only one available to her in this role. Rosalind represents the fame that could be achieved by Faucit and by Kate Terry, a fame dependent on a certain acquiescence with, and negotiation of, contemporary expectations of Victorian women and their behavior: Faucit famously swaddled her legs in a cloak rather than appear before her audience in tights. There would, as Irving may have suspected, have been something less compromising about Terry's Rosalind, something he was not prepared to see on his stage. Terry's attenuated narrative of disappointment about the role witnesses to a streak of foiled determination that belies the charm for which she was so famed, and which, ironically, was one of her primary qualifications to be Rosalind.

Nonetheless, the Rosalind-like role of Philippa Chester in Reade's play effected her re-entry onto the stage in 1874, and attracted the attention of the Bancrofts who soon afterwards engaged her to appear as Portia in *The Merchant of Venice* at the Prince of Wales's Theatre. As Terry herself suggests, this engagement embedded her within the heart of the theatrical establishment of the mid-1870s and propelled her back forcefully into the public's gaze. The production was expensive and gorgeous, designed by Edward Godwin with the fullest attention to historical research. Biographers have speculated that it was this opportunity to work again with her lover that attracted Terry to the role; but while the production did not save their foundering relationship, and was a commercial drain on the Bancrofts' theatre, it established Terry as a new star.

Reviews were enthusiastic, but Terry's own account of the play and her reception is more telling, as it reveals the dynamics of success, and her readiness to accept another's failure as its price:

> Success I had had of a kind, and I had tasted the delight of knowing that audiences liked me, and I had liked them back again. But never until I appeared as Portia at the Prince of Wales's had I experienced that awe-struck feeling which comes, I suppose, to no actress more than once in a lifetime—the feeling of the conqueror. In homely parlance, I knew that I had 'got them' at the moment when I spoke the speech beginning, 'You see me, Lord Bassanio, where I stand.'
>
> 'What can this be?' I thought. '*Quite* this thing has never come to me before! This is *Different*! It has never been quite the same before.'
>
> It was never to be quite the same again.
>
> Elation, triumph, being lifted on high by a single stroke of the mighty wing of glory—call it by any name, think of it as you like—it was as Portia that I had my first and last sense of it. And, while it made me happy, it made me miserable because I foresaw, as plainly as my own success, another's failure.[37]

Terry's terms echo those of contemporary reviewers, all of whom found Charles Coghlan's Shylock as much of a disappointment as she did.

The play was deemed notable, though, for the discovery of Terry, as this review from the *Pall Mall Gazette* makes clear:

> Fortunately for the performance of 'The Merchant of Venice' at the Prince of Wales's Theatre, the cast includes a young actress who has but now joined the company, and who brings to her impersonation of Portia sounder and safer views as to the due rendering of the poetic drama. Miss Ellen Terry, who in her early childhood served an apprenticeship at the Princess's Theatre under the rule of Mr. and Mrs. Charles Kean, is now an artist of real distinction. With all the charms of aspect and graces of manner indispensable to the impersonation of the heiress of Belmont, Miss Terry is gifted with a voice of silvery and sympathetic tone, while her elocutionary method should be prized by her fellow-actors. [. . .] Miss Terry's Portia leaves little to be desired; she is singularly skilled in the business of the scene, and assists the action of the drama by great care and inventiveness in regard to details [. . .] Thus it chanced that, probably for the first time, the portions of the play that relate to the loves of Portia and Bassanio became of more importance and interest than the scenes in which Shylock appears [. . .] Interest, however, attaches to the production because of Portia and the pictures, at once brilliant and careful, of Venetian life in the sixteenth century which occupy the stage.[38]

Terry and the splendor of the production share the laurels in reviews; a situation fraught with difficulty for Terry, as the designer, Godwin, was by then her estranged partner. Onstage, however, theirs was a powerful partnership that determined responses to the production. Not all reviewers were won over, however: 'The Man About Town' in *The Sporting Gazette* found the performance nothing but an 'upholstery exhibition.'[39] But mostly honors were shared between Terry's acting and Godwin's sets: *Bell's Life in London and Sporting Chronicle* noted that 'Mr Godwin has consulted old-established authorities' in allowing 'Venice [to appear] in all its beauty' and that '[t]he principal success of the evening was obtained by Miss Ellen Terry, whose Portia will assuredly long be remembered for the grace, intelligence, and charm with which this skilful actress invested it,'[40] a 'Portia who looks like a picture by Leighton,'[41] the Royal Academician, but who was in fact dressed by the more raffish Godwin. For *Fun*, the sumptuousness of the production signaled its being 'dished up for the stalls.' *Punch*, however, in a curiously sympathetic review, suggested that the play's 'series of pictures' precisely demonstrated 'a considerable feeling for its poetry'; indeed, *Punch* can 'remember no more striking example of all that is excellent in scenic arrangements.' Terry is similarly groundbreaking: 'such a Portia [. . .] as this generation, at least, has not witnessed [. . .] a Portia worthy of SHAKSPEARE'.[42] Thus Terry was relaunched for a new set of audiences, too young to remember the Shakespeare seasons of Samuel Phelps and Charles Kean, and eager for something more than the 'cup and saucer' dramas that the Bancrofts had pioneered. Irving's drive to bring Shakespeare to the intelligent middle classes, and vice versa, arguably is anticipated in the efforts of this production, which ran for only three weeks at the Prince of Wales's, but whose significance was longstanding.

The production had taught Terry the delight of moving an audience, of holding them in her grasp, and of keeping them in thrall to her words. It also taught her, however, that such a success was not one that could necessarily be shared, and might even depend on another's failure. Had Coghlan's Shylock been stronger, then arguably Terry's Portia would not have shone as it did, and as several reviews acknowledged. As she writes, 'it was never to be the same again'; her partnership with Irving did not give her the satisfaction of that early Portia, cast as she so often was as the foil to his starring role. Nonetheless, working with Irving gave her a more prominent theatrical and cultural position than could be achieved elsewhere.

More productively, that season also showed Terry how important might be her collaboration with the artists of her day:

> The audiences may have been scanty, but they were wonderful. O'Shaughnessy, Watts-Dunton, Oscar Wilde, Alfred Gilbert, and, I think, Swinburne were there. A poetic and artistic atmosphere pervaded the front of the house as well as the stage itself.[43]

For many visual artists, poets and musicians, Terry and the Lyceum stage would become their natural inspiration and environment. For Graham Robertson, Terry was the painters' actress, and the links with the visual arts that were such a part of her first two romantic relationships continued to play a significant part in her work and in responses to her throughout her career. Terry's relationship with Godwin was initially forged through his designing her dresses for the stage: for Portia, he provided her with 'a dress like almond-blossom' in the casket scene[44] and silk gowns which put her at the heart of a new form of appreciation for the possibilities of what the stage could represent for the new aesthetes of the approaching fin de siècle.[45] At this point, then, Terry was primed to bring with her a distinct audience and form of appreciation to the Lyceum which resulted in that theatre's unique ability to appeal to the aesthetes, among whom was counted Oscar Wilde, as well as to all ranks of society, including the bourgeoisie for whom Wilde would become in the 1890s the sign of all that was least acceptable to it. It was part of Terry's power, and perhaps that of Victorian theatre more generally, that she could unite otherwise discrete social and cultural groups in an appreciation of her art and of the personality that that art could project. In the acting of the Lyceum company, as we will see in the next section, Karl Marx and Queen Victoria could find a shared enthusiasm, Eleanor Marx could be inspired by Ellen Terry to want to go on stage, and young society women could compete for the honor of walking on with her.

Shakespeare at the Lyceum

From the Prince of Wales's, where she had been a 'useful' actress—the term is her own—for the Bancrofts, Terry moved to the Lyceum, where she and Irving would become the dominant cultural stars of their day, and the Lyceum a nexus of cultural and political influence. To that theatre, Terry brought a passion for and dedication to Shakespeare, which formed itself through a lifelong critical study of the dramatist that was often scarcely appreciated by her audiences. As she exasperatedly wrote, 'There is something more to my acting than charm.'[46] But that charm, the seductive effortlessness with which her appearances seemed to bridge the social and theatrical worlds, was part of the reason that she was so indispensable to Irving. He was the actor who carried his hard work and application as the badge of his dedication to his trade; she was the beauty from an established theatrical family who had grown up on the boards and who brought that ease to him. As she herself wrote: 'I might have deteriorated in partnership with a weaker man whose ends were less fine, whose motive was less pure. I had the taste and artistic knowledge that his upbringing had not developed in him.'[47]

The intense reciprocity of their relationship underpinned their success both onstage and off, but it was also something that both occasionally felt as a bind. Terry wrote of Irving that, 'He was always quite independent of the people with whom he acted,'[48] and recognized, though less explicitly, the extent of her own acting ambitions, which could be fulfilled neither with Irving nor any conceivable stage partner. Her conception of Beatrice could not be realized with him or any actor who could not reciprocate her mercurial brio: she felt that her Portia, though successful, was determined, weighted down, by his Shylock. Yet, for just over two decades, Irving and Terry dominated not only the Lyceum Theatre, but the London cultural scene, even the nation, and extended their renown to North America through a series of highly successful and lengthy tours.[49] They benefited undoubtedly from the burgeoning celebrity culture that emerged at the end of the nineteenth century, but also, and primarily, from the Victorian investment—financial, cultural, educational, and emotional—in the works of Shakespeare.

The Irving-Terry partnership lasted from 1878 to 1902, during which time the company produced, alongside a varied range of contemporary and popular plays, *Hamlet* (1878), *The Merchant of Venice* (1879), *Othello* (1881), *Romeo and Juliet* (1882), *Much Ado about Nothing* (1882), *Twelfth Night* (1884), *Macbeth* (1888), *Henry VIII* (1892), *King Lear* (1892), *Richard III* (1893), *Cymbeline* (1896) and *Coriolanus* (1901). (For a summary of the productions, see Richard Schoch's chapter, pp. 133–154.) Their acting partnership ended with a revival of *The Merchant of Venice* in 1902 on the day that Irving relinquished control of the theatre. Terry was thirty-one when she moved to the Lyceum and fifty-five when she left it. Like Cleopatra, however, a part she refused to play, age did nothing to weary either heror her audiences' enthusiasm; nor did it do anything to alter Irving's conception of Terry's capabilities. Reading criticism of Terry's roles at the Lyceum has a curiously vertiginous quality as one becomes embroiled within a rhetoric of timelessness. Henry James's protest that Terry might be a little old for Juliet at thirty-five is an unusually dissenting voice.[50] Many of Terry's roles are those of the young heroines—Ophelia, Portia, Viola, Cordelia and Imogen—so popular with Victorians who, however misleadingly, found in those Shakespearean roles images of an idealized femininity. The exception to the rule proved to be Terry's 1901 Volumnia, a performance much praised by John Ruskin, yet by few who saw it in the Lyceum's penultimate year.

The mismatch between Terry's offstage life and onstage roles, and the veneration that they generated, is in fact typical of the nineteenth century's reception of Shakespeare's heroines. A gloss of ideality, such as that provided most famously in Ruskin's account of the heroines in 'Of Queen's Gardens' (1865),[51] spread across and camouflaged the more unsettling experience of heroines who, like Beatrice, Juliet and Viola, were romantically declarative, and others, like Portia, who were independent in action. As Mary Ann Evans noted in an early review, before she became George Eliot, such heroines are 'inconvenient for those whose creed includes at once the doctrine of Shakespeare's infallibility and the doctrines of modern propriety.'[52] In fact, Shakespeare gave a license to break or at least to disregard those proprieties for a while and he gave the Victorians the opportunity to recognize the complexities and compromises involved in those proprieties, in that they were desirable and yet impossible to attain. In an age which gave Freud so much material but which had not yet been exposed to his remorseless unveiling of the conditions by which life is lived, the theatre could briefly articulate the complex and disruptive nature of desire, and experience in Ellen Terry one who embodied that very complexity. The rhetoric of charm which followed her throughout her career, and which is in part of course simply a lazy response on the part of reviewers, is also a way of almost silently registering this uneasiness at the heart of Terry's appeal, its simultaneous almost ethereal wistful loveliness and its fundamental sexuality. Charm registers the grounds of the irresistible and absolutely unselfconscious appeal of a child—perhaps the child-bride that Terry once was—but is also the remit of the charmer, the conscious manipulator, the witch or seductress, or the actress, whose appeal can work like a spell.

Terry is famously resentful of her reduction to being found charming by reviewers, perhaps wrongly so, as the term carries a more active, as well as the usual passive, connotation. It is an admission of strength and volition, not just aimless delight. Terry acknowledges this herself in a famous marginal annotation in one of her acting versions of *Macbeth,* where she instructs herself to 'Play with [Macbeth's] hands and *charm* him.'[53] Unlike Sarah Siddons's towering and powerful take on the role, Terry's Lady Macbeth was slight and fragile, both physically and mentally, subject to the panic of her situation, and purportedly concerned primarily for her husband's status.

The Lyceum production of *Macbeth* occupies a significant space in Terry's memory of events:

> My mental division of the years at the Lyceum is *before* 'Macbeth,' and *after.* I divide it up like this, perhaps, because 'Macbeth' was the most important of all our productions, if I judge it by the amount of preparation and thought that it cost us and by the discussion which it provoked.[54]

As part of that preparation, Irving and Terry took a trip to Scotland to drink in the atmosphere of Macbeth's homeland:

> We had great fun yesterday—we are full of our next production—Macbeth—& being in Macbethshire we "go about" to the different "spots"—well we came to the blasted heath!—Lo, a fine potato field—& a sky line of waving barley! However we had received a very warm invitation from the Thane (the Earl) of Cawdor to visit Cawdor Castle & to sleep

> there—& we went & stayed to luncheon (though *not* to sleep) & were most charmingly entertained by the old Laird and his daughter Lady Evelyn Campbell, who took us for a wonderful drive through—first an Oak forest then up higher amongst the firs then higher still where there was nothing but heather—except grouse—oh, it was lovely—lovely—& we came to the conclusion we cannot build our own 11th Century Castles & blast our own Heaths, for there's nothing left to take pattern by!—but after all, "the play's the thing", & the people like us, & with that encouragement, we'll never say die!!—I'm writing all this twaddle in bed.[55]

Macbeth was an eagerly awaited theatrical event, heavily trailed in newspapers across the country. On December 15th *The Era* gave news of Terry's first act dress which she is said to have designed herself: it is 'a woven dress of dark blue wool and threads of gold. This garment clings to the figure, and is full of serpentine gleams. A mantle of peacock-blue velvet and gold admirably carries out the tone and glitter of the gown.'[56] An approximation to the then popular, and sensational, Sarah Bernhardt clearly lurks in this description, and might alert the attentive reader to a new change of tone in Terry's dresses. *The Era*'s 'The Revival of "Macbeth" ' contains interviews with Irving and Terry on their understanding of their respective parts, and stresses that audiences are now ready for new conceptions of classic roles like Macbeth and his wife: 'Playgoers have emancipated themselves largely from the traditional fetters handed down from one Macbeth to another, and are far readier to accept the new lights which a thoughtful and studious intelligence can bring to bear.' As a measure of that readiness, the interviewer gives the following account of his 'chat on the subject of Lady Macbeth' with Terry, where she

> at once refers to Miss [*sic*] Siddons, and speaks with enthusiasm of what she is convinced must have been a 'stupendous' performance [Terry] has read volumes of commentaries, essays innumerable, psychological analyses and mental dissections, and she says, 'I get bewildered and confused, and I come back to Shakespeare at last, and there, and there alone, I seek my inspiration and my guidance.' I believe that the public will experience a keen delight in Miss Terry's performance. She will give us—it goes without saying—a lovely Lady Macbeth with a winsome face and a fascination of personal charm. Hers will be no stage-striding heroine of the conventional kind. She will be womanly, even in her iniquity; beautiful even in the stress of her remorseful dreams. Miss Helena Faucit's idea was that Lady Macbeth was not naturally a bad woman but that intense love for

> her husband prompted her to prick the sides of his intent, and urge him on to the fulfilment of his own ambitious devilry. I don't think Miss Terry intends to take quite this view. She recognizes that Lady Macbeth is not exactly a saint driven into guilt by the unavoidable force of connubial necessity. But between the extenuating conditions of Miss Faucit's Lady Macbeth and the tragic proportions of Mrs Siddons's there is the mean of womanly grace and outward softness cloaking a heart of desperate and unrelenting wickedness. Without revealing too much, these, I fancy, will be the lines upon which Miss Terry will proceed, and I venture to say that this new and striking conception will realize Shakespeare's meaning in such a way as it has never been realized in our time.[57]

What is particularly fascinating here is how novelistic expectations have replaced theatrical conventions as guides to the anticipated spectacle on stage, or rather perhaps, that the expectations of stage melodrama are allowed to infiltrate expectations of Shakespeare. The interviewer's account of Terry's Lady Macbeth sounds like nothing more than the Lady Audley of Mary E. Braddon's novel *Lady Audley's Secret* (1862), a radiantly beautiful young woman, abandoned by her first husband, who chooses to take a second rich husband to support herself, and then tries to kill the first husband to conceal her bigamy. The novel was twice successfully adapted for the stage, by George Roberts for the St James's Theatre and by Colin Hazlewood for the Britannia Theatre, Hoxton. This account of Lady Macbeth as a beautiful schemer whose main offense lies in going against the implications of her looks, stems straight from the tastes and sensibilities encouraged by Braddon. This also suggests the extent to which Terry and the Lyceum are now positioned culturally to appeal to both elite and popular London audiences. Such was the nature and extent of the Lyceum's popularity and ubiquity as a cultural icon that it came to be made available to all; subsequently, of course, it could hardly be expected to satisfy its vast range of spectators, and arguably in the conflicting views which this production engendered can be seen the beginning of the dissolution of this national institution.

Most striking in many ways in these preview pieces is the extent to which popular newspapers assume a detailed knowledge of stagecraft and theatre history in their readers, and an appetite for more. *The Penny Illustrated Paper and Illustrated Times* and *Jackson's Oxford Journal* both direct their readers to William Archer and Robert Lowe's essay 'Macbeth on the Stage,' which had just appeared in the *English Illustrated Magazine*. A 'doubtlessly transcendently beautiful revival of "Macbeth"' is anticipated,[58] but readers are also alerted to the cuts and textual restorations on which Irving is working.[59] Anticipation is heightened still further by an alleged slight delay to the opening of the production, although Irving is quoted as saying that no such delay was actually envisaged. This level of minute speculation and interest attests to the national event that was the opening of a new Lyceum production. This is witnessed also in the number and geographical spread of reviews, stretching from Aberdeen and Glasgow to Dublin, Belfast, Liverpool, Derby, Leeds, Birmingham and Bristol. In many papers, too, the event is covered not just in theatre reviews sections, but also news sections and gossip columns. The *Pall Mall Gazette* reviews the play on December 31st, when it also carries a piece on 'The House and Who Was In It. A Brilliant First Night.' The *Daily News* has a review of the first night, an article on the audience and the late-night Beefsteak Room supper which followed the performance, and a paragraph in its news section on 'The First Night of "Macbeth."' The Lyceum understood the possibilities of the press.

Terry ends *The Story of My Life* with a series of jottings from her diary, and notes of this production:

> It ('Macbeth') is a most tremendous success, and the last three days' advance booking has been greater than ever was known, even at the Lyceum. Yes, it is a success, and I am a success, which amazes me, for never did I think I should be let down so easily. Some people hate me in it; some, Henry among them, think it my best part, and the critics differ, and discuss it hotly, which in itself is my best success of all! Those who don't like me in it are those who don't want, and don't like to read it fresh from Shakespeare, and who hold by the 'fiend' reading of the character. [. . .] Oh, dear! It is an exciting time![60]

This is a slightly contradictory account—a record of success and an acknowledgement of dissent—and the same strains are apparent in reviews of Terry's Lady Macbeth and of the production as a whole. The reviews also begin to expose fault lines within the grounds upon which the Lyceum company has been so successful for the previous ten years, primarily the relationship of Irving and Terry themselves, and the appeal of their pictorial production values. Nonetheless, what is most clear of all, is the popular and financial success of this most talked about production, which saw unprecedented advance bookings and queues around the block from the first day of the production.[61]

The Era's generous review encapsulates the dilemma of critics favorably disposed towards Terry; she provides another charming spectacle, but not one appropriate to her current role:

> Miss Terry as Lady Macbeth, like one of her great predecessors, was delicate and refined, but she was not a delicate and refined fiend. Her reading of the character is one that is sure to create almost endless discussion, but even those who question its correctness will not be able to deny the grace that marks it throughout, and to question its claims as an interesting study, and Lyceum patrons, who may firmly refuse to believe that so gentle a lady and so loving a wife could have murder in her heart as upon her lips, will be hushed into silent admiration by the beauty of the sleep-walking scene, and will join in the acclamation that greets the actress for a bold effort carried out with undeniable charm.[62]

For *Punch*, 'Miss ELLEN TERRY has conceded too much to her own sweet, natural self. She has made one "blend" of *Beatrice*, *Ophelia*, and *Lady Macbeth*, in which the awful characteristics of the last have been toned down.'[63] What is in many ways most remarkable is the extent of this discussion. In 'Topics of the Week,' *The Graphic* notes that, 'This week all the world has been talking about the revival of *Macbeth* at the Lyceum,'[64] a comment which seems far from hyperbolic. 'THE CALL BOY,' in *Judy: The Conservative Comic*, professes himself intimidated, 'With so much deep and beastly clever discussion flying about as to how Shakespeare's characters of General and Lady Macbeth should or should not be played, I feel, in offering my opinion on the subject, as nervous as a horse on a frosty road.'[65] The crux of the matter lies in how far Terry is the Lady Macbeth of Shakespeare, and indeed of what that character consists. Most critical opinion of the time found against Terry in her interpretation of the role, though that it was actively an interpretation is also conceded. Nonetheless, Terry attracted reviews that were amongst the harshest of her career. The usually friendly *Graphic* writes:

> As to Miss Terry's gentle, clinging, affectionate spouse, it is obviously not Lady Macbeth–though it is probably the only sort of Lady Macbeth whom this sweetly tender and poetical actress is capable of presenting us with. [. . .] Incitements to treason and barbarous murder sit ill upon a woman who is all love and caresses, and whose voice, do what she will, is wholly wanting in the tragic note. [. . .] The effect, to put it plainly, borders on the ludicrous; though nothing could be more touching or full of sorrowful suggestions than her sleep-walking scene.[66]

In many ways, the critics are simply saying that Lady Macbeth was not Terry's part, and *Punch*'s pun neatly encapsulates the critic's dilemma in responding to Terry's performance: 'a horror-struck, nervous Lady Macbeth, listening for the result of her husband's murderous visit to Duncan's bed-room is not SHAKSPEARE'S Lady Macbeth, but Lady Macbeth Terry-fied.' It goes on: 'Miss Terry is probably right as to the fascination of the Thane's wife. But she must be the tiger-cat as well as the purring domestic cat; and when alone the tiger-cat only. Velvet and iron is *Lady Macbeth*.'[67]

Terry's celebrity status is confirmed by responses to this production—one article on 'How I Sketched Mrs Siddons's Shoes,' is a detailed account of a visit to Terry's dressing room.[68] Terry had been given the shoes in which Siddons had performed her Lady Macbeth as an act of homage to her own performance. The gift itself prompted further examination of Terry's performance, and another very poor pun:

> A Miss-Terry-ous Epigram
> (*Picked up at the Stage-door of the Lyceum*)
> [Miss Ellen Terry recently had presented to her the shoes of Mrs. Siddons]
>
> Siddons' shoes I have had the good luck to secure,
> They're my own—I can give'em or will'em;
> But the critics, alas! Don't profess to be sure
> If as Lady Macbeth I can *fill 'em!*[69]

Not only was Terry's acting called into question in ways that it had not been during her earlier performances of more congenial roles, but the very grounds of the Lyceum's popularity were also disputed. This all happens, of course, as Terry notes, against a background of heavy demand for the play. Nonetheless, the note of longer-term dissent is being struck. In 'Topics of the Week,' *The Graphic* notes that:

> Whatever may be thought of the acting of Mr. Irving and Miss Terry, there is no difference of opinion as to the splendour of the background provided for the play. Nothing more magnificent in its way has ever been seen in any theatre [. . .] but may it not be doubted whether all this display is really an advantage to lovers of the drama? Shakespeare's supreme object was surely to touch the imagination and to quicken feeling. Can it be truly said that the best way to enable his work to attain this end is to give it a gorgeous material setting? [. . .] The triumphs of the carpenter and the scene-painter may be very wonderful, but it is doubtful wisdom to force them into a sort of competition with the triumphs of the noblest dramatic art.[70]

This intriguing response pits the scenic and histrionic arts for which the Lyceum had been best known against each other; indeed, it makes them mutually exclusive in a newly unfavorable articulation of that theatre's aesthetic.

This is peculiarly ironic given that the cultural afterlife of the Lyceum *Macbeth* has been secured largely by Sargent's painting of Terry as Lady Macbeth. Currently hanging in the National Portrait Gallery in London, the work was originally displayed by Irving in the Beefsteak Room at the Lyceum. Terry herself writes that the portrait 'suggested [. . .] all that I should have liked to be able to convey in my acting as Lady Macbeth.'[71] This is a curious comment, not supported by critical accounts of the production. The figure of Lady Macbeth is Siddons-like in stature, and Terry's comments may reflect a rueful aspiration to have had Siddons's stage-dominating presence. In this rather overwhelming full-length image, Terry appears in her famous dress of shimmering green beetle wings with a crown raised above her head. Her expression, and indeed her action, are ambiguous. Critics have been unable to decide whether she is crowning herself, or taking the crown off, and her face registers the excited anguish of the moment, the terror of the achievement of her ambitions. The face is far less finished than those of Sargent's society portraits, but it blazes nonetheless out of a painting which is otherwise relieved in its gloomy beauty only by the gold of Terry's hair bindings and her girdle and the ominous shimmering of those famous beetle wings.

As Terry herself noted, the painting is Sargent's nearest approach to Pre-Raphaelitism: 'The whole thing is Rossetti—rich stained-glass effects.'[72] It captures, too, the ambivalent beauties of those paintings and the often sinister morality at their heart. It also reflects the impossibility of Terry's ambitions in representing a moment of contradictory aspirations and ambitious desires which she seems not to have been able to convey on stage, and which critics arguably would not have been able to appreciate if she had. The painting raised as much controversy as the performance, and underlined the parameters of the conditions in which Terry was working, both in the Lyceum and within the broader world of late-Victorian theatre, where she was bound into an aesthetic of pleasing, as well as possibly showing her and her audiences the limit of her own talents.

After this watershed moment, though Irving remained at the Lyceum for another fourteen years, the level of critical urgency and debate engendered by *Macbeth* was never achieved again. Rather, the theatre consolidated its institutional status and its popularity. Terry clearly felt that, following *Macbeth*, the moment ought to have been seized for something more decisive than *The Dead Heart*. But the moment was not seized, and her Shakespearean parts after that never again achieved quite the degree of public attention and critical vitality that her Lady Macbeth had aroused. One production, however, embroiled her in a private critical dispute that in its terms and in the disjunction between those terms and popular representations of the production, show up the difficulties which predetermine the best and most ambitious actress's performances. The production was *Cymbeline* (1896) when Terry played Imogen to Irving's Iachimo.

By common consent, this was deemed an actress's play by critics, which perhaps went some way to explaining why *Cymbeline* had so infrequently been seen on the nineteenth-century stage. For Terry, it enabled a starring moment in a theatre whose life was drawing to an end. *The Era* notes that for Imogen's 'sake, possibly, the play was written; for its leading female personage, it certainly continues, theatrically speaking, to exist.'[73] Reviews of the production refer back to the Imogens of Mrs Siddons and Helena Faucit and to the last London run of play in 1872, with Henrietta Hodson taking the part.[74] The pleasure of seeing Terry in a starring role determines journals' anticipation of the production: 'For Miss Terry there is still left the opportunity of completing her great gallery of Shakespearean portraits with a fine picture of Imogen.'[75] The play's stage history was otherwise felt to be undistinguished. Expectations ran high for Irving's production, though were not so enthralled as those taster articles for *Macbeth*. Rather, critics await the first night as another in the line of Lyceum triumphs, with articles expressing the thrill of the anticipation of the fulfillment of familiar responses, and also perhaps the scarcely articulated sense that the Lyceum was reaching the end of its reign—the *Pall Mall Gazette*'s reference to Terry's 'completing' her gallery of Shakespearean parts sounds an ominous note. In fact, in many respects, the production exceeded expectations, stunning audiences with the beauty of its costumes and sets, for which Sir Lawrence Alma-Tadema took some responsibility. The *Pall Mall Gazette* considered the production 'more artistic than any other we have seen at the Lyceum [. . .] we fancy we have never seen a play in this theatre so admirably staged.'[76] Terry, too, exceeded her audiences' sense of her attractiveness in the role. Reviews are full of superlatives that speak to the besotted state of the journalists:

> Miss Ellen Terry's Imogen was delightful. She admirably portrayed the most womanly woman ever depicted by Shakespeare, being in turn loving, sorrowful, trusting, doubting, scorning, suffering and triumphing. [. . .] Miss Terry possesses a keen conception of the character she portrays, and depicts the varying moods of the sorrowing but ever loving Imogen with affecting fidelity.[77]

The Era found her 'exquisite. The sweet womanly weakness of the lighter side of the character was exhibited in the daintiest way by Miss Terry.' It even manages to embed her notorious onstage quirks into her successful rendering: 'Her little fidgetty pats of the foot when worried by Cloten's importunities were as truly in the comedy vein as the scathing indignation with which she expressed Imogen's righteous wrath at Iachimo's insulting proposals was highly heroic and dramatic.' For the *Daily News* she had 'never played any part with more touching pathos, or at certain points with a nearer approach to tragic power,'[78] and for *The Times*, Terry simply finds in Imogen a part that might have been designed for her, and which she plays with 'rare grace and charm.' That newspaper finds her an appropriate vehicle for all the praise that commentators have heaped upon the character of Imogen and deems that 'the artlessness and unostentatiousness of Imogen's character are at every turn fully suggested.'[79]

How, and by what artfulness, the characteristics are suggested is not specified: it is simply enough that Terry appears in a role that enables her to appeal to her audiences as they wish her to appeal to them. As *Pick-Me-Up* succinctly puts it: Miss Ellen Terry 'practically runs the show.'[80] In her correspondence, Terry shows herself acutely aware of audiences' tendencies to make of her what they will. She writes to Shaw that her audiences love her, 'Not for what I am, but for what they imagine I am.'[81] Her description of herself as 'being fat and nearly fifty'[82] in the run-up to *Cymbeline* is not one that her spectators could have shared, so determined were they to maintain the force of a theatrical nostalgia which in some respects served Terry and the Lyceum so well. Terry was simply not allowed to grow up or to grow beyond the terms of an idealized femininity current earlier in the century and which appeared in the earliest responses to her adult appearances on the stage. In its vulnerability to the superlatives supplied by reviewers and Lyceum audiences, the part of Imogen was the ideal vehicle for Terry at a period when the Lyceum needed to bolster its reputation against the incursion of the New Drama of the 1890s, as exemplified by Ibsen, and (as suggested above) against a certain complacency in audiences' responses to it. *Cymbeline* allows company and audiences to hark back to a time of greater social and theatrical certainties and to give their nostalgia free rein. For once, as several reviews acknowledge, it seemed strategically important to Irving to allow himself to play a supporting role to Terry, whose popularity had been a constant of the Lyceum's attraction to audiences.

However, the reviews and popular depictions of the production also hint at an even more uncomfortable ground for the production's success:

Cymbeline allowed for the playing out of a scene of uncomfortable and illicit intimacy between Irving and Terry. The bed-chamber scene, in which Iachimo hides himself in a chest in Imogen's bedroom in order to fabricate information suggesting her infidelity to her husband Posthumus, obviously caught the attention of spectators. *The Westminster Budget*, the *Lady's Pictorial*, *The Gentlewoman*, and *The Queen: The Lady's Newspaper* are just some of the journals which include full page, double page or even front page images of Irving's dark-robed Iachimo looming threateningly and with evil intent over the sleeping figure of Terry's Imogen. *The Times* describes Irving as wearing a 'dark, sinister costume that testifies to his evil designs. He is almost goblin-like, ghoulish—some hideous thing of the darkness.' The illustrations capture the sexual tension that the play, in its convoluted family relations and expressions of desire, struggles to contain, and thus suggest a further ground for the play's appeal. This appeal, however, is rather to an illicit form of desire, which *Punch* describes in an unusually sensitive—and favorable—review which is illustrated with two sketches of Irving, exposed inside the chest by means of 'Rontgen Rays' and then popping out of the box above the caption, 'Jackimo in the Boximo.' The humor of the cartoons belies the more disturbing, and horribly voyeuristic, account of the play:

> ELLEN TERRY was simply charming as *Imogen*; perfectly natural, which is the same as saying 'genuinely artistic.' So thoroughly did she identify herself with the modest, virtuous, retiring-to-bed-early *Imogen*, that, when roused from her sleep by the plaudits of the audience, after the Bed-room Scene, when from her arm wicked *Iachimo* has stolen her bracelet, Miss ELLEN shyly refused to face the house, but hid her face with her hands as, in her snow-white robe de nuit, she stood by the friendly bedpost as if shrinking from the boldly-expressed admiration of a 1000 *Iachimos* in the stalls, boxes, and gallery.[83]

This is a horrible depiction of a figure essentially violated once by the scheming of Iachimo and then again by the male audience's collusion in his plans, and casts a darker light on the psychology of the Lyceum's audience. That it was also a scene that appeared prominently in popular women's magazines and papers is intriguing, and speaks to the notoriety, or at least to the frisson that the scene conjured in the late-Victorian mind, as well as to the ubiquity of its performers at this period. In the women's magazines, the actors occupy a space similar to that of fictionalized characters in a popular romantic story.

The gap between the prurient crudity of these responses and the level of critical exchange between Terry and Bernard Shaw over this production shows up starkly how little of the actress's engagement with a particular role was discernible by, or even perhaps of interest to, her regular audiences. Shaw was at this time engaged in trying to wean the actress away from the Lyceum's standard repertoire of melodrama and Shakespeare, and towards his own plays. Terry would later create the role of Lady Cicely Waynflete in *Captain Brassbound's Conversion*, but at this point she is grateful for the chance to talk on paper with Shaw and to gather his advice on a part which offered her more challenges than her audience realized, not the least of which was the fact that she received little if any advice from Irving:

> You must understand that I am the one person at the Lyceum who is never advised, found fault with, or 'blackguarded' before the production of our plays! Henry finds fault with everyone, and rehearses and rehearses and rehearses and (da capo) them over and over and over again. Then our scenes (his and mine) come on, and he generally says 'Oh, we'll skip these scenes,' and I am to be found up in the scene-dock doing it all by myself, or being heard in the words by some girl or boy.[84]

This was perhaps because of Irving's confidence in her, but when Shaw offers her the chance to go over her part with him, she greedily soaks up his advice, responding to it with an intelligent stage consciousness which leads Shaw to declare: 'I begin to doubt whether you can really be an actress. Most of'em have no brains at all.'[85] The upshot of Shaw's intervention is that the day before *Cymbeline* opens Terry is declaring to Shaw that 'I want to act a modern part. Oh, I am so ill, and stiff, and dull.'[86] Ellen Terry is also responding here to the appearance on the London stage in modern parts of international stars such as Eleanora Duse, Bernhardt and the New Actresses—Janet Achurch, Stella Campbell and Elizabeth Robins. Shaw had identified a disjunction both between Shakespeare's play and the conditions in which it was to be acted, and between the various aspects of Imogen's character. These latter were brought into marked relief by their juxtaposition with a theatre being rejuvenated by the works of Ibsen. Shaw writes:

> All I can extract from the artificialities of the play is a double image—a real woman *divined* by Shakespear without his knowing it clearly, a natural aristocrat, with a high temper and perfect courage, with two moods—a childlike affection and wounded rage; and an idiotic paragon of virtue

> produced by Shakespear's *views* of what a woman ought to be, a person who sews and cooks, and reads improving books until midnight, and 'always reserves her holy duty,' and is anxious to assure people that they may trust her with their spoons and forks, and is in a chaotic state of suspicion of improper behaviour on the part of other people (especially her husband) with abandoned females. If I were you I should cut the part so as to leave the paragon out and the woman in; and I should write to The Times explaining the lines of this operation. It would be a magnificent advertisement.[87]

In fact, however, audiences clearly responded to Terry as paragon, which, to be fair, was at least as much a Victorian as a Shakespearean creation. The same might be said also of Terry herself, whose renown was bound up with her audiences' sense of what they needed her to represent and with the extent to which her Shakespearean roles might be the vehicle for that pleasing spectacle.

These roles also dictated the terms upon which Terry became a celebrity both on and off the stage. As John Plunkett notes, this celebrity status was substantial, and second only to that of the royal family.[88] She and Irving, both in and out of costume, adorn the covers of publications as diverse as *Madame* and *The Illustrated Sporting and Dramatic News*. In celebrity features from the late-nineteenth and early-twentieth centuries a now familiar pattern of interview and snoop around the celebrity's home is taking shape, as a number of articles on Ellen Terry demonstrate. They also demonstrate how far, even in this most popular of genres, Shakespeare was readily invoked as an integral part of the actress's appeal and fame.

Interviews usually contain mention of Terry's favorite roles—Beatrice and Ophelia, according to Ethel Mackenzie McKenna's interview in *McClure's Magazine* and *The Strand Magazine*'s 'Illustrated Interview' with Terry[89]—the number of books in her various homes, and the prevalence of Shakespeare on her shelves.[90] *The Strand Magazine*, which features the most reverential of these interviews, is also the most concerned with Shakespeare, and describes the Johnston Forbes-Robertson etching of the church scene in *Much Ado* which adorns Terry's London entrance hall. It speaks also of 'the oaken table and chairs, which are an exact model of those used by Shakespeare himself!,' pencil sketches of Terry as Portia and Beatrice, and her extensive library of well-annotated books about Shakespeare.[91] The article further notes that in her tiny study-cum-sitting room, 'Ellen Terry rests and reads, living with the genius of the man who first conceived and penned the lives in that little row of books on the wall, which bear his name in golden letters—Shakespeare.'[92] Shakespeare and Terry confirm and 'sell' each other in an age of celebrity endorsement.

Post-Lyceum Shakespeare

After the management of the Lyceum was handed over to a syndicate in 1898, Terry tried her hand at different types of theatre, appearing in Ibsen's *The Vikings at Helgeland* in a production directed by her son Edward Gordon Craig, and also briefly in Shaw. But it was as a Shakespearean actress that she continued to be best known and most highly acclaimed. She appeared as Mistress Page in *The Merry Wives of Windsor* (1902) and as Hermione in *The Winter's Tale* (1906), both produced by Herbert Beerbohm Tree. She also made a cameo appearance at celebrations marking her sixty years on the professional stage in June 1906 in act one of *Much Ado about Nothing*, the finale of the jubilee evening, which was acted by twenty-three members of the Terry clan, including Ellen as Beatrice, and supported by Beerbohm Tree as Benedick. Terry's final stage appearance was as Juliet's nurse in 1919. These appearances kept her in the public eye and determined the memories already being constructed around her. These memories had been initiated by Terry herself in her early autobiographical writings in the *New Review* in 1891, where she positioned herself in professional terms, made no mention of her various romantic relationships, and cited only Ellen Kean as a mentor.

In her later writings, however, under the influence of Christopher St John, Terry identified herself more definitively with Shakespeare, as shown in 1932 in her published lectures. St John's introduction exalts the relationship between actress and playwright into something almost sacred, even transcendent:

> It has often been remarked that Ellen Terry spoke the language of Shakespeare as if it were her native tongue, and in these communings with herself there is revealed something of the process by which she arrived at that state of grace in which his words became her words.

She goes on:

> His world too became her world: she was entirely at home in it, as these lectures alone are left to testify now that she is dead. She speaks in one

> of them of its being 'more real to some of us than the actual world,' but I have never met anyone as familiar with it and its inhabitants as she. She lived on the most intimate terms with Shakespeare's men and women.[93]

Precisely the same language was used nearly thirty years earlier by Henry James in his obituary of Fanny Kemble, an actress of an earlier age, and one whom Terry had mocked (in Irving's defense) in her autobiography. James, a friend and fan of Kemble's, wrote that

> She was so saturated with Shakespeare that she has made him, as it were, the air she lived in, an air that stirred with his words whenever she herself was moved, whenever she was agitated or impressed, reminded or challenged. He was indeed her utterance, the language she spoke when she spoke most from herself. He had said the things that she would have wished most to say, and it was her greatest happiness, I think, that she could always make him her obeisance by the same borrowed words that expressed her emotion.[94]

St John's is a cruder, and more anxious, tribute, but the resonance of both tributes is strikingly similar, as is their use of Shakespeare. In each he works to venerate a recently dead actress, and links her name to one who has triumphantly survived the passage of time. Terry thus becomes part of a longer tradition of actresses whose loyalty is confirmed through their work in Shakespeare. The novelty in Terry's case is that their relationship is confirmed through a range of media outlets.

Her lectures, or 'recitals' as they were often known, propelled Terry into an exhausting series of public appearances at home and abroad. In the winter of 1911–12, she appeared in twenty-one towns during a forty-four day tour. The lectures work as a kind of footnote to her career, explaining and exemplifying, making claims for her standing as a student of Shakespeare, as well as an actress, and allowing, too, for a self-conscious positioning of herself in relation to Irving as well as to Shakespeare. Denying any clams to being a scholar, she suggests that the actress's

> task is to learn how to translate this character into herself, how to make its thoughts her thoughts, its words her words. It is because I have applied myself to this task for a great many years that I am able to speak to you

> about Shakespeare's women with the knowledge that can be gained only from union with them.[95]

Interestingly, she is a clearly revisionist writer, debunking theatrical tradition and fundamentally changing how some women characters are viewed. Bram Stoker noted Terry's strategy more generally, remarking that her example allowed actresses 'to emerge from the meshes of convention.'[96] The organization of her thoughts into four lectures on children in the plays, Shakespeare's use of letters, and the heroines who are pathetic, and those who are triumphant, further resists, as Nina Auerbach has argued, the conventional generic categories of tragedy and comedy and their implications for their heroines.[97] Citing Beatrice's indignation towards Claudio in the chapel scene, Terry is particularly determined that the character should be read in this scene as serious, and not as partially comic. Terry also famously disputes Irving's insistence that at the end of this crucial scene a time-honored gag be included. As Benedick exits, Beatrice traditionally asks him to kiss her hand again. Clearly this does not suit Terry's reading of Beatrice's sober demeanor in this scene, but Irving insisted on its inclusion, despite her tears. The actress recalls that she

> went home in a terrible state of mind, strongly tempted to throw up my part! Then I reflected that for one thing I did not like doing at the Lyceum, there would probably be a 100 things I should dislike doing in another theatre. So I agreed to do what Henry wished, under protest.
>
> I have played Beatrice hundreds of times, but not once as I know she ought to be played. I was never swift enough, not nearly swift enough at the Lyceum.[98]

This slightly ungenerous anecdote subtly undermines Irving, critiquing his status as a responsible, modern interpreter of Shakespeare, as a manager, and finally as a co-actor, but should be set against Stoker's recollection of the incident. The details vary slightly, but he insists that this is the only instance he can recall 'when her wishes were not exactly carried out.'[99]

From the letters to Shaw onwards, Terry's writings take her further and further away from her main professional relationship and into a more private individual relationship with Shakespeare. Indeed, when Irving died, she chose to record his passing in her diary with Shakespeare's words: '13 Oct 1905—Henry died today—"and now there is nothing left remarkable beneath the visiting moon"—*Cleopatra*—.'[100] As her professional life dwindles into old age, and ill health, its Shakespearean resonances maintain their hold over her own and others' accounts of her. *The Times*' review of Terry's *Lectures* notes that

> [i]n reading them it is difficult to shake off a queer impression that she who is speaking was herself one of Shakespeare's women, and that in the native country of them all, his creative mind, she had met, and talked with, and lived with them all.[101]

This is in a sense the official line promoted by Craig and St John as they sought to secure Terry's place in popular memories and in cultural history. Thus Terry is dissolved into Shakespeare and his words, the memory of her becoming one with them.

This contrasts intriguingly with a letter by Terry herself, written in 1902, where the same possibility of identification threatened self-dissolution:

> I've gotten over wishing *I* were 'Portia'—&, (as I *shd cease to be* I verily believe if I had not *some* hope) I nowadays think that in 'another & a better world than this' (!) I *may* (?) open my eyes & say, 'oh Bottom how art thou translated!!!' & find no *E. T. left*! But some creature begotten of Portia Beatrice Imogen Rosalind Volumnia Cordelia Hamlet Cesar *Silvius*!!!—& I'll say looking at some old Photograph (!!) 'that's *me*!!! *Was* me'[102]

Terry's habitually skittish punctuation aside, this is a disturbingly contorted letter, trapped within its own dilemma, no less than within its own meandering structures. The actress used to translating parts for her audiences now anticipates her own translation, or dissolution, into a melee of roles, some male, others female, some played by her, some not. Of course the irony is that the photograph which should confirm her identity is likely itself to be part of the Lyceum publicity machine. In a sense, this is Terry's final posthumous plight. It is, however, a plight that was celebrated in the words read and scripted for her by Christopher St John in response to the BBC broadcast in honor of her eightieth birthday. She recognizes that she is remembered because of Shakespeare:

> *I know I have to thank Shakespeare for it.* It is because I am associated with him in people's minds, because the parts of his I played are more enduring than 'marble or gilded monument' that I am not forgotten.[103]

The emphasis is St John and Terry's, and the sentiment is included because St John and Edy Craig claimed often to have heard Terry say it. But just as charm has its Janus qualities, so might this phrase, too—because it recognizes her not always grateful immersion within words and lives not her own. Of herself, when left to voice her own plight, the words are rather different: 'There are times,' Terry said, 'when I feel rather like Bottom,'[104] transformed and bewildered. Dementia clouded her final years, and it is this condition to which her words are taken by St John and Edy Craig to refer; but they might also stand as a final bewildered admission of the confusion of the self engendered by a prolonged immersion in Shakespeare's words—and of the enveloping of that self within a popular adoration which was at least as much for Shakespeare's heroines as for herself.

Chapter 4

Henry Irving

Richard Schoch

The actor whose knighthood from Queen Victoria was announced on the same summer day in 1895 that his friend Oscar Wilde was sentenced to two years' hard labor for gross indecency was born John Henry Brodribb, son of a travelling salesman, in the Somerset village of Keinton Mandeville, fifty-seven winters earlier, in the year of Her Majesty's coronation. Theatrical history knows him as Henry Irving. Thoroughly Victorian, he never rode in an automobile, never spoke on the telephone, never liked having his picture taken. Although his acclaimed management of the Lyceum Theatre eventually became a byword for a backward-looking visual aesthetic, Irving himself was a celebrity of the modern age. He was the last great Victorian actor-manager and the unlikely herald of theatrical modernism. What, to a great extent, explains those contradictions was Irving's long uncompromising commitment to Shakespeare.

A Theatrical Life

Having moved to London at age ten, the boy quickly fell in love with the theatre, particularly Sadler's Wells, the suburban playhouse then managed by Samuel Phelps. Before he turned eighteen Brodribb quit his clerkship in a firm of East India merchants to seek his fortune in what he regarded as a pursuit more intellectual: 'the Dramatic Profession.'[1] With a versatile wardrobe and £20 to spare, he was on his way. Yet unlike generations of leading performers—John Philip Kemble at the turn of the century; Charles Kean, actor-manager of the Princess's Theatre, then at the height of his career; or the young Ellen Terry—the aspiring actor was not born into a theatrical family. His path unpaved with kindly intercessions, Henry Irving—the name adopted for his first professional appearance at the Lyceum Theatre, Sunderland, on September 29th 1856—learned the art of acting through a customary lengthy provincial apprenticeship. It is an awesome statistic that Irving acted half of the more than 800 roles that he would ever play in the first thirty months of a career spanning six decades. Never cast in the great tragic roles that he would later attempt in London, Irving settled for a gravedigger in *Hamlet* and an Ugly Sister in a *Cinderella* pantomime and was nearly heckled off the stage in Dublin.[2] When not practicing his gestures in front of mirrors in a succession of cheap boarding houses, he comforted himself with the thought that Macready, Phelps and the elder Kean were all novices once.[3]

The London breakthrough came in 1870 when he played the shabby gentleman Digby Grant in James Albery's *The Two Roses* at the Vaudeville Theatre. In the audience on his benefit night (a custom whereby leading actors supplemented their income with a share of box office receipts) was 'Colonel' H. L. Bateman, the new lessee of the Lyceum Theatre, a respectable but hardly distinguished playhouse. The American-born impresario had taken over the theatre to launch the acting career of his seventeen-year-old daughter Isabel. As he watched Irving, the proprietor realized that he had found his leading man: someone talented enough to make a good showing but not (he thought) talented enough to upstage Isabel. In the summer of 1871 Irving joined the Lyceum's company at £15 a week. It was the pivotal moment of his career, for that establishment lodged between the Strand and Covent Garden remained Irving's artistic home for thirty years. The word 'Lyceum' came to signify a style of playwriting and *mise-en-scène* that invited acclaim and censure in equal measure, and which still today names an era in theatrical history. But at the time no one guessed how fantastically Irving would prosper, nor how soon.

It was not Bateman's goal to make Irving a star but that is what happened. After some modest success in long-forgotten comedies and melodramas, Irving persuaded the proprietor to let him act the haunted murderer Mathias in Leopold Lewis's *The Bells*. The smallish number of spectators assembled at the Lyceum on the night of November 25th 1871 could not have suspected that they were witnessing legend in the making. J. M. Levy, editor of the *Daily Telegraph*, was in the audience, as was his newspaper's drama critic, Clement Scott. 'Tonight,' he told Scott, 'I have seen a great actor at the Lyceum—a great actor. There was a poor house. Write about him so that everyone shall know he is great!'[4] Scott did write about him and soon everyone did know of his greatness. *The Bells* held the stage for an astounding 151 nights and the part of Mathias gave Irving his signature role, more lauded than his Shylock, more long-lasting than his Hamlet.

Late on the night of triumph, as the actor and his wife rode past Hyde Park Corner, Florence Irving, not forgetting her social pretensions as the daughter of the Surgeon-General, exclaimed, 'Are you going to make a fool of yourself like this all your life?' His hard efforts mocked, the husband of three years and father of two sons halted the carriage, stepped out and strode away. Although he continued to support his family, Irving never returned to his marital home and never spoke another word to the woman who remained his wife. Success lay within reach and he would not be deterred.

On the strength of *The Bells*—which made him the actor to watch of his generation—and starring roles in the costume dramas *Charles I* and *Richelieu*—Irving convinced Bateman to let him play Hamlet, which was announced for the evening of October 31st 1874. Nothing seemed less sensible, for he possessed no reputation whatsoever as a tragedian. Yet Irving defied critics who predicted disaster by turning a threadbare production costing £100 into a sensation lasting 200 nights. Such was the arresting novelty of his performance—he neglected the acting 'points' petrified into tradition; he subscribed to William Hazlitt's theatrically risky proposition that Hamlet's ruling passion was not to act, but to think; he moved with 'short and frequently jerky' steps, so unlike Kemble or Edwin Booth—that it was hailed as the beginning of an era in Shakespearean production.[5] That was an overstatement, for nobody else in the cast deserved much recognition and there was but scant *mise-en-scène*. Still, the performance must have felt shockingly modern: here was a Hamlet who made you stop and think, just as the character himself did. 'Those who hold that the cut-and-dried Hamlet is the genuine article,' *The Times* reported, 'will be grievously disappointed.'[6] Almost from nowhere Irving became the leading Shakespearean of his day. So easy a conquest tells us more about the declining standards of histrionic art than Irving's singular genius. But there was a vacuum to be filled and it was Irving who filled it.

Bateman died during the long run of *Hamlet* and the Lyceum's management passed to his widow, who sanctioned productions of *Macbeth*, *Othello* and *Richard III* with the leading roles taken by Irving and Isabel Bateman. Realizing that, for all her charm, the young actress was out of her depth, Irving pressed Mrs. Bateman to replace her. Familial pride dented, mother and daughter moved on to Sadler's Wells in 1878 and sold to Irving the lease for the Lyceum, along with a full stock of scenery and costumes and the acting rights to many plays in the theatre's repertoire.

After seven London seasons in someone else's employ, Irving became his own master, the position he most enjoyed and which he would not relinquish for decades. Determined to make the Lyceum the foremost West End theatre he assembled his own production team, renovated the playhouse, and made the smartest decision of his career in naming Ellen Terry his leading lady. It was a surprising, almost offhand, choice. Irving and Terry had shared the stage but once—a forgettable revival of Garrick's *Katherine and Petruchio* a decade earlier—and they had not seen each other since. Irving of course knew that her Portia at the Prince of Wales's Theatre (1875) had been much admired. (For an extended discussion of Terry, see Gail Marshall's chapter in this volume.) She remained at Irving's side until 1902 and together they presided over a series of fabled productions. Fabled, that is, to some. Never in his career did Irving shake off his detractors, from Henry James to William Archer to George Bernard Shaw. All were outraged that Irving settled for a tired menu of bloated Shakespeare and stale melodrama. Against them ranged committed 'Irvingites,' Clement Scott chief among them, who kept the actor's name and accomplishments before the public.

Between 1878 and 1902 Irving produced thirty-seven plays at the Lyceum, of which twelve were by Shakespeare. The rest were mainly melodramas, leavened by the occasional new drama—Tennyson's *Becket*, most notably. Costume pieces were favored, with Irving playing King Arthur, Napoleon, Peter the Great, Robespierre and Louis XI. With exceptions like Tennyson's grand verse dramas, the repertoire looked backward, and thus ran counter to emerging trends in European drama. The roles that Irving played—and the way he played them—would not have puzzled audiences at the Princess's Theatre in the days of Charles Kean. Indeed, Irving purchased from Ellen Kean the promptbook and acting rights to plays such as *The Corsican Brothers* as originally produced by her late husband.[7] Shaw was right that new plays were not central to Irving's vision. But he was wrong to presume that you couldn't have a vision without them.

Irving was frequently absent from London, especially during the late summer and autumn when he toured the provinces. Touring was highly lucrative for him personally, but also for the Lyceum, as box-office takings in Dublin, Glasgow, Edinburgh, Manchester and Bristol subsidized expensive London productions. In 1883 Irving embarked upon his first North American tour, returning seven more times over the next twenty years. Those exhausting trips lasted up to six months, and over his career Irving played to American audiences for the equivalent of four years. Because the tours took him to middle-sized cities—Nashville, Baltimore, Hartford, Cleveland, St. Louis—millions of Americans saw Henry Irving perform in their hometown. The prominence of his tours reminds us that, far from being rooted to the London stage, Irving was a national and international star of a magnitude unknown in theatrical history.

For a man who never appeared on film, and whose voice survives only on a few scratchy wax cylinder recordings, it was the direct connection with his audience that made him a star. Hostile critics accused him of destroying the ensemble tradition by surrounding himself with lesser performers (Ellen Terry, the exception), but that tradition, a casualty of the Victorian 'star system,' had been weakening for years. A more perceptive analysis comes from Gordon Craig, Terry's son, who as a youth acted alongside Irving. As befitted a pioneer of theatrical modernism, he understood that Irving's productions expressed not ego, but artistic vision. 'We apprentices in Irving's time,' Craig remembered, 'were at our best when . . . we did our bit on the night as we were told to do it by the chief.'[8] Wilde, a man of deeply contrasting aesthetics, grasped the same idea: Irving's goal 'was to realise his own perfection as an artist.'[9] Even the abrasive Shaw conceded that Irving had risen above mere showmanship: '[his] art was the whole of himself; and that was why he sacrificed himself—and everybody and everything else—to his art.'[10]

Sacrifices to art notwithstanding, the Lyceum was still a place of business, and its proprietor understood that theatre 'must be carried on as a business or it will fail as an art.'[11] With military precision, Irving commanded an entourage numbering nearly 600: prompters, ticket-takers, carpenters, men to shine the limelight, women to mend the costumes, choreographers, ballet masters, orchestra conductors, actors, and a 'super master' to look after hundreds of extras. Engaged in both the manufacture and retail of theatrical performance, Irving was vulnerable to marketplace fluctuations. The greatest threat to the Lyceum's financial health was the loss of its star performers or its scenery. In the late 1890s, Irving faced both.

Just before Christmas 1896 Irving suffered a knee injury that kept him off the stage for over two months. Terry, then in Germany, would not return for another month. Without either of its leading actors the Lyceum could not sell tickets and there was no alternative but to close temporarily. Upon her return Terry resumed the part of Imogen in *Cymbeline*, but it was no crowd pleaser. The theatre ended the season with a deficit of £10,000. A lucrative tour recouped the loss, but the misadventure proved a grim augury.

The next year was worse, beginning with the destruction of the Lyceum's enormous stock of scenery and ending with Irving forced to surrender control. On February 18th 1898 the scenery for forty-four plays—including *Much Ado about Nothing*, *Becket*, *Macbeth*, *Henry VIII*, *King Lear*, *Faust* and

Othello—went up in flames when fire engulfed the two railway arches in Southwark where it was stored. To save money Irving had reduced his insurance coverage, leaving a payout of just under £6,000, barely a tenth of the cost of replacing what had been lost. Nor could new scenery be created overnight, as master craftsmen were required for backdrops thirty feet high and forty-two feet wide. With no scenery and no quick prospect of replacement, Irving was doomed. Months later he sold his lease to a group of investors.

The Lyceum thus became a public company with Irving as principal shareholder. In return he received £26,000 cash and the syndicate (as the controlling investors were called) hired him as actor and producer. But times remained tough and by 1902 the syndicate could not afford the £20,000 worth of safety and fire prevention improvements mandated by the London County Council. Facing bankruptcy, the syndicate sold the Lyceum. For the final performance on Saturday July 19th 1902, Terry, who had by then left the theatre, returned to play Portia to Irving's Shylock for one last time. A melancholy afternoon it must have been. After thirty years Irving was homeless in the theatrical world. The Lyceum was turned into a music hall, but not before its contents were sold at auction, down to the crimson carpet that softened the path to the Royal box and the mahogany table at which Irving had hosted late-night dinner parties in the Beefsteak Room. Mercifully, he was on tour and so did not witness the death of the playhouse that he had turned into a national theatre in all but name. His own death was but a 1000 days away.

There remained a full calendar of acting engagements but the triumphs were over. After the wounding failure of *Dante* at Drury Lane in 1903, Irving took to exhausting provincial tours: three nights in Northampton, three nights in Swansea, the luxury of a full week in Southampton, with at most a day between engagements. Cash-strapped, he embarked upon a final American trip in the autumn of 1903. Before long he announced his retirement. The farewell tour ended prematurely when the actor collapsed after a performance of *Becket* on October 13th 1905. Sir Henry Irving, aged sixty-seven, died in his dresser's arms in the lobby of a Bradford hotel, barely an hour after speaking his last prophetic words on the stage: 'Into Thy hands, O Lord, into Thy hands.' Extraordinarily, the funeral service was conducted in Westminster Abbey and Irving's ashes were interred in Poet's Corner, next to the remains of David Garrick and immediately in front of the Shakespeare memorial. The coffin was carried up the nave to the strains of the funeral march composed for Irving's 1901 production of *Coriolanus*. Unmoved by the actor's death, Shaw refused his invitation to the funeral, declaring that 'Literature had no place at Irving's graveside.' Perhaps not. But Garrick and Shakespeare would do just fine as escorts into eternity.

Shakespeare on the Lyceum Stage

The following chronological account of Irving's Shakespearean productions at the Lyceum between 1874 and 1901 does not aim to reconstruct them, offer exclusively aesthetic judgments about them, or merely to contextualize them. Rather, I use this narrative (like all narratives, selective) to explore the discursive activity of these performances; to uncover the cultural 'work' they accomplished, for the actor-manager Henry Irving and for the cultural icon 'Shakespeare.' More particularly, I analyze how such performances themselves raise questions about Irving's artistic vision (and Shakespeare's place within it), his brand of Bardolatry, and his allegiance to an Anglophone cultural imperialism—topics discussed at length in the final sections of this chapter. In Romantic fashion, the story begins with Irving the neophyte ascending the highest Shakespearean summit: *Hamlet*.

Hamlet (1874)

The opening night audience sat in confused silence until the 'nunnery' scene, when the novelty of Irving's interpretation finally became apparent. Whether that interpretation deserved to be called genius was a matter quickly taken up in a war of pamphlets. Irving's performance was either the long-awaited reinvigoration of Shakespeare or the poet's decline into melodrama. But it was beyond dispute that this Hamlet was unusual. Gone was the blond wig of Charles Fechter's colloquial Scandinavian and gone was the plumed finery of Kemble's haughty aristocrat. Here, instead, was a mournfully contemplative young man dressed in black (save for a gold chain and dagger), the color set off by his wintry pale complexion. Upon long thin legs he slouched and lurched across the stage. The actor was mocked, but the edgy physicality conveyed Hamlet's anxieties: like the time, he was out of joint.

'We in the audience see the mind of Hamlet,' reported Scott. 'We care little what he does, how he walks, when he draws his sword. We can almost realize the workings of his brain.'[12] Though flattering the remark captures an important truth about Irving's relationship to Shakespeare: that the audience was led to admire less the emotional depth of any particular characterization—the melancholy of Irving's Hamlet, the ambition of his

Macbeth, the treachery of his Iago—and more the actor's intelligence in crafting that characterization. Irving's delivery in *Hamlet* was so peculiarly static that he seemed not to embody the character at all. Indeed his performance approached a conceptual reversal of theatrical norms: instead of the actor illuminating the character, the character illuminated the actor. Thus, Irving advertized himself not simply as the latest personification of an acting tradition—the heir to Burbage and Garrick—but as a complete artist of the stage, to be judged by his own standards, not those of his theatrical forefathers. Not that Irving failed to perform Hamlet but that he used Hamlet to represent himself as an uncommonly intelligent tragedian, as evocatively captured in Onslow Ford's life-size marble sculpture from 1883 of Irving the actor blended with Hamlet the thinker.

Macbeth (1875)

Expectations ran high when Irving took on the role of the ambitious Scottish thane, but the phenomenon of his *Hamlet* was not to be repeated with *Macbeth*. The largely negative reaction to this production—and to those that immediately followed—made it far from inevitable that Irving would become the greatest Shakespearean of the nineteenth century. Hamlet may have been the making of him, but Macbeth, Othello and Richard III nearly undid him. Shylock saved his reputation as a tragedian. But in 1875 that reputation was still in doubt, and it was a fair bet that a chastened Irving would soon hurry back to the melodramas in which he excelled.

But timing was on his side. Not since Charles Kean's archaeological spectacle in the 1850s had there been a major London production of *Macbeth*, while from an acting perspective the last memorable performance was Macready's in the 1840s. Macbeth traditionally had been played as 'Bellona's bridegroom,' the fierce manly warrior led astray by prophesying witches and a scheming wife. But Irving, drawing upon an 1844 essay from the *Westminster Review*, decided that Macbeth was a bloody-minded villain from the outset.[13] '[B]efore the curtain rises,' he insisted, imagining a moment that Shakespeare, at most, only implied, 'Macbeth has not only thought of murdering Duncan, but had even broached the subject with his wife.'[14]

Though the conception was novel, its execution left critics unimpressed. The *Illustrated London News* observed that on continental stages no actor would be regarded as equally suited to play Hamlet *and* Macbeth because he would be 'too heavy for the one and too light for the other.'[15] Previously enthusiastic, the *London Figaro* complained that 'an attempt [was] made to indicate the deepest feelings of the human heart by spasmodic hysteria.'[16] The *Observer* called the production 'melo-dramatic rendering of dignified tragedy.'[17] Writing for an American audience, the young Henry James judged that '[in] declamation [Irving] is decidedly flat; his voice is without charm, and his utterance without subtlety.'[18] Even the obsequious Scott admitted that the actor was 'forgetting the audience.'[19]

Despite not having given Irving a successful role, *Macbeth* holds a disproportionately large place in theatrical memory, partly because Irving left an extensive record of his thoughts on the play. That itself reveals a crucial historiographical insight: that what a performance means for later generations will depend heavily upon the archive that survives it. With a glance to posterity, Irving wrote an article on the third murderer for the *Nineteenth Century*, lectured on the play during his American tours, and composed a preface for the acting edition of the later Lyceum production.

The most striking feature of Irving's commentary was his sensitivity to the charge of staging Shakespeare as melodrama; of playing the murderer Macbeth as if he were the murderer Mathias in *The Bells.* Never raised explicitly, the grievance showed itself in Irving's defensive tone: '[V]ery many . . . think Macbeth . . . got [the crown] by the simple process of killing the owner and taking it for himself . . . [But] crowns are not to be treated in the simple manner of property in the typical low-class melodrama.'[20] Here, Irving cannily distanced himself from the charge of being a theatrical impostor: an actor who mouths Shakespeare's words but in the voice and pose of melodrama. Yet unless that charge was warranted—unless audiences glimpsed Mathias in Macbeth—why bother with the defense? Indeed, the charge was made repeatedly, for Irving's appearance in the role fourteen years later prompted one reviewer to remark that the 'shudderings,' 'cowering fears' and 'maniacal despair' of his Macbeth 'might easily be guessed by those familiar with his Mathias and his Louis XI.'[21] Irving's need to press his point reveals that he struggled against more trenchant critical opposition than his now crowning legacy might suggest.

Othello (1876)

It was risky for Irving to attempt Othello just ten months after the masterful Italian actor Tommaso Salvini had taken London by storm with his nearly bestial incarnation of the Moor. Audiences could not so quickly erase from their memory the exotic picture of Othello in turban and burnous or Salvini's raw passion when he struck Desdemona across the face with the back of his hand. Austin Brereton, one of Irving's hagiographic biographers, later described the Italian as 'the true Moor, the veritable Moor, the only Moor that ever was, could, or should be.'[22] The mocking hyperbole aims to trivialize but no doubt Irving sensed that his only option was to act the part as differently as possible. That decision led him to 'carr[y] his eccentricity of both voice and gesture to the verge of the grotesque.'[23] So negative were the reactions that Matthew Arnold ridiculed Irving's 'gibbering performance' *before* he saw it.[24]

Irving understood the depth of his failure but blamed the audience. 'They expect to see Othello as something entirely Eastern and mysterious,' he complained to Walter Pollock; 'they don't at all understand finding him dressed like other characters in the play. I ought to have thought of that and given up the idea.'[25] But he did not give up the idea. Irving returned to the play within three years of becoming the Lyceum's manager, taking advantage of an opportunity to ally himself with the American actor Edwin Booth.

Richard III (1877)

The playbill for the first performance on January 29th 1877 boasted of the single aspect of this production that matters: the text spoken by the actors was Shakespeare's *Richard III* and not Colley Cibber's. The production used 'strictly the original text, without interpolations, but simply with such omissions and transpositions as have been found essential for dramatic representation.'[26] Like all Victorian actor-managers Irving sheared texts for performance ('I'll cut—cut—cut—and cut again,' he greedily exclaimed).[27] But he was the first to overthrow entirely the adaptation that had held the stage for nearly 200 years, completing a project that Macready had begun four decades earlier.

The critic Dutton Cook judged Irving's performance a welcome return to form after a mixed Macbeth and the outright failure of Othello. The encouraging verdict seems plausible because the character—much like Iago, a part in which Irving excelled (see below)—combines a roguish sense of humor with a cruelly calculating intellect. As Irving later put it, Richard III 'needs no roar and stamp, no cheap and noisy exultation.'[28] (Acting merits notwithstanding, the play was all but exiled from the Lyceum repertoire in later years.) On the first night Irving received from a veteran actor the sword that Edmund Kean had used in the role. Thus, whether he deserved it or not, was the young actor anointed the great Kean's successor.

Irving's performance consolidated his reputation as a tragedian and, more importantly, placed him within a genealogy of revered Shakespearean actors—a genealogy whose public importance he understood even as he rejected its parochial tendency to 'compar[e] this actor with that.'[29]

Hamlet (1878)

Irving acquired the Lyceum's lease in September 1878 but did not return to London from his provincial tour until mid-December, leaving two weeks to rehearse his inaugural production. Builders and decorators occupied the theatre, refurbishing the stalls and dress circle, and adding seat backs to the hard pit and gallery benches. The auditorium was painted a fresh sage green and turquoise blue. Hawes Craven, whose greatest scenic triumphs lay ahead, designed the act drop. When the curtain rose on the night of December 30th the Lyceum's new proprietor had accumulated debts of £12,000 and held no assets other than himself and Ellen Terry. It was a time to take risks.

But Irving did not risk his interpretation of Hamlet, playing the role much as before. If anything, time polished his performance. 'I did not think Irving could have improved,' Tennyson remarked; 'he has done so—he has lifted it to heaven.'[30] Irving's ascension notwithstanding, the most notable aspect of the production was the Lyceum debut of Ellen Terry. Believing that she had been under-rehearsed—even by the accelerated pace of the Victorian stage, two weeks was not much time for a new company to produce Shakespeare's greatest play—Terry left the theatre after her last scene. It must have struck the audience as odd when she failed to appear at Irving's side in the final call. Where was she? Nearby, driving a carriage up and down the Thames embankment in nervous despair. A few hours later the morning reviews elicited from her an altogether happier reaction.

The Merchant of Venice (1879)

In the summer of 1879, while on a Mediterranean cruise aboard the yacht of his patron, Baroness Burdett-Coutts, Irving seized upon the idea of opening his second season as the Lyceum's manager with *The Merchant of Venice.* Once back in London, time was short; but Irving had already mapped out the entire production in his head. The result was a triumph: it ran for 250 nights and gave Irving his best Shakespearean role, one that outlasted Hamlet, Macbeth, Romeo, Benedick, Wolsey and Lear.

Working from Charles Kean's 1858 acting edition he cut 500 lines, mostly in Act III, so that scenes could be combined, thus reducing the number of changeovers from nineteen to a manageable twelve. Irving continued the strongly pictorial effects of Victorian Shakespeare, with violet and dove-colored costumes that might have been designed by Titian, the imposing colonnade of the Doge's palace and crimson walls and gilt carvings for the courtroom. Percy Fitzgerald likened the production to a 'gorgeous and dazzling' work by Veronese.[31]

But there were interpretive consequences to the textual cuts. Because many of the excised lines belonged to Portia, the two major roles became unbalanced. Initially, Irving restored the fifth act—the reunion of the two couples in Belmont after Shylock's trial—but frequently omitted it in subsequent performances, blithely ignoring a letter from the venerable Shakespearean F. J. Furnivall condemning such 'damnable barbarism.'[32] If *Merchant* concludes with Act V, then it is Portia's comedy in the Shakespearean sense, with Shylock a subordinate villain. But if it concludes with Act IV, then it is Shylock's tragedy, properly culminating with his courtroom defeat. Irving played the role for a quarter century, during which time his interpretation swung decisively toward tragedy.

It could not have been otherwise given Irving's belief that Shylock never regarded himself as a villain. In 1884, while on his first American tour, Irving described to the journalist Joseph Hatton that he had seen 'a Jew once, in Tunis . . . [H]e was old, but erect, even stately, and full of resource. As he walked beside his team of mules he carried himself with the lofty air of a king.'[33] The Tunisian Jew was recreated upon the Lyceum stage. Irving's Shylock seemed about sixty, feeble enough to need a cane, but still proud. The bearded man wore a fur-trimmed dark brown cloak over a tunic that reached to his ankles, the sober effect relieved only by the red and yellow striped sash at his waist from which hung a small leather pouch. The yellow mark on his tight-fitting black cap branded him a Jew. But that racial badge failed to diminish his dignity and Irving's Shylock towered above the taunting Christians who surrounded him. Indeed, Irving argued that the Christians were the play's true hypocrites because they preached mercy but never showed it.[34] 'I am sure Shylock was not a low person,' he elaborated to Hatton, 'a miser and usurer, certainly, but a very injured man . . . I look on Shylock . . . as the type of a persecuted race; almost the only gentleman in the play, and most ill-used.'[35]

Irving's sympathetic portrayal of Shylock rested upon two scenes. One was performed in silence and the other distorted Shakespeare's words. After Jessica's flight with Lorenzo the stage was engulfed by a swirl of revelers and masquers—complete with moving gondola—upon whose festivities the act curtain fell. The vibrant stage picture was met with customary applause and the audience believed that the act had concluded. But a moment later the curtain unexpectedly rose on the same pale moonlit piazza, only now the stage was empty and the already distant sounds of the guitar and barcarolle faded into silence. (Tellingly, the orchestra played throughout the action set in Belmont and carnival Venice, but never when Shylock, the outsider, entered the scene.) From the far side of the bridge appeared a dejected Shylock, leaning heavily upon his cane, slowly and wearily heading home. The unpopulated stage heightened the contrast between massive scenery and the lone figure. Expecting to find solace in his daughter's company, Shylock knocked twice at the unopened door of his house and then looked upward in confusion toward Jessica's room. The curtain dropped just as the lonely father was about to enter his house and discover what the audience already knew: that his daughter had abandoned him.

This brief interpolation unleashed an extraordinary emotional charge. For late-Victorian spectators immersed in the cult of domesticity, Jessica was more villainous than Shylock because she betrayed a parent. The *Spectator* branded her 'an odious, immodest, dishonest creature', unworthy of the 'loveliest love-lines' that Shakespeare had written for her.[36] The Lyceum audience could not help but feel sympathy for a man who had been unjustly abused in public and then returned home, where he ought to be loved and respected, only to endure the pain of abandonment. This scene of pure feeling, all the more potent for being silent, was not one that Shakespeare had written. But it was one that a Victorian audience wished he had.

The defeated Shylock's exit in the trial scene also aroused the audience's pity. Though hardly sympathetic, neither was the character monstrous, for his insistence upon a pound of flesh was a valid consequence of the law. But just when Shylock seemed to cross over into villainy by refusing to accept the debt paid three times over, Portia intervened: 'This bond doth give thee here no jot of blood.' Vengeance was turned upon the avenger. Shylock faltered, barely able to ask, 'Is—*that*—the—*law*?'[37] Instantly, he became the hounded victim, robbed of his wealth and, because forced to convert to the faith of his tormentors, stripped of his identity. Many in the audience wept.

Whether Shakespeare intended Shylock to leave the courtroom a victim was much debated. The *Era* ridiculed Irving's interpretation with its absurd claim that Shakespeare wanted to 'repeal . . . the Jewish Disabilities Bill.'[38] Shaw pronounced Irving's Shylock as neither good nor bad but 'simply not

Shylock at all.' Ignoring the text, the actor 'positively acted Shakespear off the stage.'[39] Ruskin, in a private letter, issued a similar chastisement: 'you had not yet as much love for Shakespeare as for your art, and were therefore not careful enough to be wholly in harmony with his design.'[40] Remembering Irving's performance from a distance of thirty years, the playwright Henry Arthur Jones likewise described it as 'ex-Shakespearean.'[41] Theodore Martin savaged Ellen Terry's Portia (his wife, the former Helena Faucit, had embodied that character for an earlier generation) but tried to find middle ground by declaring that Irving aroused in the audience nothing more than the 'pity which one feels for any human creature hardened by cruel usage.'[42] Meanwhile, *The Theatre* featured an essay arguing that Shakespeare 'defended' the Jews by making Shylock a sympathetic, dignified character.[43] Scott, the editor, published the piece to coincide with the Lyceum production and, indeed, to pre-empt criticism. But it was beyond quarrel that Irving's more humane Shylock proved surprisingly effective. 'How often is this part turned into melodrama', the *Washington Post* observed during Irving's final American tour in 1904, 'in which Shylock becomes merely an inhuman butcher. Irving's art pictures him here a great tragic figure.'[44]

Othello (1881)

Edwin Booth had been the first American actor to win acclaim in Britain but his engagement at the Princess's Theatre was proving a disappointment. Wishing to score a success before returning home, Booth proposed that Irving lease him the Lyceum for matinee performances. Irving proposed something bolder: that he and Booth alternate Iago and Othello in the main evening performances. The American agreed, and they played opposite each other three nights a week from May 9th to June 11th 1881. Ticket prices were raised on those evenings for the more discerning occupiers of the stalls, dress circle and private boxes. (For an extended discussion of Booth, see Gary Jay Williams' chapter in this volume.)

Irving's Othello had improved but little. Contrasting the nobility of the part with the gaucheness of the actor, one critic remarked that it was 'as though an artist painted a beautiful picture and deliberately smudged it with his sleeve.'[45] Compensating for that failure, Irving turned in a highly praised portrayal of Iago, whom he regarded as a devilish Machiavellian youth. Villains always came easier to Irving than heroes and so it cannot be surprising that he later chose Iago as one of his four favorite Shakespearean parts. To exhibit Iago's malicious zeal, but also his insecurities, Irving acted the role in a whirlwind of stage business: taunting flicks of his red cape, fidgeting with his costume, 'slapping Roderigo on the back, throwing his arm around his neck,' picking his teeth with a dagger, and rumpling his hair.[46] Terry relished the moment when the mocking Iago stood apart, leaning against a pillar, slowly eating grapes and spitting out the seeds while Cassio was preoccupied with Desdemona, each expulsion 'represent[ing] a worthy virtue to be put out of one's mouth.'[47]

No one expected much from Irving's Othello, but neither was Booth particularly effective in the role. Salvini slept safe in the knowledge that he remained his generation's reigning Othello. Yet by enabling Booth to conclude his London engagement with dignity—and a third of the profits—Irving gained a key ally ahead of his first American tour. The grateful Booth returned home full of praise for Irving and described his weeks at the Lyceum as among 'the most agreeable' of his life. 'I wish I could do as much for Henry Irving, in America,' he wrote before sailing to New York, 'as he has done for me here.'[48] It would not be long before Booth's amiable wish was granted.

Romeo and Juliet (1882)

No one remembered the acting, but everyone remembered the scenery. Romeo was forty-four, Juliet thirty-five, and the critics cruel. Florence Irving, who never let the failure of her marriage stop her from occupying a free private box on Lyceum first nights, sarcastically recorded in her diary on March 8th 1882 that the production was a 'jolly failure—Irving awfully funny.'[49] Public reactions were similar. 'I had never thought of *Romeo and Juliet* as a dull drama,' Henry James opined, 'but Mr. Irving has succeeded in making it so.' Max Beerbohm quipped that Romeo's suicide 'could only be regarded as a merciful release.' The American drama critic William Winter, who would become one of Irving's closest friends and most faithful chroniclers, observed that the actor did not so much 'impersonate' Romeo as 'expound' him. After a brief revival the following season, *Romeo and Juliet* permanently exited the Lyceum repertoire.[50]

Still, the production ran for 160 performances and the opening night was a society event, with the Prince and Princess of Wales leading the spectators. And that is what really matters about this production: that the elite audience it attracted and the scale and opulence of its *mise-en-scène* signified that the Lyceum had become Britain's unconsecrated national theatre, its foremost shrine to Shakespeare and a veritable Temple of Art. '[W]e have learned to look at the Lyceum,' Scott pronounced at the time, 'for a better unfolding of Shakespeare's genius,' 'a deeper insight into his meaning, [and] a greater respect for his conception . . . than the stage of this country has ever before presented.'[51] That exalted achievement was rendered all but permanent seven months later with another of Shakespeare's Italian plays, *Much Ado about Nothing*.

The extravagance of *Romeo and Juliet* cost nearly £10,000, the inevitable consequence of the actor-manager's belief that the drama 'proceeds from picture to picture.'[52] A series of striking pictures—eighteen in total, a combination of painted and 'built out' scenery—was precisely what Irving offered his audience. As the *Daily Telegraph* remarked, 'the outside of Capulet's house lighted for the ball, the sunny pictures of Verona in summer, the marriage chant to Juliet changed into a death dirge, the old, lonely street in Mantua, where the Apothecary dwells, the wondrous solid tomb of the Capulets—are as worthy of close and renewed study as are the pictures in a gallery of paintings.'[53] Henry James trivialized the visual effects by calling them 'little tableaux'; but his petty caricature obscured the larger truth that the production aspired to the status of a work of art.[54] Henceforth, so did all of Irving's Shakespearean revivals.

A moderately attentive observer of the theatrical scene in 1882 would have comprehended that the intricacies of Irving's production—swordfights in the street, a masked ball, torch-bearing citizens of Verona filling the stage—had been influenced by the appearance at Drury Lane a year earlier of the Duke of Saxe-Meiningen's acting troupe. The celebrated foreign company had performed *Julius Caesar* and *The Winter's Tale*, both notable for crowd scenes and requiring dexterous stage management. Irving lost no time in applying the lessons learned from watching the Meininger troupe and for the first time employed a large cast. The full significance, then, of the Lyceum *Romeo and Juliet* was that it marked the moment when Irving became known not as a typical actor-manager, but as a figure more strategic, more artistic, and, hence, more powerful: the 'master-mind and guiding spirit' who 'suggest[ed] and organize[d] what was so splendidly carried out.'[55]

Such a description reveals the emergence of modern ways of thinking about theatre and about performances of Shakespeare in particular: that a production expresses a single individual's interpretation. It is hard to overestimate how much of a conceptual shift was being demanded of nineteenth-century audiences. Theatergoers had been accustomed for generations to interpret performances as a series of well-known acting 'points,' with today's tragedians judged against those of distant yesterdays. But Irving offered an alternative. '[T]he drama of the Lyceum and the acting of Mr Irving have passed out of the region of criticism and individual taste,' one reviewer observed. 'The Lyceum is, in a sense, the cathedral of dramatic art, with Mr Irving for its high priest.'[56] Whether you liked or loathed his acting was in some ways irrelevant. What mattered was that you recognized that the production belonged to *him*. No one else could have created it.

Much Ado about Nothing (1882)

Requiring another Shakespearean drama for his planned American tour, Irving made the unlikely selection of *Much Ado about Nothing*. Although the play was never highly esteemed by Victorian audiences, the Lyceum production proved astoundingly successful and held the stage for over 200 nights from October 1882 to June 1883, contributing to the theatre's profit that season of £33,000. It remained in the repertoire for nearly fifteen years.

Although incapable of playing honeyed young lovers, Irving and Terry were well suited to the sardonic maturity of Benedick and Beatrice. Irving had taken the part at one of Lady Martin's genteel readings at her home in Onslow Square but had never performed it onstage. Terry had played Beatrice just once. Still, the roles came easily to them. Not since Garrick and Hannah Pritchard more than a century earlier had London audiences seen the roles so vividly incarnated. What gave their performances such winning charm was the deception of the characters themselves: despite their true feelings, they posed as adversaries and thus had to be dragged into romance. An unwilling love affair played to Irving's strengths as an eccentric comic actor. Indeed, Benedick gave Irving his only success in Shakespearean comedy.

The text was rearranged for performance into thirteen scenes. All but three—Leonato's house, the garden and the cathedral—were played well downstage in front of painted backdrops. Of the full-stage scenes, the high point was the marriage of Claudio and Hero in a grand Sicilian chapel. While browsing in Quaritch's, an antiquarian bookshop, Irving found a folio on 'Italian Ceremonies.' It featured a picture of an elaborate wedding ceremony 'created by a mass of vergers or javelin men . . . They were dressed in long robes and each carried a halberd. I pressed these men at once into the service of Shakespeare and his cathedral scene at Messina.'[57] Shakespeare said nothing about a cathedral, but no matter. William Telbin created an enormous three-dimensional environment through which the Lyceum cast freely moved.

As memorialized in Johnston Forbes-Robertson's painting (the actor played Claudio) the wedding chapel featured wrought iron gates twelve feet high and four feet wide and real columns thirty feet high supporting an ornamental crimson roof from which hung golden lamps. The canopied altar erected stage right was covered with flowers and tiers of flaming candles rising to a height of eighteen feet. The cathedral's walls were decorated with statuary and stained glass windows. Church pews and painted flats set diagonally created the impression of vast offstage space. Monumental sets required monumental casts, and so surrounding the wedding party were ecclesiastics bearing candles, torches, and incense, their movements underscored by organ, choir, and stringed instruments. Such was the opulence that for fear of embarrassment Irving cut Leonato's line, 'Come, Friar Francis, be brief; only to the plain form of marriage' (4.1.1–2). Nothing brief, though, about the fifteen-minute scene change to put the cathedral in place.

The Times complained that 'the action is almost overweighted with upholstery and wardrobe . . . To this we have come—that the most vivid and enduring impressions produced by a Shakespearean Play are spectacular.'[58] But spectacular Shakespeare had been around for decades, and such comments even then must have felt more like a well-nurtured prejudice than serious criticism. A more penetrating insight came from G. A. Sala, who observed that 'modern scenic artists' were able 'to model as well as to paint their scenes, to introduce really cylindrical columns and really plaster bas-reliefs.'[59] Sala hinted that *Much Ado about Nothing* epitomized Irving's artistic vision by uniting actor and setting in a single totalizing space. The contours of the stage picture were no longer, as they had been since the Restoration, painted wings, backdrops and occasional scenic units, but rather the performing ensemble itself. Remove the actor and you destroy the stage picture. That could never have been said of the productions mounted by Macready, Phelps, or Kean. It was said first of Irving.

Twelfth Night (1884)

He had never seen the play, let alone performed Malvolio. Indeed there had been no major London production for nearly forty years, not since Phelps at Sadler's Wells. For Victorians who learned their Shakespeare at the theatre, *Twelfth Night* was a near total mystery. And after watching Irving's infelicitous production, many must have felt that the mystery was not yet solved. One critic branded the play 'improbable and wearisome,' while another held that it was 'devoid of strong dramatic interest.'[60]

Produced for a brief summer season wedged between two lengthy American tours, *Twelfth Night* opened during a heat wave. Terry, playing Viola, suffered from an infected thumb that developed into blood poisoning. She withdrew after only sixteen performances, replaced by her sister Marion. The outside actors that Irving brought in for the comic roles of Toby Belch, Sir Andrew Aguecheek and Fabian failed utterly. Irving himself began well, but let his Malvolio slide into tragedy. Some spectators felt that Olivia's duped steward had turned into Shylock, a destroyed and humiliated figure granted an emotional exit ('I'll be revenged on the whole pack of you.') The contemporary fashion for exposing the dark side of Shakespearean comedy did not entice the Victorians.

Irving was booed for the only time in his career as he came forward to deliver the opening night curtain speech. A determined minority in the audience assailed him and Irving matched their feistiness with his own. Committing what Terry termed his 'only mistake' Irving berated his audience.[61] 'I can't understand,' he lectured them, 'how a company of earnest comedians and admirable actors . . . [having] the three cardinal virtues of the actor—being sober, clean, and perfect [in knowing their lines]—can have failed to please you.'[62] Being clean, sober and word perfect might earn a compliment for an amateur, but not for a theatre that regarded itself as the finest in the realm.

Though Irving's rant lasted but a few minutes it led to some of his most hurtful notices. One astute critic put the whole episode into the larger context of theatrical celebrities accustomed to cheers and puffs turning nasty when reminded that the audience was in charge:

> Mr. Henry Irving has begun to show temper . . . [There is no reason] why the principal [actor] should attempt to gag his audience and to stifle opposition, and why anger should be shown at an honest expression of opinion. . . . Time was when the drama's laws the drama's patrons gave; but they are altering all that, and are making a law which insists upon all praise, and are prepared, as in this instance, to be filled with fiery indignation directly that law is departed from.[63]

At least the agony was brief. *Twelfth Night* was withdrawn after an embarrassingly short run of thirty-nine performances and never revived at the Lyceum.

Was Irving stung by failure? He did not offer a new Shakespearean production until the revival of *Macbeth* four years later. There was no new Shakespearean role for eight years, until he portrayed Wolsey in *Henry VIII*. The hiatus in new Shakespeare must be partly attributed to the second (September 1884 to April 1885) and third (November 1887 to March 1888) American tours. Moreover, the phenomenal success of *Faust* (1886) meant that for nearly two years the Lyceum's bill was dominated by a single play. Irving continued to perform Shakespeare but only those dramas already in the repertoire. At the very moment when he appeared to be at the height of his powers, Irving consciously withdrew from Shakespeare.

Twelfth Night is not much remarked upon in scholarship on Irving but it should be. The scorn that arose when he attempted to silence a disapproving audience exposed the limit of what nineteenth-century theatergoers accepted from Shakespeareans, especially ones convinced of their own greatness. Whatever stature Irving enjoyed as his country's roving ambassador for the Bard was not entirely of his own making. Without the renewed endorsement of the 'drama's patrons,' as Dr. Johnson called the audience, Irving was nothing but an unquenched thirst for fame. The moment that he displeased his audience was the moment they reminded him of the unspoken moral contract that bound each to the other; a contract that he broke to his cost.

Macbeth (1888)

The late 1880s witnessed the zenith of Irving's career as a theatrical producer. His matured vision of integrating acting, scenery, lighting and sound was flawlessly executed. It is an indication of Irving's triumph as *metteur-en-scène* that his 1888 *Macbeth* was remembered for the dramatic intensity of its visual and aural effects to the point where the scenery attained the status of a dramatic character.

Terry played her role for the first time, with Irving reprising the role he had performed thirteen years earlier. The lasting fame of John Singer Sargent's portrait of the actress in the part—resplendent in a gown adorned with real beetle wings—belies the fact that 'Lady Mac' was not one of her memorable roles. Her softer interpretation of the character failed to disturb the legend of the late Sarah Siddons, who had last trod the boards in 1819, twenty-eight years before Terry's birth. (See Marshall's chapter, pp. 110–117.) Irving's interpretation remained unchanged: Macbeth was not a good man turned bad but a bad man who found his opportunity. The character was now richly and nobly picturesque, clad in a 'homespun tunic and shirt of mail' with a broadsword in his hand and a 'winged helmet' on his head.[64] But the real difference, as Archer put it, was that the 'grotesqueness' of the actor's earlier characterization had been eliminated by keeping 'a tight rein on those peculiarities of gesture and expression which used to run away with him.'[65] Not everyone, particularly not his American critics, felt that Irving had acquired self-mastery. '[T]he hero of Tuesday night was worse than our direst beliefs,' moaned one Boston journalist; 'he was queer, ludicrous, impossible.'[66] A Chicago newspaperman observed that 'the actor does not shine at his best' and it was the *scenery* that won the day: 'But such pictures! The action of the tragedy is in the gloom of old stone walls.'[67]

Unsurprisingly, the costumes and scenery represented the harvest of deep historical research. Yet antiquarian methods for Irving were valuable only to the extent that they yielded opportunities for striking theatrical effects. In this instance, history and histrionics coincided, from the goblets in the banquet scene copied from eleventh-century originals to stained glass windows modeled after illuminated medieval manuscripts in the British Museum. The watercolorist Charles Cattermole supervised a team of forty that designed and constructed more than 400 costumes, including 165 for soldiers and eighty for the grand coven of witches.[68] 'I have had a life of research,' Cattermole boasted (or complained) to the *Pall Mall Budget*. 'I should be sorry to say how many working drawings I have made, not only for the costumes but for the helmets, shields, spears, axes, swords, daggers, boots, [and] wigs.'[69]

Hawes Craven assumed responsibility for massive three-dimensional scenery with textured and decorated surfaces, the culmination of which was the courtyard of Macbeth's 'dark and frowning castle.'[70] Surpassing Telbin's cathedral in *Much Ado about Nothing*, it was fully habitable. On one side stood a tower, with an internal spiral staircase leading up to Duncan's chamber; on the other side a flight of steps led to a gallery along two sides of the enclosed space; in the middle was placed the Porter's gate. The flat wooden roof atop the windowless space created a feeling of entrapment. Pursuing effect, Irving violated the logic of theatrical space with 'ever punctual shafts of limelight' to suggest moonbeams.[71]

Electric lights would be installed at the Lyceum in the 1890s but Irving made little use of their 'naked trashiness,' preferring the subtleties of thick soft gaslight.[72] He started with an unlit stage and then built the lighting cues—number and location of lamps, angle, intensity, color, duration—needed to achieve the desired effect. Colored lenses placed over the limelight and independently operating footlights meant that his control over the lighting was nearly that of a 'painter us[ing] his pallette.'[73]

In *Macbeth* the lighting expressed a heavy murkiness, achieved mainly by keeping both stage and auditorium dark. 'Perhaps Mr. Irving is a little too fond of gloom,' *The Times* noted with understatement. 'Three-fourths of the action of the play passes in an obscurity which is certainly trying to the nerves from the necessity of straining eyes and ears to catch what is doing on the stage.'[74] An exception to the deepening darkness was the glaring sunlight of Birnam Wood, which prompted one relieved gallery spectator to shout 'Good Old England!'[75]

Why, having taken care to ensure the historical accuracy of the scenery, and having built it to extravagant proportions, did Irving let it 'be lost in mysterious half light?'[76] Because his audience was not supposed to be looking at the scenery. They were supposed to be immersed in an entire world, one made up of shape, color, texture, light and sound. The Lyceum *Macbeth* reminds us that Irving numbered among the first to use light—which did not simply make objects visible but possessed mass and movement of its own—to create theatrical space. If he overindulged his authority by keeping everyone and everything in semi-darkness, it was not to defy, but to challenge, his audience; to enable them to see, literally, in a different light. From Irving's perspective—the complete autonomy of art—his lighting was not a mistake but an achievement. The problem was that not everyone shared his perspective.

Despite its challenging aesthetics and less than universally praised acting, *Macbeth* ran for 150 nights, playing to capacity houses until the London season ended in June and turning a profit of £5,000. Whatever was objectionable in this production was overpowered by the sense of its being an event. By the late 1880s Lyceum Shakespeare had become a commodity desired not necessarily for the pleasure that it afforded but the status it bestowed. As Ruskin put it, 'Irving has so much power with the public.'[77] To some extent, that power placed his productions beyond judgment, criticism, or opinion. 'Mr Irving is no longer a celebrated actor,' Archer tartly observed; 'he is the actor-celebrity of the day.'[78] Of course there were bad reviews as well as good, but Henry Irving the great Shakespearean had hardened into immutable fact: something to be accepted, not argued with. His performances were of such unquestioned importance that to miss them was to miss out on culture itself. '[Irving's] management,' Hatton earnestly remarked, 'inspired you with a special sense of its responsibility to Art, and your own obligations to support its earnest endeavors.'[79] The comic magazine *Truth* noted the degree to which his productions had been transformed from a popular amusement—one among many—to a burdensome social obligation—the one thing you would never dare neglect: 'people not only talked about the new Macbeth, but went to see it, whether they liked it or not, in order that they might unite their voices to the fierce discussion at dinner-tables and in clubs.'[80] Beneath the satire lies a serious point. Within a decade of taking over the Lyceum's lease, Irving had consolidated his position as guardian of his country's theatrical tastes and he had consolidated it through Shakespeare.

Henry VIII (1892)

Because Shakespeare wrote into the action of *Henry VIII* a sequence of banquets, masques and processions, no Victorian actor-manager could be blamed for highlighting the play's rich pictorialism. Yet despite being perfectly suited to spectacular staging, the play had not received a major London revival since Charles Kean in the 1850s. Like his predecessor, Irving justified the Lyceum production's expense by aligning his desires with Shakespeare's presumed intention. 'In my judgement,' he declared, '*Henry VIII* is a pageant or nothing. Shakespeare, I am sure, had the same idea.'[81] Tellingly, Irving's own judgment took precedence, with the dramatist cited merely to corroborate a fixed opinion. Seymour Lucas, commissioned to research the costumes, became pageant master. Much publicity was generated from his antiquarian zealotry, not least by Lucas himself, who published an essay in *The Magazine of Art* detailing his endeavors. He copied King Henry's costume from a Holbein portrait in Belvoir Castle; at the College of Heralds he acquired correct designs for Tudor pages, heralds and gentlemen-at-arms; and the letters of the Spanish ambassador to the English court yielded details of the dress of ordinary men and women of the period.[82]

Once the Royal Academician's 138 chalk and outline sketches were turned into costumes worn by actors who moved around and through the scenery—from the palace at Bridewell to Wolsey's banqueting hall in York Place, and from the church of the Grey Friars to the apartments of the discarded Queen Katharine (played by Ellen Terry)—Irving omitted no opportunity for pictorial staging. Spectators confessed fatigue: 'A splendid pageant. What next? A splendid pageant. And next? A splendid pageant.'[83] Irving's first entrance was indeed an exaggerated set piece:

> The silver trumpets sound, and amidst monks, retainers, servitors, choristers, and retinue, under a gorgeous baldaquin, the haughty Cardinal appears. Never before in our memory has Mr. Irving made so wonderful a picture. He is swathed from head to foot in what is miscalled

> the cardinal's scarlet. It is not scarlet at all, but an indescribable geranium-pink, with a dash of vermilion in it.[84]

The actor took pride in that geranium-pink robe, insisting to a doubtful critic that the expected scarlet was, in fact, a color never worn by Wolsey. He was prouder still of the difficulty with which the expensive garment had been constructed. His costumiers had concocted the dye themselves, the precious tint no longer used even at the Vatican. '[G]etting into the skin of a character,' Irving explained, 'you need not neglect his wardrobe.'[85]

The wardrobe must have helped because the acting notices were largely favorable. Irving's payoff came in the play's second half, when at the moment of his public disgrace Wolsey finds within his heart the Christian priest that for so long he had forsaken. His grand moving soliloquy from Act III—'O Cromwell! Cromwell!!/Had I but served my God with half the zeal/I serv'd my King'—was delivered in a sobbing broken voice, for which a rare recording survives. The next scene with Cromwell aroused great pity from the audience, who were moved by the character's lonely grandeur. '[T]he habitually sinister aspect of the Cardinal has departed from him,' one critic observed; 'he is a feeble old man.'[86] The 'malignity' of Irving's Wolsey, the critic believed, 'almost' reached the height of his Mephistopheles. That canny remark reminds us yet again that Irving's greatest acting triumphs were in the higher reaches of melodrama. Whatever audiences responded to when Irving stood opposite them across the footlights, Shakespeare was not its essential ingredient.

Although *Henry VIII* held the stage for an impressive 172 performances between January and July 1892, the Lyceum ended the season with a loss of £4,000. It could scarcely have been otherwise. Simply to mount the play cost £12,000, to which were added weekly running costs of £1,800. With such heavy expenses the Lyceum could not make a profit even though it was full night after night.

King Lear (1892)

It was a legendary failure, lasting only sixty-seven performances. No English tragedian had made a success of *King Lear* since Garrick, who enjoyed the advantage of performing Nahum Tate's 'happy ending' version in which Lear and Cordelia survive. Shakespeare's somber version returned to the stage with Macready in the 1830s but it never much appealed to Victorian sensibilities. '*King Lear* is—well, it is not,' announced the *Illustrated London News* in its review of Irving's production. '*Lear* would not be tolerated for an hour if produced without the name of Shakespeare.'[87] Theatrical lore has it that the production failed because on opening night Irving adopted a trick of the voice that although intended to add complexity to his characterization, succeeded only in making him inaudible and 'deplorably slow.'[88] The critic from *Black and White* regretted that Irving's performance 'does not take my breath away, does not thrill my nerves, nor hurry the beating of my pulse . . . [T]he thunder drowns Mr. Irving's ravings. And by-and-by the spectacle of an old man shouting words which I cannot hear because of the thunder, tires me.'[89]

Martin Meisel has persuasively argued that Irving's drawn out manner was his attempt to frame the entire production in 'long units of effect,' like a composer indicating a passage to be played ever more slowly for heightened effect.[90] If so, that idea failed to translate into actuality. Apart from the touching reunion with Cordelia (Ellen Terry), the desired result was not achieved. Despite conjecture that Irving's performance improved during the brief run, *King Lear* never caught fire. Irving's only published comment on the production contains a rare admission of defeat:

> It broke down my physical strength after sixty consecutive nights, and when I resumed it after a brief rest I was forced reluctantly to the conclusion that there is one character in Shakespeare which cannot be played six times a week with impunity. I tried to combine the weakness of senility with the tempest of passion, and the growing conviction before the play had proceeded far that this was a perfectly impossible task is one of my most vivid memories of the [opening] night.[91]

Once, however, the production passed into theatre history, becoming vulnerable to reinterpretation, opinions began to shift. Nearly a century after being judged a failure, the production was redeemed by scholars who saw in it an unusual combination of visual arts and cultural history. When attention turned from acting to *mise-en-scène*, a conceptually new artifact emerged, an unexpected find in Shakespearean archaeology.

Irving set the play in an indeterminate period after the Romans had abandoned Britain in the fifth century AD but well before anything recognizably medieval. The aging pre-Raphaelite artist Ford Madox Brown suggested the period and provided sketches—the Romano-British interior of Lear's palace and Albany's hall and an exterior view of Gloucester's seat with a decayed Roman temple in the background—from which Joseph Harker designed the actual scenery. Irving sought guidance from Brown because his own understanding of the play was deeply indebted to the artist's *Cordelia's Portion* (1866), an engraving of which hung in his dressing room. Garrick had turned to the painter Philippe de Loutherbourg for advice and Kemble found inspiration in the classical images of Nicolas Poussin; but no one before Irving developed such close associations with artists. Yet he never embarked upon a true collaboration because his concept of the production came first. Like the script, the scenery was accounted but one element in a larger picture whose sole creator was Henry Irving.

In the Lyceum production, what remained of Roman imperial power had been reduced by neglect and nature's harshness to ruins inhabited by warriors who knew little of the race of giants that preceded them. The invading trees and clinging ivy that contended for dominion with the crumbling architecture echoed Lear's personal journey from the halls of power to the brutality of nature. By the end of the play the scenery depicting man-made structures disappeared—culture and civilization disappeared—allowing nature to reassert her primordial strength. Thus, Lear started the play as a ruler of built spaces but ended it subjected to the natural world, dying at the foot of Dover's white cliffs under a sky of pitiless sunshine. In terms of stagecraft, three-dimensional practical scenery—the most advanced form of representation then possible—gave way to the centuries-old practice of two-dimensional backdrops flanked by wings.[92]

The staging reveals not just the primacy of the visual over the historical in Irving's approach to Shakespeare but his readiness to manipulate theatrical convention. Irving renounced the heavy ornaments that had been synonymous with Lyceum Shakespeare and stripped the stage down to its essentials. The bold confidence of his gesture anticipated the modernist aesthetic still forming in the mind of Craig, his eager apprentice. It entailed a conception—not of Shakespeare, but of what the theatre could make of Shakespeare—all but inconceivable to anyone else.

Cymbeline (1896)

Not seen on a major London stage for decades, the play was an odd choice for a theatre running a deficit. Perhaps his desire to give Terry a strong leading role persuaded Irving to chance it. Too old for Posthumus (the actor-manager's role ever since Garrick), Irving had no choice but to play the villain Iachimo, to whom Shakespeare had given just a few good scenes. Writing in March 1896 while on tour in Detroit, Irving asked William Winter to craft a performance text for *Cymbeline* ('if you can spare the time & have the inclination') that, by trimming the other roles, made that of

Iachimo seem larger.[93] Fortunately there was no acting tradition for this hitherto secondary character, which allowed Irving not merely to expand the part but to act it much as he had once acted Iago: as a Machiavellian scoundrel.

Opening in September 1896, the production featured the expected historical accessories—horned helmets, Druidic symbols—and ran a respectable eighty-eight nights. At a time when his powers and his fortune were on the wane, Irving must have relished the favorable acting notices. 'Iachimo is quite in Sir Henry Irving's line,' Archer declared—twenty years after attacking Irving in his scornful essay *The Fashionable Tragedian*—'[h]e is a subtle, tenebrous, deadly creature.'[94] Shaw was remarkably complimentary, praising the actor's 'true impersonation, unbroken in its life-current from end to end, varied on the surface with the finest comedy.'[95]

Yet the same critics denounced Shakespeare's play as shockingly bad. Archer pronounced it 'constructed in plain defiance not merely of any and every set of canons, but of rudimentary common sense.'[96] Shaw, going further, dismissed it as 'stagey trash of the lowest melodramatic order' (although he would later recant much of that position in the preface to *Cymbeline Refinished*, his 1936 revision of the play's fifth act, commissioned for the Shakespeare Memorial Theatre).[97] Such remarks reveal the extent to which a nineteenth-century audience's response to a theatrical performer did *not* depend upon the quality of the drama being performed. Actors shone in tawdry roles and incoherent scripts because spectators focused on the pictorial display of emotion and temperament. Such display, although it could profit from beauties of language, never required them. That is another way of saying that as much as Irving borrowed Shakespeare's cultural authority to enhance his personal reputation and the Lyceum's social standing, Shakespeare, when it came down to the practicalities of performance, was often the one who needed help: from charismatic performers, historically conscious scene painters and visionary *metteurs-en-scène.*

Coriolanus (1901)

As Britain mourned the death of Queen Victoria in January 1901 Irving prepared his long deferred production of Shakespeare's Roman play, one that had never been popular with the late queen's subjects. It had been five years since Irving's last Shakespearean revival and during that long interval he had come close to staging *Richard II*—with scenery designed by Edwin Abbey—and *Julius Caesar*—an acting edition was produced and Sir Lawrence Alma-Tadema enlisted for the scenery. Charles Kean in the 1850s had turned the part of King Richard into a good acting role and the play's historical pageantry would have enhanced its appeal. In the 1880s the Meininger troupe was praised for its blockbuster staging of *Julius Caesar*. For Irving, either play would have made sense. What did not make sense was *Coriolanus*.

There had been no important London production since 1860 and the last successful one had been a full century earlier, when John Philip Kemble ruled Covent Garden. More immediately, how could Irving, aged sixty-three, and weakened by illness, play a virile young warrior? (What actor plays Coriolanus a decade *after* playing Lear?) The absurdity of Irving's decision was underscored by the casting of Ellen Terry—ten years his junior—as Coriolanus' mother, Volumnia. Even the sycophantic Austin Brereton conceded that Irving 'was not the Roman solider of tradition any more than Miss Terry was the Roman matron.'[98]

Whatever praise could be summoned was reserved for the scenery and the crowd scenes, which created a stunningly detailed realization of republican Rome. Irving compressed Shakespeare's five acts into three, thus enabling the entire play to be acted in only ten scenes, each with specially prepared sets—the Forum, the Senate House, the streets of Rome and the interiors of the homes of Coriolanus and Aufidius. Alma-Tadema relied on sources ranging from Vitruvius' description of an Etruscan temple to the latest archaeological discoveries in Volterra. But no amount of Roman splendor could compensate for leading actors who were miscast. Greenroom gossip had it that a wearied Lyceum stagehand, after spotting a poster outside the theatre billing the actor Sir Henry Irving, the designer Sir Lawrence Alma-Tadema and the composer Sir Alexander Mackenzie, remarked, 'Three knights! That's about all I'll give it.' Drawing spare houses, *Coriolanus* closed after thirty-six nights. As a dejected Irving soon acknowledged, 'the public don't want [it].'[99]

It was his thirteenth—and last—Shakespearean revival. It was also an outright failure. He had by then relinquished control of the Lyceum and his career as a producer of Shakespeare, having faltered for the past decade, finally came to a stop. Theatre history lingers over the glittering triumphs of the 1880s—even though the only unqualified success was *Much Ado about Nothing*—but the inarguable fact was that Shakespeare did not save either Henry Irving or his theatre from an embarrassing decline. Productions became less frequent, roles less congenial, notices less adulatory. Of the great classical roles there remained only Shylock. Whatever sustenance Irving needed in his final years did not come from Shakespeare.

Irving's Artistic Vision

Stepping back from this chronological account of Lyceum Shakespeare, I now want to provide an overall assessment of Irving's artistic vision, one less *about* Shakespeare than realized *through* Shakespeare. Moreover, my goal in this part of the chapter is to excavate the frequently hidden connection between high-Victorian Shakespeare as exemplified by Irving and the birth of modernist Shakespeare as represented by the young Gordon Craig. The conceptual sympathy between these formally distinct aesthetics explains how Shakespeare survived the transition from the nineteenth to the twentieth centuries.

Consider this example from the 1874 *Hamlet.* Irving discarded tradition by dispensing with actual portraits of old Hamlet and Claudius in the closet scene. Instead he gestured toward the audience, as if the portraits hung on the stage's imaginary fourth wall. The 'counterfeit presentments' were thus either part of the illusory theatrical world or hallucinations in Hamlet's tortured mind. The scene made sense either way because both options demanded that the audience remain conscious of the performance *as* a performance. In the first scenario, the audience is invited to obey the rules of theatrical illusionism: if Hamlet sees something, then it must be there. In the second, the audience is privy to the distorted reality of the character Hamlet: the portraits may be hallucinations, but the character is genuinely hallucinating.

Irving's handling of the scene provides early evidence that Shakespeare's text was *not* the performance's centerpiece. The monumental aesthetics of his *Romeo and Juliet* and *Much Ado about Nothing* made the same point on a grander scale. Thus in his first Shakespearean leading role Irving adhered to the conviction that even the most hallowed texts are malleable; that they are necessarily conditioned by the demands of their performance. Indeed, Irving explained that his use of 'imaginary' portraits arose from a desire not to protect Shakespeare's words from scenographic distractions but to capture his audience's imagination. When 'practical difficulties' make 'literal conformity with the text' impossible, he argued, he had 'complete justification' to depart from the text. 'It is not a question of violating the poet's ideal', Irving elaborated, 'but of choosing from amongst certain effects those which will create the most vivid impression.'[100] The Shakespearean text, then, is a function of its possibilities in performance, not the other way around.

To put the matter differently, it was not Shakespeare who was the artist and Irving his humble servant, but the reverse: Irving was the artist and

Shakespeare his raw material. Other raw materials included actors, scenery, costumes, lighting and sound—all united to from a complete world onstage. No longer would scenery, however luxurious, however archaeologically correct, be regarded as separate from the moving body of the actor. As Irving's secretary, Louis Austin, remarked of *The Merchant of Venice*: 'I recall those pictures, not on account of any scenic magnificence, but because they live in the imagination together with the noble figures that moved in them.'[101] No longer would the Lyceum ensemble stand in front of scenic backgrounds; henceforth, they would inhabit a three-dimensional scenic milieu. Shaw's accusation that Irving 'never in his life conceived or interpreted the characters of any author except himself' is much more than an indictment of theatrical ego.[102] It recognizes that even Shakespeare was vulnerable to Irving's artistic desires.

Where in all this, a Victorian critic would instinctively ask, was history? It was both there and not there. Lyceum Shakespeare did not forsake historicism—that would have been a shocking deviation from precedent—and so there was no shortage of diligent archival research to create period-perfect scenery and costumes. But historical accuracy was not for Irving the shibboleth that it had been for Charles Kean. Gone were the pedantic historiographical essays that Kean had written for programs at the Princess's Theatre. Gone was the obsession with courting the approval of professional historians. Gone, too, was the fear of anachronism.

The loosening of historicism's grip upon Victorian Shakespeare began in the mid-1870s when E. W. Godwin (Terry's lover and father of Gordon Craig) published an influential series of articles on 'The Architecture and Costume of Shakespeare's Plays.' In identifying the precise historical period of various dramas he expressed a crucial caveat: that archaeological accuracy must be compromised for the sake of theatrical effect. Godwin's declaration that art trumps history became gospel truth for Irving, who in an 1885 lecture at Harvard offered an anecdote revealing his less than slavish devotion to 'archaeology on the stage':

> I received a letter complaining of the gross violation of accuracy in a scene [in *Much Ado about Nothing*] which was called a cedar-walk. 'Cedars!' said my correspondent,—'why, cedars were not introduced into Messina for fifty years after the date of Shakespeare's story!' Well, this was a tremendous indictment, but unfortunately the cedar-walk had been painted. Absolute realism on the stage is not always desirable. . . .[103]

'Archaeology must give way to beauty,' Irving insisted.[104] And so it did. The final scene from *Romeo and Juliet* is a case in point. Irving used two sets: a gloomy churchyard for the duel between Romeo and Paris and then the Capulets' crypt. Throughout the first part of the scene the audience was shown an exterior view of steps leading down into the burial vault. Then, after a changeover, the audience was presented with the interior view of the white-robed Juliet asleep at the foot of the same flight of steps. Romeo appeared at the top of the massive staircase, visible in the moonlight shining through the door that he had forced open. Slowly, he descended into the depths of the tomb, dragging Paris's corpse behind him, the staircase stained with the dead man's blood. The thrill of the scene lay in pictorial seamlessness—Romeo leaves the churchyard and then enters Juliet's tomb—even though the second scene violated the spatial logic of the first by presenting discontinuous spaces as if they were integrated. Archaeology had indeed given way to the beautiful realization of dramatic space and time.

The ironic paradox of Irving's aesthetic, ironic because neither foreseen nor intended, was that it overthrew itself and paved the way for theatrical modernism. The union of actor and scenery brought about the demise of theatre as 'illustration' by acknowledging that theatrical space mattered more than the depiction of any particular space, whether historical or fanciful. Irving anticipated twentieth-century innovations in scenery and lighting by placing his attention not on actors but on the space containing them. All that is now taken for granted. But it was revolutionary at the time to understand how theatrical space could be manipulated.

Emphasizing the continuities between Irving and Craig forces us to rethink the traditional segmentation of Shakespeare's theatrical afterlife into self-contained periods of which the two most antithetical—and yet chronologically adjacent—are 'Victorian' and 'modern.' A comparison of the wedding scene from *Much Ado About Nothing* in the productions of Irving (1882) and Craig (1903) is enlightening on the point. While the Lyceum's impresario incorporated mammoth three-dimensional columns and wrought iron gates into his scenery, the young director-designer created the same dramatic space with a plain backdrop of folded gray curtains and a lone crucifix hung above a simple altar, enhanced through dramatic lighting effects. Each man knew how different a style the other championed. 'It was very pleasant to come and see the interior of a Cathedral at Messina,' Craig conceded. 'But somehow all this made the younger people . . . and I was one of them—a little impatient.'[105] Irving, softly muttering, sat in a private box for Craig's production, while his protégé crouched nervously behind him. Whether the integration of actor and setting was in Irving's lavish spectacles or Craig's bare suggestive settings, the underlying precept was the same: that the vitality of a performance lay in the conscious arrangement of theatrical space to create a distinctive milieu.

Modernism was the alternative to Victorian spectacular Shakespeare, but not its opposite. Craig, applying the formal principles of Adolphe Appia, began to use light and scenery not to represent particular historical sites within Shakespeare's plays but to create symbolic worlds in which the plays unfolded. Just as progressive painters of the time argued for pure pictorialism—a picture without a referent—Craig created abstract performance spaces out of line, color, rhythm and light. They referred to nothing but themselves and their theatrical potential. Not representing a particular time or place, such spaces captured the play's thematic essence. In another instance of stage modernism, the actor and playwright William Poel (1852–1934), founder of the Elizabethan Stage Society, returned Shakespeare to his emblematic origins through the use of a platform stage, curtains and screens.

Once Victorian Shakespeare articulated its own theory of the theatre, as it were, that theory was put into practice across a range of theatrical styles—spectacular, minimalist, pseudo-Elizabethan. Thus began the long slow death of Shakespeare as archaeology. It is astonishing to reflect that Poel staged *Hamlet* (using the 1603 First Quarto text, rather than the one in the 1623 First Folio) at St. George's Hall within weeks of the Meininger troupe's visit and only three years into Irving's management of the Lyceum. It is no contradiction to observe that the decline of high-Victorian Shakespeare began *before* its climax was reached, because it was exemplified and negated by the same person. His name was Henry Irving.

Bardolatry

Craig remarked that Henry Irving *had* nothing—no inborn talent, no handsome aspect, no elegant stride, no power to his voice—but *was* everything—a man possessed of a 'powerful will and a determination not to fail, spite of all his shortcomings.'[106] To which appraisal we may add that he possessed little originality of thought. '[O]ne may search through all of Irving's public utterances,' the dramatist Henry Arthur Jones candidly, yet judiciously, remarked, 'without discovering or recalling much that is really profound, penetrating or illuminative of any great subject. But there is much that is correct, much that is just above commonplace, much that is well said, much that is personally interesting.'[107] To acknowledge Irving's shortcomings, to refuse him the intellectual eminence that he sought, and that so many of his contemporaries attributed to him, is, in fact, to acknowledge a yet more remarkable attribute: the raw strength of his desire to perform that eminence.

From the outset of his London career Irving willed himself to become—first to pose as, but then actually to become—something more than a celebrated actor. Central to Irving's exalted vision for himself was an inward union with Shakespeare, an almost structural bond that enabled each to strengthen and in turn be strengthened by the other. To a degree unparalleled at the time, and rarely matched since, Irving crossed over into the 'Shakespeare trade,' borrowing and profiting from its rising cultural value. He delivered speeches in Stratford, officiated at commemorative events, penned essays for learned journals, befriended (but never kowtowed to) the most acclaimed scholars, assembled a Shakespeare library and lent his name to an eight-volume edition of the plays. Not since Garrick had an actor-manager been so completely absorbed within the cult of Shakespeare.

Yet his love for the Bard was fundamentally a form of self-love. By that I mean no criticism. Irving's well-phrased, but intellectually safe, essays and speeches on Shakespeare command our attention for what they reveal about Irving: that he used Shakespeare not just to uphold his vision of the theatre but also to fulfill his personal ambition of becoming a public man of letters. In 1877 he published his first 'Note on Shakespeare' in the *Nineteenth Century*.[108] Within three years of playing Hamlet for the first time he was reinventing himself as a credible commentator upon the plays. Revealingly, Irving's private correspondence rarely touched upon Shakespeare (other than pertaining to the business of the Lyceum Theatre) even though many of the letters he received from friends, acquaintances and perfect strangers attempted to initiate such a conversation. When replies were necessary it was usually Bram Stoker, his chief of staff, or his secretary Louis Austin who drafted them, Irving simply adding his signature. Naturally, the actor's public devotion to all things Shakespearean was couched in the familiar language of humble service to genius unsurpassed. But the icons named Henry Irving and William Shakespeare were evenly matched.

Consider Irving's speech delivered in 1885 to the Goethe Society in New York. The core of his argument was that 'Shakespeare commands the homage of all the arts' and that the stage's highest honor was to blend acting, music and painting to create a 'strong and truthful impression of his work.' The word to pause on is 'commands,' for it indicates not gentle toleration but driven compulsion. Staging Shakespeare through the union of the arts was not one option among many, but the only option. Irving's preferred style of staging Shakespeare aligned perfectly, so ran the argument, with the dramatist's own intent. Victorian actor-managers regularly asserted that historicist and spectacular *mise-en-scène* enabled them to realize Shakespeare's true but hitherto unrealizable design. But none behaved in so audaciously self-aggrandizing a manner as Irving.

Curiously, the importance of Shakespeare for Irving's public image revealed itself in a speech on Christopher Marlowe. In September 1891 Irving unveiled Onslow Ford's monument to the playwright in Canterbury, Marlowe's birthplace. Figure 3 shows Irving delivering his speech, a rare photograph of the actor as public intellectual—addressing a street corner throng, one hand waving his notes, the other planted on his hip in the orator's characteristic pose. Throughout his remarks Irving deliberately constructed an anti-theatrical identity for Marlowe by invoking a distinction between literature and theatre, something he rejected when discussing Shakespeare. He insisted that Marlowe was a poet whose works were to be savored in bookish silence while Shakespeare was a dramatist whose glories were most fully visible upon the stage. Marlowe appealed to scholars, Shakespeare to actors. 'Whatever may be thought of his [Marlowe's] qualities as a dramatist . . . he stands first and foremost as the poet who gave us . . . the literary form which is the highest achievement of poetic expression.' As the speech progressed, Shakespeare's contemporary was vaporized, reduced from embodied historical personage to elemental purity: 'it is not with Marlowe the man that we need busy ourselves . . . [but] the ideal of the poet.'[109] Irving unveiled a memorial to Marlowe only to render it an empty signifier. How appropriate that the bronze sculpture of the dramatist was rather small. Though doubtless aware of the falsity of his remarks, Irving had no choice: Marlowe was a threat. Irving needed a Shakespeare without rival.

The well-known fact that Shakespeare earned his living in the theatrical marketplace appeared in many of Irving's writing and speeches. If well known, why was the point belabored? Because it applied to Irving himself. Earlier in the century leading actor-managers often felt ambivalent towards their profession. Macready frequently succumbed to self-loathing while Charles Kean did his utmost to convert the theatre into a sedate tutorial. Irving, by contrast, felt proud to be a man of the theatre and he campaigned ceaselessly to promote not just the respectability of the legitimate theatre and its parity with the fine arts, but also its social importance. He addressed hundreds of learned societies and charities, spoke at countless civic

FIGURE 3 Henry Irving unveils the Christopher Marlowe memorial in Canterbury, September 16th 1891. By permission of the Folger Shakespeare Library.

luncheons, unveiled public monuments and lobbied aristocrats, politicians and clergymen. Shakespeare was Irving's most powerful weapon in that campaign. Thus, in a eulogistic letter to the son of the actor Edward Compton, Irving stressed a Shakespearean role that his late colleague had played as evidence of his 'high position in [the] profession.' That the role was minor—'First Gravedigger' in *Hamlet*—made Irving's strategy only more apparent.[110] A polemical essay from 1883 similarly underlined the value of Shakespeare in the commercial theatre's continuing fight for social prestige:

> Shakespeare is our shield and buckler against a great deal of prejudice. If he had not written plays, if he had not been an actor . . . the player would have had a much harder fight for social recognition. The fact that Shakespeare wrote primarily for the stage is our salvation.[111]

The battle for salvation, he believed, was gradually being won. Irving used a speech delivered at the dedication of an elaborate public drinking fountain in Stratford to observe with gratitude that at the present day the 'actor's art . . . comes much nearer to Shakespeare's estimate of its importance in the intellectual life of the community' than it did in the dramatist's time, 'when the Corporation of Stratford refused to permit the performance even of his own plays.'[112] More than a touch of self-congratulation rested within those words, for Irving had in effect declared that the genuinely Shakespearean moment was right now—1887—when, because of Irving's own efforts, the acting profession had begun to receive the respect that for centuries it had been denied. As much as Shakespeare was the 'salvation' of actors, Irving was the salvation of Shakespeare.

The affirmation of Shakespeare as a commercial theatre artist, moreover, explains why Irving long opposed a subsidized national theatre: because it would reduce Shakespeare the marketplace entrepreneur into a ward of the state. Matthew Arnold, writing after the Comédie-Française performed at London's Gaiety Theatre in the summer of 1879, argued that 'the performances of the French company show us plainly . . . what is to be gained by organizing the theatre.'[113] By 'organizing' he meant state financing or control. Irving, an unyielding proponent of theatrical free trade, dissented strongly: 'the stage is . . . entitled to make its own bargain with the public without the censorious intervention of well-intentioned busybodies.'[114] The ideal model for theatrical laissez-faire, he offered, was the Elizabethan public playhouse—because it produced the greatest playwright in the English language. Still, Irving recognized that those prejudiced against the theatre frequently regarded Shakespeare as a purely literary figure: 'The actor, it is contended, has no claim to be regarded as an interpreter of Shakespeare . . . he is at best a poor kind of illustrator . . . far inferior to the student who . . . illumines the poet's pages with the cold light of critical inquiry.'

Countering that argument, Irving upheld the superiority, not just the parity, of the stage, insisting that actors could give the public what 'critical investigations' never could: 'the tones of a human voice vibrating with passion, tenderness, and mockery, together with the subtle play of look and gesture which impart form and color to the thought.'[115] True, but that scarcely amounted to a thesis, given that it was irrational to blame an essay for not behaving like an actor. Irving stood on firmer ground when he pointed out the ridiculousness of those who believed that Shakespeare was 'nature's child . . . a sort of chance phenomenon who wrote these plays by accident.' The truth, as Irving saw it, was that the dramatist wrote them to be performed and to make him money.

'Shakespeare belongs to the stage for ever,' Irving preached, 'and his glories must inalienably belong to it.'[116] A man who professed that was unlikely to hold Shakespeare scholars in awe. Indeed, Irving regarded their efforts as parasitic upon performance: 'the commentator did not precede the actor but followed in his footsteps.'[117] In a deeply sarcastic letter to Furnivall—who had accused him of using Shakespeare only to make money—he expressed his indebtedness to the quarter of a million people who had seen him in *The Merchant of Venice*. With the public on his side he would willingly forfeit the approval of the New Shakspere Society, the scholarly organization that Furnivall had founded in 1873.[118] At the dawn of modern academic study of Shakespeare Irving insisted that the playwright must never be divorced from the living theatre. In the academic world today such arguments have lost their force because many scholars understand that performance functions not as an animated version of a dramatic text but as a signifying entity in its own right—one that incorporates, but also exceeds, a textual dimension. Irving's *mise-en-scène* provided an early instance of just that insight, showing yet again that the practice of theatre usually precedes its articulation in theory.

As if to assert his own credibility as a Shakespearean, Irving collaborated with his old friend Frank Marshall, a dramatist and journalist, on a complete edition of the plays for a popular readership. The result was the eight-volume *Henry Irving Shakespeare*, published in installments between 1888 and 1890.[119] Overlooked in most accounts of Irving's career, the grandly titled edition warrants inspection, not least because the magnitude of the enterprise was so unlike the single-play editions that Victorian actor-managers, Irving included, regularly published to advertize and commemorate their productions. This work, intending to be timeless, only glanced at Irving's stage management. 'I feel . . . such a horror,' Marshall confided, 'of anything like puffing or seeming to puff you in this edition.'[120] Instead, the various prefaces covered the textual and theatrical history of each play and offered a general critical overview.

Marshall, who had been ill for some time, and died before the final volume appeared, prepared the introductions and edited the texts, but gradually handed over responsibility to other literary figures, including Joseph Knight and Arthur Symonds. Apart from the prestige value of his name, Irving's contribution was modest. For the first volume he wrote a 'not very remarkable essay' repeating his standard thesis that Shakespeare was best appreciated in the theatre and that the theatre was best appreciated when it joined 'the sister arts of music and painting.'[121] For the final volume he penned a tribute to Marshall. And for each play he advised on the recommended textual cuts (far less drastic than for Lyceum productions).

It was not a scholarly tool comparable to the massive Variorum editions overseen by Horace Howard Furness. Glosses were held to a minimum, as were stage directions, and the occasional bracket surrounded lines that might be safely omitted in performance. As *The Times* noted with understatement, 'necessary guidance is given in the simplest possible way.'[122] Privately, Marshall complained to Irving that the notes prepared by some of the replacement editors were useless.[123] Nor was this an edition that appealed to actors: the volumes were large, heavy, published in installments, and altogether unsuitable for use onstage or in parlor theatricals. Irving's edition possessed, then, no obvious utility. It was decorative, a collectible, something for casual display, not deep investigation. Over a century later, the volumes are rarely studied and it remains doubtful whether they were much studied when new. Reviews at the time were polite but unenthusiastic. That, however, was beside the point—because the work's usefulness lay not in exploring Shakespeare's plays but in appropriating his cultural value. Owning the volumes meant that the owner had been admitted into the polite middle class cult (or 'humbug,' to use the detractors' preferred term) of Victorian Shakespeare.

Because the ritual center of Victorian Shakespeare was the Lyceum Theatre, no one should be surprised that the *Henry Irving Shakespeare* was as much about Henry Irving as Shakespeare. The various prefaces, not written by Irving, but still subject to his approval, validated his interpretation of the plays. Thus, Irving's sympathetic reading of Shylock was justified as being authentically Shakespearean. Shylock's 'greedy usury' was recast as the dramatist's secret strategy of 'yield[ing] to popular prejudice' just enough to keep the audience on his side, but then challenging their bigotry by allowing Shylock to voice 'eloquent pleas against the social injustice of which he is the victim.'[124] Similarly, the discussion of *Macbeth* aligned itself with Irving's belief that Macbeth had decided upon his regicidal course before the play started. '[I]s it not curious,' Marshall asked, that when Macbeth heard the witches' prophecy 'his thoughts should turn with such astonishing promptitude to the idea of murder?' His conclusion echoed Irving's own: 'The tinder, it is evident, is lying ready.'[125]

Yet it was not solely to sanction his artistic vision that Irving relied upon Shakespeare. He also used the national poet as a weapon in his hate campaign against the New Drama, as represented by Henrik Ibsen (whose plays Irving condemned for their unhealthy preoccupation with 'sexual sins'), as championed by Shaw (whose essay, 'The Quintessence of Ibsenism,' Irving found absurd) and as performed by J. T. Grein's Independent Theatre (whose work Irving ridiculed for being anything but independent, given that Grein borrowed actors and scenery from 'self-supporting' theatres that made their money from a rather different repertoire.)[126] But at least Irving could claim that he had seen Ibsen's work, for he accepted an invitation from the actress Janet Achurch to attend a matinee of *A Doll's House* in June 1889.[127] Dramaturgical quarrels quickly became a matter of cultural nationalism, for Irving repeatedly constructed Shakespeare as the morally upright poet who embodied an ideal of the nation's character and the wholesomeness of its artistic preferences. In opposition stood the (then) avant-garde genre of dramatic realism, branded by its opponents as morally suspect and, therefore, unpatriotic. Irving denounced Ibsen's dramas as 'absolutely foreign to British codes of morals, manners and social usage' and predicted that they would never thrive on British soil. Though wrong, the prophecy turned on a decidedly nationalistic invocation of Shakespeare, one that justified Irving's own practice by attributing to it a fidelity to 'English life and character.'[128]

Anglophone Cultural Imperialism

As has been well documented in biographies and traditional theatre histories, Irving undertook overseas tours partly to win an international reputation and partly to secure income for himself and the Lyceum. His desire must have been strong, for the tours presented daunting logistical complexities, the traveling personnel numbered near seventy and hundreds of pieces of scenery filled three railroad cars.[129] Yet Irving's careerist imperatives should not blind us to the wider implications of his actions. If domestic Shakespeare was largely about validating Irving's artistic stature, then foreign Shakespeare became a vehicle for cultural imperialism.

Irving' first visit to the United States in 1883 took place against the faded backdrop of the 1849 Astor Place Riot, when the rivalry between the American actor Edwin Forrest and the British tragedian W. C. Macready left twenty-five dead and more than 100 wounded in the streets of New York. (See Edward Ziter's chapter, pp. 47–50.) Far from being a matter of parochial interest, the riot embodied a deep quarrel within American culture: should it be native and homegrown or should it look to Britain for inspiration? By the 1880s the terms of the debate had moved on. Booth and Irving's joint appearance in *Othello*, a sort of prelude to Irving's appearance across the Atlantic, symbolized a new harmony between American and British theatre. It was a sign of changed times that while touring in Philadelphia, Irving was presented with Forrest's watch, the latest treasure added to his theatrical reliquary. Yet the gift was less an emblem of sudden reconciliation than a redrawing of the battle lines. In this latest iteration of the culture wars, the now reconciled enemies Britain and America fought on the same side in the name of Anglo-Saxon superiority. The blatantly imperialist discourse surrounding Irving's tours confirmed that the great weapon in the arsenal of the English-speaking peoples (though a weapon directed against a vague unnamed enemy) was Shakespeare.

The cultural logic of the American tours was announced in London during a banquet for 500 men—watched over by 400 ladies in the gallery, Ellen Terry chief among them—held in Irving's honor on July 4th 1883, the last night of the season before his and Terry's first crossing to New York. Like the tours themselves, the occasion celebrated Anglo-American amity, with Lord Coleridge, the Lord Chief Justice, declaring that Irving's impending visit was Britain's birthday gift to a 'great and generous' America. In their respective speeches, both Irving and the poet James Russell Lowell, then American minister to Court of St. James's, referred not simply to the 'English-speaking race' and 'English-speaking' people but to the role of theatre—and Shakespeare particularly—in shaping that transnational identity.[130] Such an appropriation looked back to Thomas Carlyle's passionate vision from 1840 of a global Shakespeare, 'radiant aloft over all Nations of Englishmen a 1000 years hence.'[131] But it was something new for the popular theatre, as distinct from literature, to be lauded for championing that worldwide Anglo-centric vision.

On October 19th 1883 Irving arrived in New York harbor aboard the steamer *Britannic* as the conquering hero of the British theatre, the man whom Wilde and Lillie Langtry had waved goodbye at the Liverpool docks eight days earlier. But he was also more than that as one American newspaper observed: 'Genius on the stage is cosmopolitan, and the American people are ever ready to acknowledge it.'[132] In immediate acknowledgment two vessels rushed over the waves to greet the *Britannic* as soon as she dropped anchor. Irving appeared on deck waving his hat while on one of the escorting vessels the Metropolitan Opera House orchestra played 'God Save the Queen.' Aboard the other was William Winter (already friends with Irving from his visit to London the year before), who later recorded his impression of the moment: 'I saw prefigured that cordial union of brotherhood and art which has since been established between the theatres of England and these States.'[133] As predicted at the London farewell banquet, Irving's arrival spurred no antagonism. Nor was his welcome a sign of America's infantilized subservience to Britain. Rather, in a transcending dialectical moment, past differences were overcome, shared global interests acknowledged, and the Shakespearean stage became the embodiment of internationalist concerns. At a banquet in New York near the end of his second tour—undertaken after an absence of only five months—Irving declared that 'upon the broad platform of a noble art the two greatest sections of the English-speaking race are one nation.'[134]

Not that the greatest English-speaking playwright featured prominently in Irving's American repertoire, which followed its British counterpart in giving pride of place to 'the high walks of melodrama.'[135] On the inaugural tour the only Shakespearean plays were *Hamlet, The Merchant of Venice* and *Much Ado about Nothing*—even though *Othello* and *Romeo and Juliet* were also in the repertoire. Cautiously, Irving chose Mathias in *The Bells* for his maiden appearance before an American audience. After a week, he attempted Shylock. But not until the return engagement months later did he dare to play Hamlet in New York, perhaps fearing failure, perhaps deferring to the stature of his friend Edwin Booth. In Chicago, the fourth city on the tour, he appeared as Benedick. Only two more Shakespearean roles were added during the subsequent seven tours—Macbeth and Wolsey—making a less than grand total of five.[136]

Nor did Shakespeare provide Irving with his most acclaimed roles. American and British audiences liked him best as Becket, Faust, Louis XI and Mathias. 'Mr. Irving's Hamlet will not be popular in America,' a New York critic predicted after witnessing the first performance at the not quite fashionable Star Theatre on 13th Street. Why not? 'It is Mathais of *The Bells*, not Hamlet'—a charge first heard in London a decade earlier.[137] (That verdict did not, however, prevent Irving from boasting that 'Hamlet has never been so enthusiastically received in England.'[138]) His Benedick left critics complaining that '[h]e should leave the lovers for younger men.'[139] Macbeth was attacked for being 'painfully' mannered.[140] Not even Shylock was guaranteed to please: 'He vaults from guttural to falsetto and decimates the lines . . . till the text dissolves itself into a blur of crooning and guffawing.'[141]

If newspaper reviews were the only documentary source of theatre history then later generations would wonder how Shakespeare could be central to Irving's reputation, let alone his vision of Anglo-American cultural supremacy. But the very absence of critical consensus that Irving was a worthy heir to the mantle of Garrick, Kemble and Kean makes the point that the actor's vision for a worldwide Anglophone culture far exceeded debates on histrionic merit. To praise or blame Irving for his broken voice, his angular gait, his contorted posture, or any such eccentricity, was to lower one's sights. It was to miss entirely what he strove to accomplish, both on the stage and in the wider world. For that enlarged perspective we must look beyond his performance in any particular play.

Except for *The Merchant of Venice*. Unlike any other Shakespearean drama in Irving's repertoire, this one play elicited responses that spoke directly to the importance of racial pride and the belief in the global superiority of Anglo-Saxon culture that underlay the actor's commitment to international Shakespeare. Irving's production was hailed as a worthy rival to both the Comédie Française and the Meininger troupe, equally deserving of their 'international reputation.' Protesting against the common presumption that 'Shakespeare cannot be played here with the general excellence achieved elsewhere,' *The Theatre* pointed to the Lyceum as proof that the English needed no lessons from foreigners.[142]

More curiously, though, a similar national pride was aroused by Irving's performance. The starting point for such responses was the recognition that the actor's sympathetic portrayal of Shylock—a man proud of his heritage and subjected to the vicious intolerance of hypocritical Christians—was itself a proud sign of moral supremacy. Only a civilization devoted to tolerance, only a civilization in the ascendant, could produce such an enlightened interpretation. In the United States the play became a pointed moment of reckoning for the united Anglophone world. *The Merchant of Venice* 'could not be played in any century but the nineteenth,' affirmed the *Chicago Tribune*, 'and it could not be played by any but an English-speaking actor.' The distinctive characteristic of Irving's Shylock—so distinctive that only an American or British audience could appreciate it—was its 'modernity.' '[B]y modernity,' the critic elaborated, 'one means the liberality of the conception.'[143] Such remarks make explicit the conjunction between Shakespeare and contemporary political consciousness. But it was always there, the underlying recurrent theme of those eight American tours.

Perhaps nowhere was the indivisibility of Anglo-American Shakespeare more apparent than in Irving's own remarks. On October 17th 1887, just before his third American tour, Irving spoke at the dedication of a monumental stone drinking fountain in Stratford-upon-Avon, the gift of a Philadelphia philanthropist, the newspaper owner G. W. Childs, to mark Queen Victoria's Golden Jubilee. Irving's dedicatory speech elaborated on how Anglo-American cultural unity was anchored in and best expressed by a love for Shakespeare: 'On this spot of all others Americans cease to be aliens, for here they claim our kinship with the great master of English speech . . . The simplest records of Stratford show that this is the Mecca of American pilgrims, and that the place which gave birth to Shakespeare is regarded as the fountain of the mightiest and most enduring inspiration of our mother tongue.' The Union Jack and the Stars and Stripes affixed to the exteriors of the surrounding buildings supplied visual complement to the orator's theme. Irving, who had just been elected a trustee of Shakespeare's house in Henley Street, reached extravagant heights, imagining that among the spectators at the Globe had been men who later settled in the New World; men who sired generations that still preserved in their colloquial speech 'phrases which have come down from Shakespeare's time.'[144]

In a toast at the lunch afterwards Irving pressed his theme further, describing his impending American tour as a diplomatic mission whose purpose was to cement the 'bond' uniting 'two great nations.' That indissoluble bond was neither political nor economic, but cultural: the Bard himself. In a speech aware of the power of language, Irving deliberately employed the language of power, referring to 'the world-wide sphere of Shakespeare's influence.' Shakespeare behaved exactly like a nation-state that sought to advance its interests beyond its borders and fend off rivals for global dominion.

Similarly, consider Irving's speech at a London banquet celebrating his return from an overseas tour:

> Go also to America and learn how easy it is admire it and love her people and yet remain a Briton. It was indeed a pleasure for me entering this

> *salon* to see, as I last saw in Delmonico's, the Stars and Stripes interlacing in decoration the Union Jack. They portray the union of sentiment in both lands. Indeed, I do not realize that I have been abroad . . . I feel that I have been in another England, visiting cousins, all of us sharing in the English glories of the past. I believe from my visit that if ever dear, honest John Bull shall find himself in a tight place that equally dear, honest Uncle Sam will be at his side.[145]

The overstated tone, far from invalidating the message, underscored its seriousness. The 'union of sentiment in both lands' was less an objective fact to be encountered by transatlantic travelers than an emergent consciousness that appealed to each nation's pride, sense of moral worth and paternal responsibility to the (so it was believed) less civilized regions of the globe. In public, Irving ridiculously pretended to have forgotten that he had been abroad. In private he boasted of invasion and conquest: 'our triumph has been complete and the country captured.'[146] But his intent throughout was less to give a factual account of his sojourn than to reframe it as the convergence of 'Anglo-Saxon peoples' around Shakespeare; a convergence that, once achieved, would be an example to the world.[147] Although the 'American nation [was] too young,' Irving remarked, to produce 'great dramatic plays,' it could nonetheless assume its place upon the world stage by forging an alliance with Britain.[148]

Correspondingly, the banquet at Delmonico's in New York—referred to in Irving's London speech—conveyed precisely the same message. Setting the scene for his readers, a newspaper critic pointed out the contrast between the night decades earlier 'when Macready was driven from the stage of a New York theatre amid a storm of jeers and curses' and the previous night when Irving '[sat] down at a bounteous feast, with garlands of flowers around and above him.'[149] The rapprochement signaled not a cessation of theatrical rivalry (Booth and Irving had never been antagonists) but the 'full blossom' of 'friendship' that had grown between the two countries. 'I cannot feel that I am a stranger,' Irving declared that night:

> We have no distinctions in our art, and I know now that all English actors are welcome in America. Nobody can be more sensitive than the actor of the great unity between these two great peoples. Whatever political clouds are on the horizon the actors are always received with the heartiest welcome. I have witnessed the great affection which you have for the English people, and I think our people at home scarcely realize the strength of this sentiment . . . [L]et an alien attack English institutions and from my observation I think you are pretty sure to 'wipe the floor with him.'[150]

He began by asserting the indivisibility of English and American theatrical culture—'I cannot feel that I am a stranger'—and then enlarged his perspective, recasting the absence of competition between actors as the paradigm for a broader sympathy—'the great unity'—between the peoples themselves. For evidence of the harmonious blending of the two nations, one must look, Irving suggested, not to diplomatic missions but to the hearty welcome that an actor from one country receives in another. Or in today's parlance, soft power matters more than hard power. Raising his rhetoric to global level, Irving concluded with a triumphant vision of a united Anglo-Saxon imperial race successfully defending itself from 'alien' foes. The same rhetoric inspired an imagined testimonial banquet at which Uncle Sam presents Irving with 'An International Loving Cup/About Which There Can Be No Dispute.' (Figure 4) Tellingly, the Stratford bust of Shakespeare appears as the apex of the diplomatic triangle, uniting both countries in a shared dramatic culture. The image carried credibility because it played upon the actual event when Irving received a loving cup from the Lotos Club in New York in 1895.[151]

Irving's grand dream of a *pax Shakespeareana* enforced by the combined might of Britain and America did not go unchallenged. A Philadelphia critic, far from extending a fraternal welcome to British actors, lambasted them as 'carpet-baggers' who 'pick up American dollars and then fly off home to invest their earnings in English securities and give their American cousins the grand laugh, treating them and considering them as a lot of greenhorns.' The bamboozler-in-chief was Sir Henry Irving, who excelled his confreres in persuading 'cockney-loving Americans' to part with their cash. But Irving would not have enjoyed such success, the critic argued, were it not for the 'fashionable American snobs who worship anything English,' particularly a knighthood. They dupe themselves by paying 'sickening homage to English actors and everything English.'[152]

A more vindictive critic denounced Irving's 'aggressiveness' in regarding himself as Shakespeare's foremost interpreter. 'By what right of conquest,' a New York journalist asked, 'does Mr. Irving declare that while the bones of Shakespeare rest in Stratford, the poet's spirit remains in the Lyceum?' However much he succeeded in tyrannizing his countrymen through his Shakespeare monopoly, he possessed no right to attempt a similar 'conquest' on foreign soil. No people—not English, not American—could be free 'so long as Henry Irving lives to shackle us with his genius.'[153]

The rhetoric of ancient grudge was as high-blown as the rhetoric of fresh concordance. It would be easy to dismiss such comments as saber rattling; a jingoistic invocation for old times' sake of half-forgotten minor controversies. But there is more to it than that. The point is not that there was open

FIGURE 4 'Here's to Sir Henry. Right Royally Knighted He Who Has So Royally Nighted Many of My Countrymen . . .', *c.* 1896. By permission of the Folger Shakespeare Library.

disagreement about Irving's narrative of cultural and racial imperialism—like all narratives, it was contested—but that the issues were framed on both sides in precisely the same way. The full realization of a mighty Anglo-Saxon race united in its love for Shakespeare, a love personified in the greatest Shakespearean of the day, could be embraced or resisted. It could be denounced. It could even be overthrown. But it could not be ignored.

Notes

Introduction

[1] *Westminster Review* 18 (1833), p. 35.
[2] Quoted in the *Athenaeum* November 16, 1878.
[3] Review of *Henry VIII*, Princess's Theatre, London, *The Times*, May 16, 1855.
[4] *Athenaeum* April 24, 1875.
[5] '*The Taming of the Shrew* at the Haymarket,' *Bentley's Miscellany* (April 15, 1844), pp. 414–415.
[6] Charles Dunphy, a letter to Charles Kean, March 17, 1857, Y.c. 830 (2), Folger Shakespeare Library, Washington, DC. Further material from the Folger will be abbreviated 'FSL.'
[7] Emma Hamilton Smith, a letter to Ellen Kean, (1857), Art vol. d4, FSL.
[8] *Westminster Review* 37 (1842), p. 78; Charles Kean, a letter to Sir William Snow Harris, June 17, 1856, Y.c. 393 (247), FSL.
[9] Henry Irving, 'The Stage as It Is,' *The Drama: Addresses by Henry Irving* (New York: Tait, Sons & Co., 1892), p. 24.
[10] William Bodham Donne, 'Poets and Players,' *Fraser's Magazine* 44 (1851), p. 512.
[11] H. C. G. Mathew, ed. *The Gladstone Diaries* vol. V (1855–60) (Oxford: Clarendon Press, 1978), p. 222.
[12] *Era* July 13, 1895.
[13] *Westminster Review* 18 (1833), p. 35.
[14] *New York Herald* January 6, 1870.
[15] Quoted in Peter Rawlings, ed., *Americans on Shakespeare 1776–1914* (Aldershot: Ashgate Publishing, 1999), pp. 59, 282.
[16] *Report from the Select Committee on Dramatic Literature* . . . (London: House of Commons Sessional Papers, 1832) and *Report From the Select Committee on Theatrical Licenses and Regulations* . . . (London: House of Commons Sessional Papers, 1866).

Chapter 1

[1] William Charles Macready, *Macready's Reminiscences and Selections from his Diaries and Letters*, ed. Frederick Pollock (New York: Macmillan and Company, 1875), p. 27.
[2] Alan S. Downer, *The Eminent Tragedian: William Charles Macready* (Cambridge: Harvard University Press, 1966), p. 47. The biographical details here and in the following two paragraphs are taken from *Eminent Tragedian*.

[3] *Illustrated London News* March 1, 1851.
[4] See John Ripley, *Coriolanus on Stage in England and America* (Cranbury, NJ: Associated University Press), pp. 95–207.
[5] Thomas Carlyle, *On Heroes, Hero Worship and the Heroic in History* (London: ElecBooks, 2001), p. 129.
[6] Carlyle, *On Heroes*, p. 94.
[7] Carlyle, *On Heroes*, p. 130.
[8] Carlyle, *On Heroes*, p. 131.
[9] For a contrary reading of this passage, see Robert Sawyer, 'Carlyle's Influence on Shakespeare,' *Victorian Newsletter* 111 (Spring 2007), p. 4.
[10] Quoted in William Archer, *William Charles Macready* (1890; New York: Benjamin Blom, 1971), pp. 117–118.
[11] Sawyer, 'Carlyle's Influence on Shakespeare,' p. 1.
[12] *Era* January 2, 1842.
[13] Charles Lamb, 'On the Tragedies of Shakespeare, Considered with Reference to their Fitness for Stage Representation,' *The Works of Charles Lamb with a Sketch of His Life and Final Memorials*, ed. Thomas Noon Talfourd, 2 vols. (New York: Derby and Jackson, 1857), 2:351.
[14] Lamb, 'On the Tragedies of Shakespeare,' 2:352.
[15] Lamb, 'On the Tragedies of Shakespeare,' 2:351.
[16] Lamb, 'On the Tragedies of Shakespeare,' 2:351.
[17] William Hazlitt, *Characters of Shakespear's Plays* (1817; London: J. Dent and Company, 1906), p. 79.
[18] Hazlitt, *Characters of Shakespear's Plays*, p. 86.
[19] Hazlitt, *Characters of Shakespear's Plays*, p. 80.
[20] Lamb, 'On the Tragedies of Shakespeare,' 2:349.
[21] Lamb, 'On the Tragedies of Shakespeare,' 2:350.
[22] Macready, *Reminiscences*, p. 27.
[23] William Charles Macready, *William Charles Macready's Diaries, 1833–1851*, 2 vols. Edited by William Toynbee (New York: G. P. Putnam's Sons, 1912) 1:212.
[24] Macready, *Diaries*, 1:239.
[25] Macready, *Diaries*, 1:463.
[26] Macready, *Reminiscences*, p. 27.
[27] Macready, *Diaries*, 1:504.
[28] Macready, *Diaries*, 1:55.
[29] Hazlitt, *Characters of Shakespear's Plays*, p. 135.
[30] George Vandenhoff, *Leaves from an Actor's Notebook; with Reminiscences and Chit-Chat of the Green-room and the Stage, in England and America* (New York: D. Appleton and Company, 1860), p. 18.
[31] Alan S. Downer, 'Players and the Painted Stage: Nineteenth–Century Acting,' *PMLA* 61.2 (June 1946), p. 545.
[32] William Hazlitt, *A View of the English Stage; or, A Series of Dramatic Criticisms*, ed. W. Spencer Jackson (London: George Bell and Sons, 1906), p. 257.
[33] Archer, *William Charles Macready*, p. 173.
[34] See for example, Paul Kuritz, *The Making of Theatre History* (Englewood Cliffs, NJ: Prentice Hall, 1988), p. 268 and Virginia Mason Vaughan, *Othello: A Contextual History* (Cambridge: Cambridge University Press, 1996), p. 140.

[35] Quoted in Downer, 'Players on the Painted Stage,' p. 545. In *The Eminent Tragedian,* Downer explains the 'Macready Pause' was 'a slowing down of the reading of speeches to give the effect of a man thinking, particularly in the soliloquies, where Macready was often praised for making one thought seem the natural consequence of its predecessor' (p. 71).

[36] Vandenhoff, *Leaves from an Actor's Notebook,* p. 16.

[37] Macready, *Diaries,* 1:12, 1:62, 1:349.

[38] W. T. Price, *A Life of William Charles Macready* (New York: Brentanos, 1894), p. 83.

[39] Letter quoted in Theodore Martin, *Helena Faucit* (Edinburgh: William Blackwood and Sons, 1900), pp. 48–49.

[40] Macready, *Diaries,* 1:413.

[41] J. R. Planché, *The Recollections and Reflections of J.R. Planché,* 2 vols. (London: Tinsley Brothers, 1872).

[42] *Report from the Select Committee on Dramatic Literature* . . . (London: House of Commons Sessional Papers, 1832), pp. 134–135.

[43] Macready, *Diaries,* 1:307.

[44] *Morning Chronicle* May 30, 1832.

[45] *Jackson's Oxford Journal* May 3, 1836.

[46] *Examiner* May 1, 1836, p. 282.

[47] *The Times* June 30, 1836.

[48] *Examiner* May 15, 1836.

[49] Archer, *William Charles Macready,* p. 104.

[50] Downer, *Eminent Tragedian,* p. 154.

[51] Macready, *Diaries,* 1:212.

[52] *Examiner* July 23, 1837.

[53] Benjamin Webster, ed. *The Acting National Drama, Comprising Every Popular New Play, Farce, Melodrama, Opera, Burletta, Etc.* (London: Sherwood, Gilbert, and Piper, 1840), p. 4.

[54] *Morning Chronicle* September 2, 1837.

[55] Downer, *Eminent Tragedian,* p. 185.

[56] *The Times* September 25, 1837.

[57] See Jean I. Marsden, *The Re-imagined Text: Shakespeare, Adaptation, and Eighteenth-Century Literary Theory* (Lexington KY: University Press of Kentucky, 1995), pp. 83–86.

[58] See volume 9 of John Philip Kemble, *John Philip Kemble Promptbooks,* ed. Charles Harlen Shattuck. The Folger Facsimiles. 11 vols. (Charlottesville: University of Virginia Press). In asserting that Macready followed Kemble's version of the play, I rely on the research of Dennis Bartholomeusz in *The Winter's Tale in Performance in England and America, 1611–1976* (Cambridge: Cambridge University Press, 1982), p. 44.

[59] Figures taken from Archer, *William Charles Macready,* pp. 103–104.

[60] *Morning Chronicle* February 23, 1838.

[61] *The Times* October 2, 1837; *Literary Gazette* October 7, 1837; *Examiner* October 8, 1837.

[62] *Examiner* October 8, 1838.

[63] *The Times* March 31, 1838.

[64] *Morning Chronicle* April 6, 1838.
[65] Macready, *Diaries*, 1:449.
[66] *Examiner* October 22, 1837.
[67] *Morning Chronicle* October 2, 1838.
[68] *Examiner* October 22, 1837.
[69] *Morning Chronicle* October 5, 1838.
[70] Quoted in Downer, *Eminent Tragedian*, p. 166.
[71] *Morning Chronicle* May 1, 1838.
[72] *Examiner* May 13, 1838.
[73] Quoted in Downer, *Eminent Tragedian*, p. 247.
[74] Quoted in Archer, *William Charles Macready*, p. 122.
[75] *Morning Chronicle* June 11, 1839.
[76] *The Times* June 11, 1839.
[77] Samuel Taylor Coleridge 'Second Lecture,' *Coleridge's Essays and Lectures on Shakespeare and Milton: And Some Other Old Poets and Dramatists* (New York: EP Dutton, 1907), p. 404.
[78] Macready, *Diaries*, 1:438.
[79] Cited in Downer, *Eminent Tragedian*, p. 170.
[80] *The Times* January 26, 1838.
[81] *Examiner* February 4, 1838.
[82] Quoted in Archer, *William Charles Macready*, p. 113.
[83] *Morning Chronicle* March 13, 1838.
[84] *Morning Chronicle* March 22, 1838.
[85] *Morning Chronicle* March 13, 1838.
[86] *Morning Chronicle* March 13, 1838.
[87] *The Times* October 15, 1838; *Examiner* October 21, 1838; *Morning Chronicle* October 15, 1838.
[88] Quoted in Stephen Orgel, 'Introduction,' in William Shakespeare, *The Tempest* (Oxford: Oxford University Press, 1998), p. 10.
[89] *Morning Chronicle* June 4, 1839.
[90] *The Sunday Times* July 21, 1839.
[91] To accept the existence of a widespread nationalist reading of Shakespeare in the Romantic period is not to deny the existence of various politically nuanced appropriations of Shakespeare, as compellingly documented in Jonathan Bate's *Shakespearean Constitutions: Politics, Theatre, Criticism 1730–1830* (Oxford: Clarendon Press, 1989).
[92] Full inscription in Macready, *Diaries* 1:441, paraphrased in *The Times* January 26, 1838.
[93] *Morning Chronicle* June 7, 1838.
[94] Macready, *Diaries*, 1:16.
[95] *Morning Chronicle* July 22, 1839.
[96] For a discussion of burlesque as a defense of Shakespeare, and a form that similarly mobilized club culture to define a band of male bohemian defenders, see Richard Schoch's *Not Shakespeare: Bardolatry and Burlesque in the Nineteenth Century* (Cambridge: Cambridge University Press, 2002), pp. 107–150.
[97] Macready, *Diaries*, 2:11.

[98] Macready, *Diaries*, 2:129. Archer, *William Charles Macready*, p. 129.

[99] The *Satirist*, the *Age*, and *John Bull* continued to publish pointed barbs against Macready. These papers were widely described as scandal sheets.

[100] Quoted in Sybil Rosenfeld, 'The Grieve Family,' *Anatomy of an Illusion: Studies in Nineteenth-Century Scenic Design* (Amsterdam: Scheltema and Holkema, 1969), p. 41.

[101] Samuel Taylor Coleridge, *Lectures and Notes on Shakspere and Other English Poets* (London: George Bell and Sons, 1893), p. 479.

[102] *The Times* October 25, 1842.

[103] Downer, *Eminent Tragedian*, p. 242.

[104] *Era* January 2, 1842.

[105] *Morning Chronicle* January 21, 1843.

[106] *The Times* January 23, 1843.

[107] The *Post* critique is mentioned in Downer, *Eminent Tragedian*, p. 216. For evidence of Macready's restoration of the First Lord's speech, see *Mr. Macready Produces As You Like It: A Prompt-Book Study* by Charles H. Shattuck (Urbana: Beta Phi Mu, 1962), p. 27.

[108] *The Times* December 30, 1841.

[109] *Morning Chronicle* December 30, 1841.

[110] *Morning Chronicle* January 21, 1843.

[111] *The Times* February 1, 1842.

[112] On Queen Victoria's patronage of lowbrow entertainment, and the criticisms made against her for a failure to patronize the legitimate drama, see Richard Schoch, *Queen Victoria and the Theatre of her Age* (Basingstoke: Palgrave Macmillan, 2004).

[113] *Era* May 7, 1843.

[114] *The Times* October 6, 1843.

[115] *Examiner* December 25, 1841, p. 823.

[116] *Report from the Select Committee on Dramatic Literature* . . . (London: House of Commons Sessional Papers, 1832), p. 134.

[117] *The Times* June 15, 1843.

[118] *Examiner* June 17, 1843.

[119] The subscription for this statuary actually dated from the 1839 public dinner celebrating Macready's Covent Garden management, but the monies had been raised and the statue completed in time to celebrate his second management of a patent theatre. Consequently, the inscription lauded his Covent Garden management but made no reference of Drury Lane.

[120] See Downer, *The Eminent Tragedian*, pp. 253–310; Richard Moody, *The Astor Place Riot* (Bloomington: Indiana University Press, 1958); Bruce A. McConachie, *Melodramatic Formations: American Theatre and Society, 1820–1870* (Iowa City: University of Iowa Press, 1992), pp. 144–155; Dennis Berthold, 'The Astor Place Riot and Melville's 'The Two Temples,' *American Literature* 71.3 (September 1999), pp. 429–461.

[121] *Examiner* November 6, 1836.

[122] *Examiner* March 5, 1837.

[123] Macready, *Diaries*, 1:358.

[124] *The Times* April 4, 1846.

[125] Michael Kimmel, 'Birth of the Self-made Man,' *The Masculinity Studies Reader*, eds. Rachael Adams and David Savran (Malden, MA: Blackwell Publishers, Inc., 2002), p. 146.

[126] Macready, *Diaries*, 2:408.

[127] Quoted in Downer *Eminent Tragedian*, p. 298.

[128] *The Times* December 8, 1848.

[129] *Examiner* June 2, 1849.

[130] *The Times* March 29, 1849.

[131] Macready, *Diaries*, 2:431.

[132] *The Times* October 9, 1849.

[133] *The Times* October 25, 1849.

[134] *The Times* October 29, 1850.

[135] Julia Thomas, 'Bidding for the Bard: Shakespeare, the Victorians, and the Auction of the Birthplace,' *Nineteenth-Century Contexts* (30.3), p. 219.

[136] Macready, *Reminiscences*, p. 651.

[137] Macready, *Diaries*, 2:475–476.

[138] *The Times* February 27, 1851.

[139] George Henry Lewes, *On Actors and the Art of Acting* (London: Smith, Elder and Company, 1875) p. 41.

[140] *The Spectator* 12 (1849), 966–967. Quoted in Downer, 'Players and the Painted Stage,' p. 545.

[141] Westland Marston, *Our Recent Actors: Being Recollections Critical, and in Many Cases, Personal of Late Distinguished Performers of Both Sexes.* 2 vols. (Boston: Roberts Brothers) 1:79.

[142] *Examiner* March 8, 1851, p. 151.

[143] *The Times* February 24, 1851.

[144] Frederick Pollock, *Remembrances*, 2 vols. (London: Macmillan and Company, 1887) 1:292. Pollock wrote that 2,000 applications had been made for tickets.

[145] *Examiner* March 8, 1851.

[146] *Examiner* March 8, 1851.

[147] Quoted in Downer, *Eminent Tragedian*, p. 252.

[148] Charles Knight, *The Comedies, Histories, Tragedies and Poems of William Shakespeare.* 8 Volumes (London: Charles Knight, 1851) 1. Front matter.

[149] Quoted in Downer, *Eminent Tragedian*, p. 340.

Chapter 2

[1] 'The Old Bowery, A Reminiscence of New York Plays and Acting Fifty Years Ago,' *Boston Herald* August 16, 1885, in *Collected Writings of Walt Whitman: Prose Works 1892*, ed. Floyd Stovall (New York: New York University Press, 1963), 2:597.

[2] Shattuck was a professor in both the English and Theatre departments at the University of Illinois at Urbana, where he directed sixty-five productions between 1943 and 1963. His contributions to the study of Shakespeare in performance were recognized in his election to the presidency of the Shakespeare Association of America in 1979.

[3] Shakespeare in performance studies today raises fundamental questions about what it means to be 'faithful' to Shakespeare's texts or about what interpretive 'authority' is being invoked in a particular production. See, for example, W. B. Worthen, *Shakespeare and the Authority of Performance* (Cambridge: Cambridge University Press, 1997). For discussions of the actor's body being in play in complex ways, see Ellen Donkin's 'Mrs. Siddons Looks Back in Anger: Feminist Historiography for Eighteenth-Century British Theatre,' in *Critical Theory and Performance,* eds. Janelle G. Reinelt and Joseph R. Roach (Ann Arbor: University of Michigan Press, 1992), pp. 276–290, and my discussion of Elizabeth Vestris's cross-dressed Oberon in 1840, in *Our Moonlight Revels: A Midsummer Night's Dream in the Theatre* (Iowa City: University of Iowa Press, 1997), pp. 92–97.

[4] Benjamin McArthur discusses Booth's pursuit of respectability in establishing the Players in his *Actors and American Culture 1880–1920* (Iowa City: University of Iowa Press, 1984), pp. 76–83. Lisa Merrill explores the relationship between Booth and critic Adam Badeau in her 'Appealing to the Passions: Homoerotic desire and Nineteenth Century Criticism,' in Kim Marra and Robert A. Schanke, eds, *Staging Desire: Queer Readings in American Theatre History* (Ann Arbor: University of Michigan Press, 2002), pp. 242–244. Thomas Postlewait offers insights about Lincoln's assassination and Whitman's readings in his 'The Hieroglyphic Stage: American Theatre and Society, Post-Civil War to 1945,' in Don B. Wilmeth and Christopher Bigsby, eds. *The Cambridge History of American Theatre, Volume Two: 1870–1945* (Cambridge: Cambridge University Press, 1999), pp. 107–111.

[5] Shattuck, *The Hamlet of Edwin Booth* (Urbana, IL, Chicago, and London: University of Illinois Press, 1969), p. v.

[6] Leigh Woods, 'Actors' Biography and Mythmaking: The Example of Edmund Kean,' in *Interpreting the Theatrical Past,* eds. Thomas Postlewait and Bruce McConachie (Iowa City: University of Iowa Press, 1989), pp. 230–247.

[7] A recent study generally germane to my purposes is Amy Cook's 'Interplay: The Method and Potential of a Cognitive Scientific Approach to Theatre,' *Theatre Journal* 59:4 (December 2007), pp. 584–86. On presence in live performance, see David Krasner and David Z. Saltz, eds. *Staging Philosophy* (Ann Arbor: University of Michigan Press, 2006).

[8] Daniel J. Watermeier followed Shattuck (his mentor) with his informatively edited *Edwin Booth's Performances: The Mary Isabella Stone Commentaries* (Ann Arbor and London: UMI Research Press, 1990), which includes her accounts of Booth's Hamlet between 1879 and 1884.

[9] By the 1860s and 1870s, the practice of lowering the house lights throughout a performance was a new factor contributing to a relatively 'private' theatre experience.

[10] Shattuck, *Hamlet,* p. 62.

[11] Shattuck, *Hamlet,* p. xxvi.

[12] Shattuck, *Hamlet,* pp. xxv, xxvi.

[13] For the larger picture, see Shannon Jackson's *Professing Performance: Theatre in the Academy from Philology to Performativity* (Cambridge and New York: Cambridge University Press, 2004). See also James Bulman's introduction to his edited volume *Shakespeare, Theory and Performance* (London and New York: Routledge,

1996) and especially essays by Worthen, Richard Paul Knowles, and Cary M. Mazer. For a critique of the ahistoric 'variorum' mode of scholarship on Shakespearean performance, see my review of Marvin Rosenberg's *The Masks of Macbeth* in *Journal of English and Germanic Philology* 78 (1979), pp. 550–555. Shattuck spoke to me of wanting his 'Shakespeare straight,' which he believed he had found in Glen Byam Shaw's productions at Stratford-upon-Avon in the 1950s. See his 'Setting Shakespeare Free?', *Journal of Aesthetic Education* 17:4 (Winter 1983), pp. 107–123. He ends this essay with a call for productions in which the plays and performances are 'perfectly fused,' where 'Shakespeare's mind and art and language, and all that he intended, and all that we should ever expect from it are simply *there*' (p. 122).

[14] Shattuck (*Hamlet,* p. xvi) mentions some of these qualities as appealing to audiences whose sights needed raising.

[15] Horace Traubel, *With Walt Whitman in Camden* (New York: Appleton, 1908), 1:356.

[16] Clement Scott, *Daily Telegraph* (London), November 8, 1880: 'The days of the old classical school are dead and buried . . .' Booth looked as if he has just 'stepped out of some old theatrical print in the days of elocution and before the era of zeal and natural acting.'

[17] Cited in Eleanor Ruggles, *Prince of Players, Edwin Booth* (New York: W.W. Norton, 1953), p. 287.

[18] Booth to Winter, February 24, 1884, in Daniel J. Watermeier, ed., *Between Actor and Critic: Selected Letters of Edwin Booth and William Winter* (Princeton: Princeton University Press, 1971), p. 256.

[19] Horace Howard Furness, *A New Variorum Edition of Shakespeare: Othello* (New York: J. B. Lippincott & Co., 1886), Booth's notes, pp. 146, 214.

[20] Mowbray Morris, review of *Othello,* Lyceum Theatre, London, *Macmillan Magazine* [1881], in Morris's *Essays in Theatrical Criticism* (London: Remington & Co., 1882), pp. 101–102. See also Charles H. Shattuck, *Shakespeare on the American Stage, from the Hallams to Edwin Booth* (Washington, D. C.: The Folger Shakespeare Library, 1976), pp. 140–142.

[21] Ellen Terry, *The Story of My Life* (New York: Doubleday, Page, & Co., 1909), pp. 224–225.

[22] For an acute assessment of the sentimentality in Booth's Lear, see Otto Braham's comments, cited in Shattuck, *Hamlet,* pp. 298–299.

[23] Watermeier, *Stone Commentaries,* p. 147, staging dated 1883.

[24] Edward Bulwer-Lytton, *Richelieu, or the Conspiracy,* in *British Plays of the Nineteenth Century,* ed. J. O. Bailey (New York: Odyssey Press, 1966), p. 102.

[25] The recording is available in a CD set from Naxos AudioBooks, entitled *Great Historical Shakespeare Recordings and Other Miscellany* (NA220012).

[26] Richard Lockridge, *Darling of Misfortune, Edwin Booth* (New York and London: The Century Co., 1932), pp. 338–340.

[27] In Eugene O'Neill's autobiographical *Long Day's Journey into Night,* James Tyrone (modeled on James O'Neill, Sr.), tells Edmund (Eugene) that in 1874 in Chicago he played opposite Booth in several roles, including Othello to Booth's Iago. Tyrone/O'Neill says that Booth, watching from the wings, commented to the stage manager, 'That young man [Tyrone/O'Neill] plays Othello better

than I ever did.' *Long Day's Journey into Night* (New Haven and London: Yale University Press, 1956), p. 150.

[28] William Winter, *Life and Art of Edwin Booth* (New York, London: Macmillan and Co. 1893), p. 101.

[29] Winter, *Edwin Booth,* pp. 101–102.

[30] Winter, *Edwin Booth,* pp. 45–51, provides a detailed description; see also Shattuck, *Hamlet,* pp. 65–66.

[31] Minutes of the first meeting of the Players, December 31, 1888 (New York: n. p. 1908), pp. 5–6, cited in McArthur, *Actors and American Culture,* p. 97.

[32] Asia Booth Clarke, *Booth Memorials: Passages, Incidents, and Anecdotes in the Life of Junius Brutus Booth* (New York: W. W. Carleton, 1866), pp. 41–55; Stephen Archer, *Junius Brutus Booth* (Carbondale and Edwardsville: Southern Illinois University Press, 1992), pp. 24–46; Stanley Kimmel, *Mad Booths of Maryland* (Indianapolis: Bobbs-Merrill, 1940), pp. 24–26.

[33] Asia Clarke claimed that Junius and Mary had married on January 18, 1821 'at the residence of the Hon. Mrs. Chambers' (*Memorials,* p. 64). Later biographers suspect that Asia was attempting to legitimize the relationship. It would not have been a recognized marriage in any case. In Asia's introduction, she refers to it as a 'boyish *mésalliance*' (p. viii).

[34] Archer, *Junius Brutus Booth,* pp. 22, 67, 196–197. On Junius' financial support to Adelaide and Richard, see the same work, n. 9, pp. 318–319.

[35] Shattuck, *Hallams to Edwin Booth,* p. 44.

[36] 'Things Theatrical,' *Spirit of the Times,* March 11, 1848.

[37] Thomas Gould, *The Tragedian: an Essay on the Histrionic Genius of Junius Brutus Booth* (New York: Hurd & Houghton, 1868), p. 60.

[38] Clarke, *The Elder and the Younger Booth* (Cambridge, MA: J. R. Osgood, 1881; Boston: American Actor Series, Vol. 5, 1982, Laurence Hutton, ed.), p. 119. Edwin's middle name, Thomas, was after actor Thomas Flynn, another friend of Junius's.

[39] Clarke, *Booth Memorials,* p. 110; Kimmel, *Mad Booths,* p. 41.

[40] See Booth's letter in Archer, *Junius Brutus Booth,* pp. 126–127; Kimmel, *Mad Booths,* pp. 54–55. For his erratic behavior thereafter in 1830s and 1840s, see the various reports cited by Archer, *Junius Brutus Booth,* pp. 160–176.

[41] *Spirit of the Times* April 5, 1851.

[42] Two brief, anonymously authored biographies of Booth had been published in about 1817; see Archer, *Junius Brutus Booth,* pp. 41–42.

[43] Thomas Ford, *The Actor; Or, A Peep behind the Curtain. Being Passages in the Lives of Booth and Some of his Contemporaries* (New York: Wm. H. Graham, 1846), p. 179.

[44] See, for example, in Clarke, *The Elder and the Younger Booth,* pp. 69, 74, 89, 114–115.

[45] Junius's father Richard wanted Junius to study law and provided for what Asia Clarke called a 'classical education' (*Booth Memorials,* p. 16), and what Ford called 'a finished education' (*The Actor,* p. 6), but where is not known. Junius's own library included Greek and Latin authors, and Richard, in his declining years, worked on a translation of the *Aeneid.*

[46] Clarke, *Booth Memorials,* p. 80.

[47] Ford, *The Actor*, p. 95. Asia remembered rustic shelves on the farm bearing the Bible, the Qu'ran, Plutarch and other classical authors, *The Divine Comedy*, and works by Shakespeare, Racine, Byron, Shelley, Keats, and Coleridge. Clarke, *The Elder and the Younger Booth*, p. 69; *Booth Memorials*, p. 111; Asia describing the farm, *Booth Memorials*, p. 74.

[48] Clarke, *Booth Memorials*, pp. 88–89; *The Elder and the Younger Booth*, pp. 76–78. The dispute over whether he performed it in French is summarized in Archer, *Junius Brutus Booth*, pp. 108 and 304, n.8.

[49] On their education, see Clarke, *Booth Memorials*, pp. 131–132, 159; Kimmel, *Mad Booths*, pp. 70–71, 55, 58,78.

[50] Winter, *Edwin Booth*, p. 3.

[51] Clarke, *The Elder and the Younger Booth*, p. 121.

[52] Kimmel, *Mad Booths*, pp. 68–71.

[53] See for example Clarke, *Booth Memorials*, p. 114. Clarke dedicated her biography of her father to her mother.

[54] Edwin Booth, 'Junius Brutus Booth,' in Brander Matthews and Laurence Hutton, eds. *Actors and Actresses of Great Britain and the United States* 5 vols. (New York: Cassell & Co., 1886), 3:99.

[55] Based on Archer's 'Appendix of Recorded Performances,' *Junius Brutus Booth*, pp. 271–278; see also pp. 238–239.

[56] E. C. Stedman, in the circle of journalists who knew Booth well, writes of young Edwin listening from his father's dressing room, his father rarely permitting him to watch him act. See 'Edwin Booth,' *Atlantic Monthly*, May 1866, p. 587.

[57] Clarke, *The Elder and the Younger Booth*, p. 125; Colley Cibber, *Richard III*, in *The Dramatic Works of Colley Cibber* (London: Rivington & Sons, 1777), 1:8–17 (1.i). This version, first played in 1700, renders Richard a more noxious villain and was widely regarded as superior to Shakespeare's play in its melodramatic compactness. Samuel Phelps restored much of Shakespeare's original in 1845 but returned to Cibber. Edwin was still using a Cibberized version in London in 1876, tried Shakespeare's play in 1877–78, but went back to Cibber for his 1886–87 tour. See Shattuck, *The Shakespeare Promptbooks* (Urbana and London: University of Illinois Press, 1965), entries 59, 69, 66, 74, and 79.

[58] Edwin Booth, 'Junius Brutus Booth,' *Actors and Actresses*, 3:101.

[59] Clarke, *The Elder and the Younger Booth*, pp. 129–130.

[60] Clarke, *The Elder and the Younger Booth*, p. 131.

[61] Booth to Elizabeth Stoddard, March 12, 1863, in the *New York Herald*, November 1, 1863, magazine section, cited in Shattuck, *Hamlet*, p. 9.

[62] Shattuck, *Hamlet*, pp. 48–50; see also p. 28 for a Badeau letter of 1860 lecturing Booth on drinking, smoking and—apparently—venereal disease.

[63] *The Transcript*, April 21, 1857; *The Traveller*, May 2, 1857.

[64] Shattuck, *Hamlet*, p. 12.

[65] George C.D. Odell, *Annals of the New York Stage* (New York: Columbia University Press, 1931), 8:14–15; Lockridge, *Darling of Misfortune*, p. 68.

[66] Badeau (1831–95) served as General Grant's secretary during the Civil War. He wrote the three-volume *Military History of Ulysses S. Grant* (1868–81), *Grant in Peace* (1887), and served as Grant's amanuensis for his memoirs.

[67] *The Albion*, April 1857, cited in Kimmel, *Mad Booths*, p. 140.

[68] *Herald*, April 6, 1857.
[69] Adam Badeau, 'American Art,' in *The Vagabond* (New York: Rudd and Carleton, 1859), p. 121.
[70] Badeau, 'Edwin Booth,' *The Vagabond*, pp. 288, 287.
[71] Badeau, 'American Art,' *The Vagabond*, p. 121.
[72] Badeau to Booth, June 15, 1857, Hampden-Booth Library, The Players, New York.
[73] Shattuck, *Hamlet*, pp. 21–29, gives much attention to Badeau as a source for Booth's literary and artistic refinement. Some thirty-six letters from Badeau to Booth survive at The Players.
[74] William Hazlitt, *The Complete Works* (London: J.M. Dent and Sons, 1930), 4:232–257.
[75] J. W. von Goethe, *Wilhelm Meister's Apprenticeship*, trans. Thomas Carlyle (New York: P.F. Collier & Son, 1917), Vol. 14, Book IV, Chapter 13, excerpts from paragraphs 17, 18.
[76] Badeau, 'Edwin Booth. On and Off the Stage,' *McClure's Magazine* 1 (August 1893), p. 259; Shattuck, *Hamlet*, p. 25, citing a Badeau letter of September 12, 1863 to James Harrison Wilson, Special Collections, Princeton University Library.
[77] Badeau, 'American Art,' *The Vagabond*, p. 122.
[78] Shattuck, *Hamlet*, p. 29. Shattuck registers dismay at the sexual possessiveness he sees in Badeau's letters to Booth and is appalled that Booth tolerated it or that he might have been using Badeau.
[79] Merrill, 'Appealing to the Passions,' *Staging Desire*, especially pp. 242–244. One wishes for more on how this influenced Badeau's imaging of Booth. The relationship between Oakes and Forrest is explored in Merrill's essay and in Ginger Strand's 'My Noble Spartacus: Edwin Forrest on the Nineteenth Century Stage,' in *Passing Performances: Queer Readings of Leading Players in American Theater History*, ed. Robert A. Schanke and Kim Marra (Ann Arbor: University of Michigan Press, 1998).
[80] Odell, *Annals*, 7:56.
[81] Devlin letter to Booth, August 24, 1859, in L. Terry Oggel, ed., *The Letters and Notebooks of Mary Devlin Booth* (New York, Westport, CT, and London: Greenwood Press, 1987), pp. 10–11. This and other of her letters are in the Billy Rose Theatre Collection, New York Public Library for the Performing Arts (hereafter NYPL TC). On Cushman, see Joseph Leach, *Bright Particular Star: The Life and Times of Charlotte Cushman* (New Haven and London: Yale University Press, 1970), p. 306. Devlin was a favorite of Cushman and developed a close, perhaps intimate relationship with Emma Crowe (married to Cushman's nephew) to judge from Devlin's letter to Crowe of about November 10, 1862. Oggel, *Letters*, pp. 84–85.
[82] Devlin letter to Booth, undated, NYPL TC, cited in Shattuck, *Hamlet*, p. 31.
[83] Mary's letter to Edwin, February 12, 1860, in Oggel, *Letters*, pp. 36–37. See also Edwina Booth Grossman, *Edwin Booth: Recollections by his daughter and letters to her and his friends* (London: Osgood, McIlvaine & Co., 1894), pp. 27, 28. As Oggel explains (*Letters*, pp. xv–xvi), Grossman cut, edited, and combined letters.

[84] Grossman, *Letters*, p. 25. Her source would have been her father; Edwina was only two months old when her mother died.
[85] Cushman to Crow, February 7, 1863, Charlotte Cushman papers, Box 2, 530, Library of Congress. See also Leach, *Bright Particular Star*, p. 323.
[86] Oggel, *Letters*, pp. 45–46. Mary's letter to Booth, March 19, 1860, NYPL TC. Cousins was the author of *Du vrai, du beau, et du bien* (1836). This was a revision of his 1818 Sorbonne lectures, in which he spoke of the need for 'religion for the sake of religion, of morals for the sake of morals, and art-for-art's sake.' See René Wellek, *A History of Modern Criticism: 1750–1950, Volume 3, The Age of Transition* (New Haven and London: Yale University Press, 1965), p. 30.
[87] Oggel, *Letters*, p. 31, Mary to Edwin, January 24, 1860, NYPL TC.
[88] Oggel, *Letters*, Mary to Edwin, February 11, 1860, pp. 35–36; Grossmann, *Letters*, pp. 27–28.
[89] See his fervent letter to Mrs. Richard F. Cary, February 9, 1865, in Grossman, *Letters*, pp. 168–170.
[90] *Boston Advertiser*, September 12 and 21, 1860.
[91] *New York Herald*, November 29 and 30, 1860; Odell, *Annals*, 7:314–315.
[92] Winter, *Edwin Booth*, p. 87; Leach, *Bright Particular Star*, p. 305; Winter, *Edwin Booth*, p. 185, discusses this characterization as an 'ancient' view in a customary defense of Booth.
[93] See Oggel, *Letters*, p. 78, Mary to Emma Cushman, May 11, 1862: '. . . to make any money now in England is out of the question. The prejudice against Americans is very great—at this present time.'
[94] Katherine Goodale, *Behind the Scenes with Edwin Booth* (Boston: Houghton Mifflin, 1931), p. 96.
[95] Mrs. Thomas Bailey Aldrich provides an account of the first meeting of the Stoddards and the Booths in September 1862 and describes the salon in her *Crowding Memories* (Boston: Houghton Mifflin Co., 1920), pp. 12–24. The intermediary was James Lorimer Graham, whom the Booths had met in England in the previous winter. Oggel, *Letters*, p. xxvii.
[96] *New York Herald*, September 20; Odell, *Annals*, 7:475–476.
[97] Aldrich, *Crowding Memories*, pp. 30–35
[98] Aldrich, *Crowding Memories*, pp. 35. Booth's discovery of this letter resulted in a break with the Stoddards.
[99] Mary's letter to Elizabeth Stoddard, January 19, 1863, makes clear that Edwin had yet to control his 'demon.' Oggel, *Letters*, pp. 98–99.
[100] Shattuck and Oggel are eager to defend Booth. Oggel, *Letters*, pp. xxix–xxx, reproduces the two letters to make the case that Booth could not have known of Mary's impending death soon enough to be at her side on the 20th. Shattuck refers to other optimistic letters from her doctor (*Hamlet*, p. 49). Still, Edwin's drinking was a contributory factor.
[101] Booth's letter to Badeau, June 6, 1863, in Grossmann, *Letters*, p. 149.
[102] Both are reproduced in Aldrich, *Crowding Memories*, pp. 39–40. In 1883, Booth had his friend, painter Eastman Johnson, do a portrait of her from a photograph. It is now in the National Heritage Museum, Lexington, MA.
[103] In 1882 Winter warned him about excessive drinking. See Watermeier, *Between Actor and Critic*, p. 209.

[104] A photograph of the bust, now at The Players Club, is reproduced in Winter, *Edwin Booth,* opposite p. 104; see also Shattuck, *Hamlet,* p. 52, citing Booth's letter to Badeau, July 30, 1863, NYPL TC.

[105] Boston *Courier,* November 12, 1863.

[106] *New York Herald,* September 22, 1863; Odell, *Annals,* 7:553–554.

[107] Odell, *Annals,* 7:561–562; Oggel, *Letters,* pp. 113–114: Notebook entry for November 10, 1860.

[108] *Spirit of the Times,* May 21, 1864.

[109] *New York Herald* and *New York Times,* November 28, 1864, cited in Odell, *Annals* 7:640.

[110] Badeau, 'Edwin Booth,' in *The Vagabond,* p. 288.

[111] On Kemble and Booth's readings of 'father,' see Winter, *Shakespeare on the Stage, 1st Series* (1911; New York: Benjamin Blom, 1969), pp. 345–347. That Booth fell to his knees on 'father' is clear from J. B. Pittman's handwritten direction in the 1879 Winter promptbook edition, Furness Memorial Shakespeare Library, p. 29. On Kemble's kneeling, see James Boaden, *Memoirs of the Life of John Philip Kemble* (London: Longman et al., 1825), 1:98. On the locket, see Shattuck, *Hamlet,* pp. 5–6, 124, 142. Winter does not mention the image of Junius but says that Booth's practice varied. Sometimes the picture was in a locket worn by the Queen, sometimes on the wall, and sometimes no actual picture was used (*Edwin Booth,* pp. 346–347).

[112] John Doran, *'Their Majesties Servants': Annals of the English Stage, from Thomas Betterton to Edmund Kean* (Philadelphia: David MacKay, 1890), 2:306.

[113] William Curtis, 'Editor's Easy Chair,' *Harper's New Monthly Magazine* 30 (April 1865), pp. 674–675.

[114] Letter from Booth to Badeau, October 14, 1864, Folger Shakespeare Library, Y.c. 215 (16).

[115] Curtis, *Harper's,* April 1865, pp. 674–675.

[116] Aldrich, *Crowding Memories,* p. 61.

[117] Winter, *Edwin Booth,* pp. 43–44n, citing an 1874 manuscript note signed 'E. B.'

[118] David Herbert Donald, *Lincoln* (New York: Simon & Schuster, 1996), pp. 512–513, 528.

[119] Donald, *Lincoln,* p. 514.

[120] Donald, *Lincoln,* pp. 15, 337.

[121] Letter of Booth to Emma Carey, November 11, 1864, NYPL TC.

[122] Noah Brooks, *Washington D. C. in Lincoln's Time,* ed. Herbert Mitgang (1895; Athens: University of Georgia Press, 1989), pp. 221–224; *The Evening Star,* April 14, 1865; James Ford Rhodes, *History of the Civil War 1861–1865* (New York: Macmillan, 1917), pp. 436–437. Nast's print was published in *Harper's Weekly,* May 20, 1865.

[123] The literature on the assassination and the trial is vast. A basic summary of the shooting, accompanied by Mathew Brady's photographs of the original theatre, is in George J. Olszewski, *Restoration of Ford's Theatre* (Washington, D.C.: U.S. Department of Interior, National Park Service, 1963), pp. 53–60; see also Donald, *Lincoln,* pp. 585–587, 594–599. Michael W. Kauffman doubts the story that was Booth tripped up by 'Old Glory' and broke his leg in the leap; he thinks

it happened later. See his *American Brutus: John Wilkes Booth and the Lincoln Conspiracies* (New York: Random House, 2004), pp. 272–274.

[124] Booth's Diary, Lincoln Museum, Ford's Theatre. Kauffman reproduces it in *American Brutus,* pp. 399–400; see also pp. 271–272. Albert Furtwangler offers a view of the assassination in the light of tyrannicide in the history of drama in *Assassin on Stage: Brutus, Hamlet, and the Death of Lincoln* (Urbana: University of Illinois Press, 1991).

[125] Donald, *Lincoln,* p. 588.

[126] Reward Poster for the capture of John Wilkes Booth and accomplices, Smithsonian American Museum of Art.

[127] 'Besides this Duncan/ Hath borne his faculties so meek, hath been/ So clear in his great office, that his virtues /Will plead like angels, trumpet-tongued against /The deep damnation of his taking–off. . . .' (*Macbeth,* 1.7.16–25).

[128] James L. Swanson, and Daniel R. Weinberg, *Lincoln's Assassins: Their Trial and Execution* (New York: William Morrow, 2006); see color reproductions, pp. 55, 57.

[129] Booth letters to Henry C. Jarrett, April 15, 1865 and Badeau, April 16, 1865, in Asia Booth Clarke, *John Wilkes Booth, a Sister's Memoir,* ed. Terry Alford (Jackson: University Press of Mississippi, 1996), pp. 112–113. Booth letter to James Lorimer Graham, mid-April 1865, Heritage Auction Galleries, 3500 Maple Avenue, Dallas, TX.

[130] *The Chicago Tribune,* April 25, 1865 (headed 'From the *New York Times*'); and 'Gen. Badeau's Letter,' *The Washington Post,* November 28, 1886. These sources, which scholars have not noted heretofore, provide the earliest known of several versions of the story. My summary of the incident derives from Badeau's account, the most detailed and, I think, most reliable version. Biographers usually cite the 1909 'Edwin Booth and Lincoln,' *Century Magazine* 77 (April 1909), pp. 919–920, which contains Robert Lincoln's letter to editor Richard Watson Gilder recounting the incident, but in less detail. The least precise version is in William Bispham's 'Memories and Letters of Edwin Booth,' *Century Illustrated Magazine* 47.1 (November 1893), p. 133. My dating of the incident at about a month before the April *Tribune* story derives from the fact that Robert told Badeau the story shortly after Robert had arrived in Washington, D. C., at which time he and Badeau traveled to Grant's headquarters at City Point, VA, with President Lincoln. This would have been on March 24; see Donald, *Lincoln,* p. 571.

[131] Badeau, *Washington Post,* November 28, 1886.

[132] Charles Bailey Seymour, 'Dramatic Feuilleton,' *New York Saturday Press,* December 30, 1865 and January 6, 1866; *New York Herald,* January 3, 1866.

[133] Odell, 8:19–20; see also Odell for Booth's New York performances in the 1866–67 season: 8:146–147, 215.

[134] Goodale, *Behind the Scenes,* pp. 176–178, describes a similar reception in San Francisco in 1887.

[135] Stedman, *Atlantic Monthly,* May 1866, p. 589.

[136] Stedman, *Atlantic Monthly,* May 1866, pp. 585–587; 585; 590.

[137] See Giles Fauconnier and Mark Turner, *The Way We Think: Conceptual Blending and the Mind's Hidden Complexities* (New York: Basic Books, 2002), especially Chapter 3, and on the kind of blending that underlies perception in the theatre,

pp. 266–267. See also Bruce McConachie, 'Falsifiable Theories for Theatre and Performance Studies,' *Theatre Journal* 59.4 (December 2007), pp. 556–561. Cook (see note 7) provides many citations of important works in the field.

[138] Mark Antony De Wolfe How, ed., *Memories of a Hostess: A Chronicle of Eminent Friendships Drawn Chiefly from the Diaries of Mrs. James T. Fields* (Boston: Atlantic Monthly Press, 1922), p. 199.

[139] Winter, *Edwin Booth,* pp. 42–43, 271.

[140] Winter, *Edwin Booth,* p. 42.

[141] Odell, *Annals,* 8:567–568.

[142] Clarke manuscript, notes on 5.2, column 186, Folger Shakespeare Library. See also Shattuck, *Hallams to Booth,* pp. 142–145, and *Hamlet,* chapter 6, *passim.*

[143] *Chicago Tribune,* April 24 and 26, 1879; Ruggles, *Prince of Players,* pp. 260–261.

[144] Clarke, *Sister's Memoir,* p. 119; Lockridge's biography is *Darling of Misfortune;* 'Child of Tragedy' is a running head of Book Five, Chapter 1 in Kimmel's *Mad Booths*; Clara Morris, *Life on the Stage* (New York: McClure, Phillips, & Co., 1901), p. 162.

[145] David S. Reynolds, *Walt Whitman's America: A Cultural Biography* (New York: Vintage Books, 1996), pp. 440–443.

[146] 'Death of Abraham Lincoln, Lecture deliver'd in New York, April 14, 1879, Philadelphia 1880, and Boston, '81,' in Floyd Stovall, ed. *Collected Writings of Walt Whitman: Prose Works* (New York: New York University Press, 1963–64), 2:497–509. Stovall's text is a collation of various versions, performed and printed, though he does not draw on Whitman's very similar article, 'Poetry today in America—Shakespere—The Future,' published in the *North American Review* (February 1881). See Whitman's proofs, Folger Shakespeare Library, which my comments reflect.

[147] Hamlin Garland (1860–1940) cited in Shattuck, *Hamlet,* p. 304, from a typescript of a Garland lecture, Garland Collection, University of Southern California Library.

[148] John Rankin Towse, *Sixty Years of Theatre* (New York: Funk and Wagnall's, 1916), p. 180.

Chapter 3

[1] Edward Gordon Craig, 'Preface' to *Ellen Terry and Her Secret Self* (London: Sampson Low, 1932), pp. vii–viii.

[2] Ellen Terry, *The Story of My Life* (n.p.: Dodo Press reprint, n.d.; 1908), p. 45.

[3] Terry, *Story,* p. 69.

[4] Terry writes: 'Mr Godwin, the architect and archaeologist, was living in Bristol when Kate and I were at the Theatre Royal, and we used to go to his house for some of the Shakespeare readings in which our Bristol friends asked us to take part. This house, with its Persian rugs, beautiful furniture, its organ, which for the first time I learned to love, its sense of design in every detail, was a revelation to me, and the talk of its master and mistress made me *think.*' (*Story,* p. 39) The romantic, aesthetic and cerebral are conflated in a characteristically enveloping response.

[5] Terry, *Story*, p. 4.

[6] Other members of the deliberately diverse and inclusive Stratford Hall of Fame are: Kenneth Branagh, Judi Dench, Leonardo DiCaprio, Charles Dickens, David Garrick, Ben Jonson, Akira Kurosawa, Laurence Olivier, Paul Robeson, Patrick Stewart, David Tennant, and Sam Wanamaker.

[7] Faucit and Kemble's accounts of playing Juliet can be found respectively in Helena Faucit (Lady Martin), *On Some of Shakespeare's Female Characters* (Edinburgh and London: Blackwood, 1885), p. 90, and *Records of a Girlhood*, 3 vols. (London: Bentley, 1878), 2: 7–16, 59.

[8] On being asked for an autograph, Macready had spotted Faucit's own name on the same page, newly changed to Helena. He saw the gesture as proof of the 'conceit and arrogance attributed to her.' Macready, *The Journal of William Charles Macready, 1832–1851*, ed. J. C. Trewin (London: Longmans, 1967), p. 240.

[9] Terry, *Story*, p. 12.

[10] Terry, *Story*, p. 14.

[11] Terry, *Story*, p. 40.

[12] At Sadler's Wells, Samuel Phelps was engaged in a similar proselytizing activity, albeit with a different audience demographic in mind. See Jim Davis and Victor Emeljanow, *Reflecting the Audience: London Theatre-going, 1840–1880* (Hatfield: University of Hertfordshire Press, 2001).

[13] 'Drama,' *Daily News*, October 16, 1856.

[14] 'Public Amusements,' *Lloyd's Weekly Newspaper*, April 12, 1863. *Reynolds's Newspaper*'s notice of Terry's appearance on the same day, notes that with it, she 'added fresh laurels to those which she so deservedly wears.'

[15] 'Drama. Princess's,' *Daily News*, June 22, 1863.

[16] 'Public Amusements: "Othello" and "Romeo and Juliet" at the Princess's Theatre,' *Reynolds's Newspaper*, June 28, 1863.

[17] Terry, *Story*, p. 59.

[18] Terry, *Story*, pp. 59–60.

[19] 'The New Juliet,' *The Era*, December 15, 1867.

[20] 'The London Theatres,' *The Era*, October 27, 1867.

[21] 'Miss Kate Terry's Farewell of the Stage,' *The Era*, October 6, 1867. Kate Terry's marriage was recorded in, amongst other papers, *Jackson's Oxford Journal*, October 26, 1867; 'The Ladies' Column,' in the *Manchester Times*, October 26, 1867; *Penny Illustrated Paper*, October 26, 1867; *The Examiner*, October 19, 1867; *Liverpool Mercury*, October 21, 1867; and the *Pall Mall Gazette*, October 19, 1867.

[22] Terry, *Story*, p. 68.

[23] Terry, *Story*, p. 66.

[24] 'New Queen's Theatre,' *The Times*, December 30, 1867.

[25] Terry, *Story*, p. 73.

[26] Michael Holroyd, *A Strange Eventful History: Ellen Terry, Henry Irving, and their Remarkable Families* (London: Chatto & Windus, 2008), p. 68.

[27] Terry, *Story*, p. 76.

[28] Terry, *Story*, p. 103.

[29] Terry, *Story*, p. 35. The pairing of these roles might seem perverse, but it was a pairing which Helena Faucit also produced in her writing on Rosalind in

On Some of Shakespeare's Female Characters (London and Edinburgh: Blackwood, 1885), pp. 225–285.

[30] Terry, *Story*, p. 86.
[31] Terry, *Story*, p. 96.
[32] Terry, *Story*, p. 178.
[33] Terry, *Story*, p. 289.
[34] Terry, *Story*, p. 295.
[35] Holroyd, *Strange Eventful History*, p. 193.
[36] Ellen Terry, *Four Lectures on Shakespeare* (London: Hopkinson, 1932), p. 97.
[37] Terry, *Story*, pp. 96–97.
[38] 'The Merchant of Venice,' *Pall Mall Gazette*, April 20, 1875.
[39] 'The Man About Town,' *The Sporting Gazette*, April 24, 1875.
[40] 'The Merchant of Venice,' *Bell's Life in London and Sporting Chronicle*, April 24, 1875.
[41] 'The "Merchant of Venice." A Tale of Tottenham Court Road,' *Fun*, May 1, 1875.
[42] 'At the Prince of Wales's,' *Punch*, May 1, 1875.
[43] Terry, *Story*, p. 100.
[44] Terry, *Story*, p. 97.
[45] There is, however, some disagreement between Terry and Squire Bancroft's versions of who was most responsible for the production's aesthetic effects. Terry states that '[t]he artistic side of the venture was to be in the hands of Mr. Godwin, who had designed my dress for Titania at Bristol' (*Story*, pp. 93–94), whereas Bancroft firmly states that '[t]he scenic artists also consulted a great authority, E. W. Godwin, who kindly gave them help, which was acknowledged [. . .] in all programmes. To attribute further assistance in the production to Mr Godwin is an error.' Squire Bancroft and Marie Bancroft, *The Bancrofts: Recollections of Sixty Years* (London: John Murray, 1909), pp. 205–206.
[46] Terry, *Lectures*, p. 13.
[47] Quoted in Holroyd, *Strange Eventful History*, p. 199.
[48] Terry, *Story*, p. 115.
[49] The Lyceum was sometimes regarded as a pseudo-national theatre. See for instance, *The Referee*'s review of *The Merchant of Venice*, which ends: 'to those who prate about the necessity of a state theatre the best reply will be "Go and see 'The Merchant of Venice' at the Lyceum"' ('Lyceum', *The Referee*, November 2, 1879.
[50]. [Henry James], 'London Pictures and London Plays,' *Atlantic Monthly* 50 (1882), 253–263 (p. 262). He also found her 'too voluminous, too deliberate, too prosaic, too English, too unversed in the utterance of poetry [. . .] not Juliet.' Irving fared less well in the critics' eyes than did Terry, but the production nonetheless was a popular success and ran for twenty-four weeks.
[51] John Ruskin, 'Of Queen's Gardens,' in *Sesame and Lilies* (London: George Allen, 1911).
[52] The review, of Marc Girardin's *Cours de littérature dramatique* (1855), is reproduced in Joseph Wiesenfarth, ed., *George Eliot: A Writer's Notebook, 1854–1879, and Uncollected Writings* (Charlottesville VA: University of Virginia Press, 1981), pp. 253–255 (p. 254).

[53] Terry's acting edition of the play is housed in the Ellen Terry Memorial Museum, Smallhythe, Kent.
[54] Terry, *Story*, p. 165.
[55] Terry, letter to Mrs Malleson, Inverness, [August 2, 1888], Y.c.1392 (2a), Folger Shakespeare Library, Washington, DC.
[56] 'Theatrical Gossip,' *The Era*, December 15, 1888.
[57] 'The Revival of "Macbeth,"' *The Era*, December 15, 1888.
[58] 'Our London Letter,' *The Penny Illustrated Paper and Illustrated Times*, December 15, 1888.
[59] '"Macbeth" at the Lyceum,' *Birmingham Daily Post*, December 22, 1888.
[60] Terry, *Story*, pp. 293–294.
[61] See 'Today's Tittle Tattle,' *Pall Mall Gazette*, January 1, 1889 and 'Gleanings,' *Birmingham Daily Post*, January 5, 1889.
[62] '"Macbeth" at the Lyceum,' *The Era*, January 5, 1889.
[63] 'Lambs at the Lyceum,' *Punch*, January 19, 1889.
[64] 'Topics of the Week,' *The Graphic*, January 5, 1889.
[65] 'THE CALL BOY,' *Judy: The Conservative Comic*, January 9, 1889.
[66] 'Theatres,' *The Graphic*, January 5, 1889.
[67] 'Shakespeare in Town,' *Punch*, January 12, 1889.
[68] 'How I Sketched Mrs Siddons's Shoes,' *Pall Mall Gazette*, January 11, 1889.
[69] *Funny Folks*, January 5, 1889.
[70] 'Topics of the Week,' *The Graphic*, January 5, 1889.
[71] Terry, *Story*, p. 293.
[72] Terry, *Story*, p. 294.
[73] 'The London Theatres,' *The Era*, September 26, 1896.
[74] 'Lyceum Theatre: Production of *Cymbeline*,' *The Times*, September 23, 1896.
[75] 'In View of To-night,' *Pall Mall Gazette*, September 22, 1896.
[76] 'Lyceum Theatre: Production of *Cymbeline*,' *Pall Mall Gazette*, September 23, 1896.
[77] 'Cymbeline at the Lyceum,' *Freeman's Journal and Daily Commercial Advertiser*, September 23, 1896.
[78] 'Cymbeline at the Lyceum,' *Daily News*, September 23, 1896.
[79] 'Cymbeline at the Lyceum,' *The Times*, September 23,1896.
[80] '*Cymbeline* at the Lyceum,' *Pick-Me-Up*, October 24, 1896.
[81] Terry, a letter to Shaw, September 23, 1896, in *Ellen Terry and Bernard Shaw: A Correspondence* (London: Reinhardt & Evans, 1931), p. 70.
[82] September 7, 1896; *Terry-Shaw Correspondence*, p. 48.
[83] 'Restoration of King Cymbeline,' *Punch*, October 3, 1896.
[84] September 24, 1896; *Terry-Shaw Correspondence*, p. 73.
[85] September 8, 1896; *Terry-Shaw Correspondence*, p. 49.
[86] September 22, 1896; *Terry-Shaw Correspondence*, p. 67.
[87] September 6, 1896; *Terry-Shaw Correspondence*, p. 42.
[88] John Plunkett, *Queen Victoria: First Media Monarch* (Oxford: Oxford University Press, 2003), p. 161.
[89] Ethel Mackenzie McKenna, 'Ellen Terry,' *McClure's Magazine* 2 (1894), pp. 457–465 (p. 460), and 'Illustrated Interviews: No. XVII. Miss Ellen Terry,' *The Strand Magazine* 4 (n.d.), 489–503 (p. 501).

[90] See McKenna, 'Ellen Terry,' p. 459; and Baroness von Zedlitz, 'A Chat with Ellen Terry,' *The Englishwoman*, 4 (1896), pp. 274–280 (pp. 274–275). Other interviews include '"Our Ellen": A Personal Impression of Her at Home,' *The Sphere*, April 28, 1906, iv–vi.

[91] 'Illustrated Interviews,' *Strand Magazine*, pp. 490, 491, 501.

[92] 'Illustrated Interviews,' *Strand Magazine*, p. 490.

[93] Terry, *Lectures*, pp. 15, 16.

[94] Henry James, 'Frances Anne Kemble,' in *Essays in London and Elsewhere* (London: Osgood, McIlvaine, 1893), pp. 86–127 (p. 98).

[95] Terry, *Lectures*, p. 80.

[96] Bram Stoker, *Personal Reminiscences of Henry Irving*, 2 vols. (London and New York: Macmillan, 1906), 2:202.

[97] Nina Auerbach, *Ellen Terry: Player in Her Time* (London: Dent, 1987), p. 225.

[98] Terry, *Lectures*, pp. 96–97.

[99] Stoker, *Henry Irving*, 2:197–198.

[100] Quoted in Auerbach, *Ellen Terry*, p. 220.

[101] Quoted in *Ellen Terry's Memoirs*, eds. Edith Craig and Christopher St John (London: Gollancz, 1933), p. 294.

[102] Terry, a letter to Charles Coleman, 1902; quoted in Auerbach, *Ellen Terry*, p. 222.

[103] Terry, *Memoirs*, p. 336.

[104] Terry, *Memoirs*, p. 336.

Chapter 4

[1] Henry Irving to Mary Ann Wilkins, August 18, 1856, Honnold/Mudd Library, Claremont Colleges.

[2] Henry Irving to J.L. Toole, [March 1860], Y.c. 485 (94a–b), FSL.

[3] Jane Smith to Henry Irving, March 28, 1874, Victoria and Albert Museum, London; Henry Irving to Charles Richard Ford, November 24, 1856, Honnold/Mudd Library, Claremont Colleges.

[4] Laurence Irving, *Henry Irving: The Actor and his World* (London: Faber and Faber, 1951), p. 199.

[5] *Athenaeum* November 7, 1874.

[6] *The Times* November 2, 1874.

[7] Ellen Kean to Henry Irving, March 5, 1879, Victoria and Albert Museum, London.

[8] Edward Gordon Craig, *Henry Irving* (London: J.M. Dent & Sons, 1930), p. 100.

[9] Oscar Wilde, 'The Soul of Man under Socialism,' *The Writings of Oscar Wilde* (New York: A.R. Keller & Co., 1907), p. 165.

[10] George Bernard Shaw, *Pen Portraits and Reviews* (London: Constable, 1932), p. 167.

[11] 'The Stage as It Is,' *The Drama*, p. 25.

[12] Clement Scott, *From 'The Bells' to 'King Arthur'* (London: John MacQueen, 1896), p. 62.

[13] George Fletcher, '*Macbeth*: Knight's Cabinet Edition of Shakespeare,' *Westminster Review* 41 (1843), pp. 1–72.
[14] 'A Note on the Character of Macbeth,' in Jeffrey Richards, ed. *Sir Henry Irving: Theatre, Culture and Society* (Keele: Keele University Press, 1994), p. 245.
[15] *Illustrated London News* December 15, 1875.
[16] Quoted in Austin Brereton, *The Life of Henry Irving*, 2 vols. (London: Longmans, Green, and Co., 1908), 1:190.
[17] *Observer* September 26, 1875.
[18] Quoted in Laurence Irving, *Henry Irving*, p. 264.
[19] Scott, *'The Bells' to 'King Arthur,'* p. 76.
[20] 'A Note on the Character of Macbeth,' in Richards, *Theatre, Culture and Society*, p. 246.
[21] Unattributed newspaper clipping, January 5, 1889, Art File Flat a26, folio 37, FSL.
[22] Brereton, *Life of Irving*, 1:199.
[23] Brereton, *Life of Irving*, 1:203.
[24] March [?] 1876, in *Letters of Matthew Arnold*, ed. George W. E. Russell (London: Macmillan and Co., 1895) vol. 2, p. 148.
[25] Laurence Irving, *Henry Irving*, p. 272.
[26] Playbill, Lyceum Theatre, London, January 29, 1877, Victoria and Albert Museum, London.
[27] Henry Irving to William Winter, June 26, 1896, Y.c. 485 (174), FSL. The reference was to *Cymbeline*.
[28] 'Four Favourite Parts,' *English Illustrated Magazine* (September 10, 1893), p. 927.
[29] Unattributed newspaper clipping, Art vol. b18, fol. 171, FSL.
[30] Quoted in Laurence Irving, *Henry Irving*, p. 316.
[31] Percy Fitzgerald, *Henry Irving: A Record of Twenty Years at the Lyceum* (London: Chapman & Hall, 1893), p. 60.
[32] F. J. Furnivall to Henry Irving, May 22, 1880, Victoria and Albert Museum, London.
[33] Joseph Hatton, *Henry Irving's Impressions of America* 2 vols. (Boston, 1884) 1:269.
[34] 'An Actor,' 'The Round Table. The Character of Shylock,' *The Theatre* (December 1879), p. 255.
[35] Hatton, *Impressions of America*, 1: 226–228.
[36] *Spectator* November 8, 1879.
[37] Fitzgerald, *Irving*, p. 135.
[38] *Era* November 9, 1879.
[39] Shaw, *Our Theatres in the Nineties*, 3 vols. (London: Constable, 1932) 2:198.
[40] Quoted in Laurence Irving, *Henry Irving*, p. 346.
[41] Henry Arthur Jones, *The Shadow of Henry Irving* (New York: William Morrow & Co., 1931), p. 53.
[42] Theodore Martin, 'Theatrical Reform: *The Merchant of Venice* at the Lyceum,' *Blackwood's Magazine* 126 (December 1879), p. 654.
[43] Frederick Hawkins, 'Shylock and Other Stage Jews,' *The Theatre* (November 1879), pp. 191–198.
[44] *Washington Post* January 3, 1904.

[45] Alfred Watson, *A Sporting and Dramatic Career* (London: Macmillan, 1918), p. 62.
[46] *Academy* May 7, 1881.
[47] Ellen Terry, *Ellen Terry's Memoirs* (London: Gollancz, 1933), p. 161.
[48] William Winter, *Life and Art of Edwin Booth* (New York: Macmillan, 1893), pp. 115–116.
[49] Quoted in Laurence Irving, *Henry Irving*, p. 389.
[50] All quotations cited in E. J. West, 'Irving in Shakespeare: Interpretation or Creation?', *Shakespeare Quarterly* 6.4 (Autumn 1955), p. 419.
[51] Scott, *'The Bells' to 'King Arthur,'* p. 229.
[52] Terry, *Memoirs*, p. 162.
[53] *Daily Telegraph*, quoted in Brereton, *Life of Irving*, 1:356.
[54] West, 'Irving in Shakespeare,' p. 419.
[55] Scott, *'The Bells' to 'King Arthur,'* p. 233.
[56] Quoted in Richards, *Sir Henry Irving*, p. 7.
[57] Quoted in Laurence Irving, *Henry Irving*, pp. 401–402.
[58] *The Times* October 12, 1882.
[59] *Illustrated London News* October 28, 1882.
[60] Quoted in Richards, *Sir Henry Irving*, p. 134.
[61] Ellen Terry, *The Story of My Life* (London: Hutchinson, 1908), p. 232.
[62] *Era* July 12, 1884.
[63] Review of *Twelfth Night*, July 13, 1884, Scrapbook C.3.1 (Henry Irving), FSL.
[64] Brereton, *Life of Irving*, 2:138.
[65] William Archer, *The World*, quoted in Brereton, *Life of Irving*, 2:142–143.
[66] *The Boston Budget* April 13, 1896.
[67] *Chicago Record* March 10, 1896.
[68] Michael Booth, *Victorian Spectacular Theatre, 1850–1910* (London: Routledge & Kegan Paul, 1981), p. 47.
[69] *Pall Mall Budget* January 3, 1889.
[70] *The Times* December 31, 1888.
[71] Jones, *Shadow of Henry Irving*, p. 60.
[72] Terry, *Memoirs*, p. 134.
[73] Bram Stoker, 'Henry Irving and Stage Lighting,' *The Nineteenth Century and After* 69 (May 1911), p. 911.
[74] *The Times* December 31, 1888.
[75] Laurence Irving, *Henry Irving*, p. 503.
[76] Quoted in Richards, *Sir Henry Irving*, p. 226.
[77] Richards, *Sir Henry Irving*, p. x.
[78] William Archer, *Henry Irving: Actor and Manager* (London: Field and Tuer, 1883), p. 42.
[79] Joseph Hatton, 'Henry Irving at Home,' *Harper's New Monthly Magazine* 64.381 (February 1882), p. 389.
[80] *Truth*, quoted in Brereton, *Life of Irving*, 2:136–137.
[81] Quoted in Brereton, *Life of Irving*, 2:166.
[82] Seymour Lucas, 'The Art of Dressing an Historical Play,' *Magazine of Art* (1894), pp. 278–279.
[83] Review of *Henry VIII*, *The Star*, quoted in *The Player*, January 13, 1892.

[84] Scott, *'The Bells' to 'King Arthur,'* p. 338.
[85] Brereton, *Life of Irving,* 2:166–167.
[86] *The Times* January 6, 1892.
[87] *Illustrated London News* November 19, 1892.
[88] *Athenaeum* November 19, 1892.
[89] *Black and White* November 19, 1892.
[90] Martin Meisel, *Realizations: Narrative, Pictorial, and Theatrical Arts in Nineteenth-century England* (Princeton, NJ: Princeton University Press, 1983), p. 427.
[91] 'Four Favourite Parts.' p. 929.
[92] See J. S. Bratton, 'The Lear of Private Life: interpretations of *King Lear* in the nineteenth century,' in *Shakespeare and the Victorian Stage,* ed. Richard Foulkes (Cambridge: Cambridge University Press, 1986), pp. 130–131 and Hughes, *Henry Irving, Shakespearean,* pp. 123, 139.
[93] Henry Irving to William Winter, March 29, 1896, Y.c. 485 (170a–c), FSL.
[94] Archer, *The Theatrical 'World' of 1896* (London: W. Scott, 1897), pp. 272–273.
[95] Shaw, *Saturday Review,* September 26, 1896.
[96] Archer, *Theatrical 'World' of 1896,* p. 260.
[97] Shaw, *Saturday Review,* September 26, 1896.
[98] Brereton, *Life of Irving,* 2:288.
[99] Henry Irving to William Winter, September 28, 1901, Y.c. 485 (187b), FSL.
[100] Irving, 'An Actor's notes on Shakespeare. No. 3: "Look here, upon this picture, and on this"', *The Nineteenth Century* (1879), p. 262.
[101] Louis Austin, 'Sir Henry Irving,' *North American Review* 181.5 (November 1905), p. 773.
[102] Shaw, review of *Cymbeline, Saturday Review,* January 2, 1897.
[103] Irving, 'Thc Art of Acting,' *The Drama,* p. 89.
[104] *Pall Mall Gazette* September 13, 1886.
[105] Craig, *Index to the Story of My Days* (London: Hulton Press, 1957), p. 249.
[106] Craig, *Index,* pp. 54–55.
[107] Jones, *Shadow of Henry Irving,* p. 93.
[108] Henry Irving, 'Shakespearian Notes 1. The Third Murderer in *Macbeth,*' *The Nineteenth Century* 1 (1877): 327–330.
[109] *The Times* September 17, 1891.
[110] Henry Irving to Edward Compton, June 3, 1878, Y.c. 485 (15a-b), FSL.
[111] 'Shakespeare on the Stage and in the Study,' *Good Words* (January 1883), in Richards, *Theatre, culture and society,* p. 294.
[112] Richards, *Theatre, culture and society,* pp. 276–277.
[113] 'The French Play in London,' *The Nineteenth Century* 6 (August 1879), p. 242.
[114] 'The Stage as It Is,' *The Drama,* p. 28.
[115] 'Shakespeare on the Stage and in the Study,' Richards, *Theatre, culture and society,* p. 294.
[116] 'The Stage as it is,' *The Drama,* pp. 41–42.
[117] 'Shakespeare on the Stage and in the Study,' Richards, *Theatre, culture and society,* p. 299.
[118] F. J. Furnivall to Henry Irving, May 22, 1880, Henry Irving to F. J. Furnivall, May 22, 1880, Huntington Library, San Marino, CA.

[119] *The Works of William Shakespeare*, eds. Henry Irving and Frank A. Marshall 8 vols. (London: Blackie & Son, 1888–90).
[120] Quoted in Laurence Irving, *Henry Irving*, p. 523.
[121] *Liverpool Mercury* November 30, 1887; 'Shakespeare as a Playwright,' *The Henry Irving Shakespeare*, 1: xxi.
[122] *The Times* January 5, 1891.
[123] Frank Marshall to Henry Irving, March 20, 1889, Victoria and Albert Museum, London.
[124] Preface, *The Merchant of Venice*, The Henry Irving Shakespeare, 3: 350, 351.
[125] Preface, *Macbeth*, The Henry Irving Shakespeare, 5: 256.
[126] *Boston Journal* October 1, 1895.
[127] Janet Achurch to Henry Irving, [*c.* June 27, 1889], Victoria and Albert Museum, London.
[128] Quoted in Harry Furniss, *Some Victorian Women* (London: John Lane, The Bodley Head, 1923), pp. 73–74.
[129] Hatton, *Impressions of America*, 2: 264.
[130] *Daily Telegraph* July 5, 1883.
[131] Thomas Carlyle, *On Heroes, Hero-Worship and the Heroic in History*, ed. Archibald MacMechan, 1840 (Boston: Ginn & Co., 1901), p. 131.
[132] Unattributed clipping (New York City, *c.* October 18, 1883), Scrapbook C.3.1 (Henry Irving), FSL.
[133] Laurence Irving, *Henry Irving*, p. 419.
[134] *Era* November 3, 1884.
[135] *Boston Gazette* October 27, 1895.
[136] Irving did play Malvolio in America, but only for a handful of performances on a single tour.
[137] Review of *Hamlet*, Star Theatre, New York City [1883], Scrapbook C.3.1 (Henry Irving), FSL.
[138] Laurence Irving, *Henry Irving*, p. 432.
[139] *Boston Gazette* October 27, 1895.
[140] *Evening Sun* (New York) October 30, 1895.
[141] *Washington Post* January 14, 1896.
[142] Review of *The Merchant of Venice*, *The Theatre* (December 1879), p. 292.
[143] *Chicago Tribune* October 1, 1893.
[144] *The Times* October 18, 1887.
[145] Unattributed clipping, Scrapbook C.3.1 (Henry Irving), FSL.
[146] Quoted in Laurence Irving, *Henry Irving*, p. 432.
[147] *The Free Press* (Detroit) March 27, 1896.
[148] *The Free Press* (Detroit) March 27, 1896.
[149] Unattributed clipping, Scrapbook C.3.1 (Henry Irving), FSL.
[150] Unattributed clipping, Scrapbook C.3.1 (Henry Irving), FSL.
[151] Henry Irving to Gen. Daniel Sickle, November 25, 1895, Y.c. 485 (80), FSL.
[152] *Taggart's Times* (Philadelphia) December 29, 1895.
[153] *The Press* (New York City) October 30, 1895.

Selected Bibliography

Archer, William. *William Charles Macready.* 1890; New York: Benjamin Blom, 1971.

Auerbach, Nina. *Ellen Terry: Player in Her Time.* London: Dent, 1987.

Bartholomeusz, Dennis. *Macbeth and the Players.* Cambridge: Cambridge University Press, 1969.

Bate, Jonathan and Russell Jackson, eds. *Shakespeare: An Illustrated Stage History.* Oxford: Oxford University Press, 1996.

Booth, Michael. *Victorian Spectacular Theatre, 1850–1910.* Boston and London: Routledge & Kegan Paul, 1981.

Brereton, Austin. *The Life of Henry Irving,* 2 vols. London: Longmans, Green, and Co., 1908.

Carlisle, Carol J. 'Macready's Production of *Cymbeline,*' *Shakespeare and the Victorians.* Ed. Richard Foulkes. Cambridge: Cambridge University Press, 1986, pp. 138–152.

Carlson, Marvin. *The Italian Shakespearians: Performances by Ristori, Salvini, and Rossi in England and America.* Washington, DC: Folger Shakespeare Library, 1985.

Clarke, Asia Booth. *Booth Memorials: Passages, Incidents, Anecdotes in the Life of Junius Brutus Booth (the Elder) by His Daughter.* New York: W. W. Carlcton, 1866.

—. *John Wilkes Booth: A Sister's Memoir,* L. Terry Oggel, ed. Jackson: University Press of Mississippi, 1996. (Originally published in 1938 as *The Unlocked Book.*)

—. *The Elder and the Younger Booth.* Cambridge MA: J. R. Osgood, 1881; Boston: American Actor Series, Vol. 5, 1982, Laurence Hutton, ed.

Clary, Frank Nicholas. 'Maclise and Macready: Collaborating Illustrators of Hamlet,' *Shakespeare Bulletin: A Journal of Performance Criticism and Scholarship* 25.1 (Spring 2007), pp. 33–59.

Courtney, Krystyna Kujawińska and John M. Mercer, eds. *The Globalization of Shakespeare in the Nineteenth Century.* Lewiston, NY: Edwin Mellen Press, 2003.

Craig, Edward Gordon. *Ellen Terry and Her Secret Self.* London: Sampson Low, 1932.

—. *Henry Irving.* London: J. M. Dent & Sons, 1930.

Davis, Jim and Victor Emeljanow. *Reflecting the Audience: London Theatre-going, 1840–80.* Hatfield: University of Hertfordshire Press, 2001.

Downer, Alan S. 'Players and the Painted Stage: Nineteenth-Century Acting,' *PMLA* 61.2 (June 1946), pp. 522–576.

—. *The Eminent Tragedian: William Charles Macready.* Cambridge: Harvard University Press, 1966.

Fitzgerald, Percy. *Henry Irving: A Record of Twenty Years at the Lyceum.* London: Chapman & Hall, 1893.

Foulkes, Richard. *Performing Shakespeare in the Age of Empire.* Cambridge: Cambridge University Press, 2002.

—. *The Shakespeare Tercentenary of 1864.* London: Society for Theatre Research, 1984.

Foulkes, Richard, ed. *Henry Irving: A Re-Evaluation of the Pre-Eminent Victorian Actor-Manager.* Aldershot: Ashgate Publishing, 2008.

—. *Shakespeare and the Victorian Stage.* Cambridge: Cambridge University Press, 1986.

Grossman, Edwina Booth. *Edwin Booth: Recollections by his daughter and letters to her and his friends.* London: Osgood, McIlvaine & Co., 1894.

Hazelton, Nancy J. Doran. *Historical Consciousness in Nineteenth-Century Shakespearean Staging.* Ann Arbor: UMI Research Press, 1987.

Hazlitt, William. *A View of the English Stage; or, A Series of Dramatic Criticisms.* Ed. W. Spencer Jackson. London: George Bell and Sons, 1906.

Holroyd, Michael. *A Strange Eventful History: Ellen Terry, Henry Irving, and their Remarkable Families.* London: Chatto & Windus, 2008.

Hatton, Joseph. *Henry Irving's Impressions of America.* 2 vols. Boston, 1884.

Hughes, Alan. *Henry Irving, Shakespearean.* Cambridge: Cambridge University Press, 1981.

Irving, Henry. *The Drama: Addresses by Henry Irving.* New York: Tait, Sons & Co., 1892.

Irving, Laurence. *Henry Irving: The Actor and his World.* London: Faber and Faber, 1951.

Jones, Henry Arthur. *The Shadow of Henry Irving* New York: William Morrow & Co., 1931.

Kimmel, Stanley. *The Mad Booths of Maryland.* Indianapolis: Bobbs-Merrill, 1940; rev. and enlarged, New York: Dover, 1969.

Lewes, George Henry. *On Actors and the Art of Acting.* London: Smith, Elder and Company, 1875.

Lockridge, Richard. *Darling of Misfortune.* New York and London: The Century Co., 1932; rpt. New York: Benjamin Blom, 1971.

Macready, William Charles. *Macready's Reminiscences and Selections from his Diaries and Letters.* Ed. Frederick Pollock. New York: Macmillan and Company, 1875.

—. *The Diaries of William Charles Macready, 1833–51.* Ed. William Toynbee. 2 vols. New York: G. P. Putnam's Sons, 1912.

Marshall, Gail. *Shakespeare and Victorian Women.* Cambridge: Cambridge University Press, 2009.

Marshall, Gail and Adrian Poole, eds. *Victorian Shakespeare: Theatre, Drama and Performance.* 2 vols. Basingstoke: Palgrave Macmillan, 2003.

Meisel, Martin. *Realizations: Narrative, Pictorial, and Theatrical Arts in Nineteenth-century England.* Princeton, NJ: Princeton University Press, 1983.

Odell, G. C. D. *Shakespeare from Betterton to Irving.* 2 vols. New York: Charles Scribner's Sons, 1920.

Oggel, L. Terry. *Edwin Booth, a Bio-Bibliography.* New York, Westport, CT, and London: Greenwood Press, 1992.

Oggel, L. Terry, ed. *The Letters and Notebooks of Mary Devlin Booth.* New York, Westport, CT, and London: Greenwood Press, 1987.

Pollock, Walter Herries. *Impressions of Henry Irving.* London and New York: Longmans, Green, 1908.

Poole, Adrian. *Shakespeare and the Victorians.* London: The Arden Shakespeare, 2004.

Rawlings, Peter, ed. *Americans on Shakespeare 1776–1914.* Aldershot: Ashgate Publishing, 1999.

Richards, Jeffrey. *Sir Henry Irving: A Victorian Actor and his World.* London and New York: Hambledon and London, 2005.

Richards, Jeffrey, ed. *Sir Henry Irving: Theatre, Culture and Society.* Keele: Keele University Press, 1994.

Rowell, George. *Theatre in the Age of Irving.* Oxford: Blackwell, 1981.

Ruggles, Eleanor. *Prince of Players, Edwin Booth.* New York: W. W. Norton, 1953.

Saintsbury, H. A and Cecil Palmer, eds. *We Saw Him Act: A Symposium on the Art of Sir Henry Irving.* New York: Blom, 1969.

Schoch, Richard. *Not Shakespeare: Bardolatry and Burlesque in the Nineteenth Century.* Cambridge: Cambridge University Press, 2002.

—. *Queen Victoria and the Theatre of her Age.* Basingstoke: Palgrave Macmillan, 2004.

—. *Shakespeare's Victorian Stage: Performing History in the Theatre of Charles Kean.* Cambridge: Cambridge University Press, 1998.

Scott, Clement. *From 'The Bells' to 'King Arthur.'* London: John MacQueen, 1896.

Shakespeare, William. *The Works of William Shakespeare,* eds. Henry Irving and Frank A. Marshall. 8 vols. London: Blackie & Son, 1888–90.

Shattuck, Charles H. 'Edwin Booth's Iago.' *Theatre History Studies* 6 (1986), pp. 32–55.

—. 'Edwin Booth's Richelieu.' *Theatre History Studies* 1 (1981), pp. 1–19.

—. *Mr. Macready Produces 'As You Like It.' A Prompt-Book Study.* Urbana, IL: Beta Phi Mu, 1962.

—. *Shakespeare on the American Stage, from Booth and Barrett to Sothern and Marlowe.* Washington, D.C.: The Folger Shakespeare Library; London and Toronto: Associated University Presses, 1987.

—. *Shakespeare on the American Stage, from the Hallams to Edwin Booth.* Washington, D.C.: The Folger Shakespeare Library, 1976.

—. *The Hamlet of Edwin Booth.* Urbana, IL, Chicago, and London: University of Illinois Press, 1969.

—. 'The Theatrical Management of Edwin Booth,' in *The Theatrical Manager in England and America,* ed. Joseph W. Donohue, Jr. Princeton: Princeton University Press, 1971, pp. 143–188.

Shattuck, Charles H., ed. *Between Actor and Critic, Selected Letters of Edwin Booth and William Winter.* Princeton: Princeton University Press, 1971.

—. *William Charles Macready's 'King John'; a facsimile prompt-book.* Urbana, IL: University of Illinois Press, 1962.

Shaw, George Bernard. *Our Theatres in the Nineties.* 3 vols. London: Constable, 1932.

Shaw, George Bernard and Ellen Terry, *Ellen Terry and Bernard Shaw: A Correspondence.* London: Reinhardt & Evans, 1931.

Stoker, Bram. *Personal Reminiscences of Henry Irving.* 2 vols. London and New York: Macmillan, 1906.

Stokes, John, and Michael R. Booth and Susan Bassnett. *Bernhardt, Terry, Duse: The Actress in Her Time.* Cambridge: Cambridge University Press, 1988.

Taylor, Gary. *Reinventing Shakespeare: A Cultural History, From the Restoration to the Present.* Oxford: Oxford University Press, 1989.

Terry, Ellen. *Ellen Terry's Memoirs*, ed. Edith Craig and Christopher St. John. London: Gollancz, 1933.

—. *Four Lectures on Shakespeare.* London: Hopkinson, 1932.

—. *The Story of My Life.* London: Hutchinson, 1908.

Thomas, Julia. 'Bidding for the Bard: Shakespeare, the Victorians, and the Auction of the Birthplace,' *Nineteenth-Century Contexts* 30.3 (September 2008), pp. 215–228.

Trewin, J. C. *Mr. Macready: 19th Century Tragedian.* London: Harrap, 1955.

Watermeier, Daniel J., ed. *Edwin Booth's Performances, The Mary Isabella Stone Commentaries.* Ann Arbor and London: UMI Research Press, 1990.

Wells, Stanley, ed. *Nineteenth-Century Shakespeare Burlesques.* 5 vols. London: Diploma Press, 1977.

Wells, Stanley and Sarah Stanton, eds. *The Cambridge Companion to Shakespeare on Stage.* Cambridge: Cambridge University Press, 2002.

Wilson, Francis. *John Wilkes Booth: Fact and Fiction of Lincoln's Assassination.* Boston: Houghton Mifflin Co., 1929.

Winter, William. *Life and Art of Edwin Booth.* New York and London: Macmillan and Co., 1893.

—. *Shakespeare on the Stage.* First, Second, and Third Series. New York: Moffat, 1911–16.

Index